MW00901341

THE

INVISIBLE

STORM

JUANIMA HIATT

ISBN-13: 978-1477430583
ISBN-10: 147743058X

Book Cover Design by Reinke Creative
Author Photography by Timothy J. Park

Printed in the United States of America

For my daughters, Lacey and Jordan

When the weight of life feels like more than you can take, have courage. You were created to overcome, and God will never leave your side. Remember to love, even when you're hurting, and never give up fighting for all that God has promised you. Your Mom and Dad will believe in you always.

FOREWORD

As a young woman I drove out to visit my grandma at her elder care home. Her Alzheimer's was progressing and I was prepared for the convoluted turns in conversations, and for sometimes having to play another person's part. I wasn't prepared, however, for the quiet, panicked hiss: "The barn!"

Puzzled, I too lowered my voice. "What about the barn?"

"They are killing people in the barn."

I looked into my grandma's frightened blue eyes. "Who is?"

"The Nazis."

I felt a little relieved, yet as a young psychologist I had already heard so many unlikely horrors, I couldn't be sure. The gracious owners of the elder home must have thought me eccentric when I asked to walk out to the barn and photograph it.

Later that night I quizzed my father closely about any unexplained disappearances from the elder home. There were none. Fifty years earlier Grandma had responded to news of Nazi atrocities but had buried her imaginings deep in her subconscious. Now, as her brain's pathways became blocked and twisted, the old imaginings were released to torment her. While the threat was fifty years old my grandma's terror was present and real.

Then I cried because I couldn't help her.

I researched PTSD (Post-Traumatic Stress Disorder) in the elderly and my grandma's experience contributed to my metaphor of the black bag where we hide our secret, and not-so-secret, horrors. Like a shark, secret trauma cruises just below our conscience awareness. When we are tired, hungry or ill, the trauma bumps us, and our black bag leaks out thoughts and feelings we thought we had stuffed away forever. Protecting our black bag from bumps can becomes a full-time job. How unfair that after fifty years of sticking, stapling, tying and duct-taping her black bag closed, my grandma's black bag leaked when she was at her most vulnerable. With real and present danger you can watch and plan; you can sometimes avoid it or you can seek to manage it. But one thing is true about PTSD: *It hijacks you at your weakest moments.*

Just as it did for Juanima. Just as it does for all of us. You push it to the darkest corner, turn out the light and pray it molders away to nothing. But sooner or later we all "pay the piper." Things that we thought we had stuffed away forever leap out at us; suddenly as real as the moment they first happened. Juanima didn't wait fifty years though. She chose to fight through layers and layers of other people's garbage that they had deposited on her. That is why sexual abuse is called "soul murder." But Juanima didn't die and she would not yield her soul. She chose to fight through the pain and safeguard her children. She chose to not be one of the sexually abused whose children are ten times more likely to be victimized (www.apa.org). And, if her girls do go through hard times, she has left them with a road map—a legacy of healing.

This young woman who could not whisper her secrets has now shared them with the world. Let's honor her courage with resolve. Report ALL SEXUAL ABUSE! It's not your job to assess if abuse is occurring. If you suspect it, report it. If the survivor is an adult, listen until you can't and then help them find a professional who cares. I promise there are those of us that do. Finally, ask humbly what you can do to help. You might be relieved to know that the very best thing you can do is clean the house or bring a meal. We do not all share the same giftings, and God surrounded Juanima with a husband with humor, a dear friend who strolled boldly in the mire with her, and two little girls who held the hope of joy in their tiny hands. May God bless each of you as you traverse your own path of healing and support others on their paths.

Sincerely,
Kali Miller, Ph.D.
Licensed Psychologist

AUTHOR'S NOTE

This memoir reflects the author's best recollection of events over a period of years. Journal entries, other documentation, and eyewitness accounts were utilized to ensure accuracy of events. Most names have been changed to protect the individual's privacy. Dialogue and events have been recreated to the best of the author's ability, and in some cases, have been compressed to capture the substance of what was said or what occurred.

ACKNOWLEDGEMENTS

In the midst of PTSD, I was oblivious to the numerous ways family and friends came to my rescue. However, I know now what they did for me; what they sacrificed for me so I could keep moving forward. Sam and Traci, Dad, Gail, Mom, Art, Jim, Susan, Cris, Kevin, John, Becky, Josh, Kristen, and Tom... I am here today because of your amazing gifts of love, and I will forever be grateful.

Michael Hiatt, my forever love. You are my champion, and a pillar of strength. Your three angels are so blessed to have you leading the way. Thank you for believing in me through our darkest times. My dreams of our future are too big to contain.

Traci Mathies, this story would not exist without you. Thank you for seeing beautiful me, for standing beside me, and for holding me up. *For saving my life.* You are a warrior and best friend. We are forever connected, and the memories will always remain.

Uncle Jim and Aunt Susan, your love and generosity astound me. Because of you, I received the help I needed. I love you both so much!

Sandy Neale, thank you for getting angry about the abuse I endured as a child. Because of you, I found my voice.

Kali Miller, you gave me the focus I needed to press forward, and helped me learn to love myself—one of the greatest gifts a person could receive.

My dad, John Sr. My heart could not love you more. Your unfailing love brought me out of the dark more than once. You will always be a winner in my book. You will always be the perfect dad.

My mom, Cathy, I see you for the courageous, resilient woman you are. I am so blessed to call you Mom. You told me I *had* to tell my story, no matter what. *That* is love, and shows your true character and selfless heart. You are an irreplaceable gift in my life, and cherished by so many.

My stepmom, Gail, one of my closest and dearest friends. Thank you for walking beside me, and for always knowing what I needed. You held onto my heart through those darkest years. You felt my pain. You understood, and always had open arms. God used you in mighty ways, and you will always be precious to me.

My stepdad, Art. It makes a difference to me, just knowing you *get it.* You are so valuable to me, and I love you Daddy Art.

My brother, John Jr. I let all childhood grievances go the day you stood up to protect me when I was fifteen. You became the big brother I've always wanted. If only you lived closer to me.

My brother, Joshua. You helped me keep *fun* in my life, when I didn't think I could experience it anymore. Just one night of karaoke, and I caught a glimpse of the Nima I thought was lost. Thanks for always being such a great friend to me. Rock on!

My sister, Cris. I see your love, and I hold it dear. I believe that through this journey, you and I will find a friendship we never would have known otherwise. My heart is wide open to whatever God wants to do in our lives; and knowing God, it will be astounding.

My sister-in-law and amazing graphic designer, Rebecca. You are not only gifted with stamina, patience, and incredible vision, but also with a beautiful heart of compassion. You made me believe I can make a difference with my story, and you captured the essence of it brilliantly in the cover of this book. My hero!

Andy, you have been a bright light through this difficult journey. I am forever grateful we reconnected after all these years. Your constant validation lifted me above the darkness, and you understood my pain in a way no one else has. You are truly one of the most compassionate people I know. I treasure you!

My daughters, Lacey and Jordan. No words can express the love and gratitude I feel for you. Lacey, you are wise beyond your years, and have given me so much understanding and compassion. You are my confidant for life. Jordan, you brought laughter and rainbows into my world when they were missing. My kitty forever!

Nancy LaTurner, thank you for your thorough editing. You encouraged me, and set me on the path to stronger writing. I am forever grateful.

Thanks to all my readers. Each of you gave me remarkable insight, and I so appreciate every single thought you shared. My heart brims with gratitude for all your love and support, and your encouragement to get this book out.

"He stilled the storm to a whisper;
the waves of the sea were hushed."
~Psalm 107:29

1

METAMORPHOSIS
OF THE MIND

❧ 2003 ❧

It was a mirror image of the past. Helplessness...
hopelessness... pain... shame... unheard cries of desperation,
and it awakened a dark, horrifying life of long ago that
I could no longer deny.

Pain surged through my spine with the rush of an exploding dam. My back jolted into a frozen arch, and the tears came instantly.

"Help—" I said in a choked whisper.

My husband, Mike, who sat behind me in my hospital bed, jumped to his feet. "What is it?"

The pain radiated into my face, paralyzing me, trapping the air in my throat. I felt like someone had stabbed a three-foot-long skewer into my spine and shoved it up through my head.

"Something's wrong!" I gasped. "Something's wrong—"

Mike called out to the anesthesiologist who was opening the door to leave. "Excuse me, can you check this? I think something's wrong with the epidural."

The tall man in blue scrubs turned back to us and said, "There's nothing wrong, I did it right," and stepped through the doorway.

The panic on my face caused Mike to change his tone. "I think you need to check this now. Something's hurting her."

The man sighed, returned to my bedside, and pulled the blanket aside to expose my back. His fingers pricked like little blades against my skin as he examined the needle he'd inserted into my spine. I cried out. A bright pain ripped across my face, and I remained unable to move.

"Oh—" he muttered, and slowly pulled the needle out. The pain shrunk away and I filled my lungs to capacity gratefully. When I was able to sit up, he repeated the entire epidural procedure, but this time correctly. When he finished, he left the room without as much as an apology. I lay there in shock over what had just happened to my body, and the smug arrogance of the anesthesiologist and his reluctance to help. Disappointment draped over me as I cupped my hands around my protruding belly. I had hoped for a joyous childbirth. A replica of my first.

So far, the only similarity was that both pregnancies had stretched a week past the due date. With the first baby, however, just one day before my scheduled induction, she decided to come into the world on her own. I remember waking with a jolt at 1:00 A.M., and within the hour my husband and I were en route to the ER. Once there, the nurses made me as comfortable as possible for the journey ahead. When the contractions came, I puffed through them as I'd learned in birthing classes. Later, as I waddled into the bathroom of my hospital room, I cheerfully hollered out to Mike, "Hey! I think I could do this again!" We'd discussed three or four children at one point, and though I didn't enjoy gaining sixty pounds during the course of my first pregnancy, the process was something to behold. A gift from God. And the pain didn't seem too bad.

Then back labor pains hit me a couple of hours later, and the words spewing from my mouth were, "No way in hell am I doing this again!" Thank God for epidurals. Despite my strong aversion to needles, when the doctor came to confirm that I still wanted the epidural as we'd previously discussed, my eyes bulged and my mouth bellowed a crazed "Yes!" To my relief, the procedure went easily, and I never had to see the needle. I waited, pain-free, for my cervix to dilate enough, and when it finally came time to push, Dr. Phelps watched the graphed contraction readings and simply told me to bear down. I never felt a thing.

Suddenly, I held a sweet, eight-pound, fourteen-ounce baby girl in my arms with deep blue eyes and small tufts of caramel-brown hair. Mike and I wept together as Lacey squawked and blinked at the bright lights. Her finger immediately grasped onto mine, and my heart melted. I looked at Mike. "We did it, Baby," I cried, "We did it!"

Not one thing went wrong that day. Every nurse that came in my room was a budding humanitarian gifted with humor. I wondered how they'd found such a team of amazing women. They alleviated every worry that crept in about the unknowns of childbirth. I never felt alone. I never felt afraid.

But I felt afraid now, waiting silently for the epidural to kick in with baby number two, still feeling pain in my spine where the first needle had pierced a nerve. Mike caressed my arm, and I smiled.

"You okay?" he said.

"Yeah, but it seems different this time. The epidural's not kicking in as fast." My belly squeezed painfully with contractions, and the dull, thick pain of back labor crept in.

Mike buzzed the nurse and asked to speak to the anesthesiologist. We assumed he'd made a mistake and given me too small a dosage. When he arrived, he assured us it was correct. "But... I'm still really hurting," I lamented.

"Yes, that's normal," he said, shifting his weight to his other leg.

"I don't understand. When I had my first baby I didn't feel these. The epidural took away the pain. I *still* have pain."

The anesthesiologist sighed and checked my chart. "Mrs. Hiatt, I did what your doctor requested."

Mike narrowed his eyes on the man, "Then we'd like to see the doctor, please."

The anesthesiologist left and several moments later, Dr. Phelps entered the room with a smile. "Hi, Juanima! How's it going?"

"Not good. These contractions are pretty bad. And I'm getting back labor pains that—" another contraction was starting, "—that *really* hurt."

That's when Dr. Phelps delivered *his* plan. "Well, Juanima, we can't give you the full epidural this time. This baby is much bigger than Lacey was, so it's going to be important that you're a full-on part of this. That you're aware of your contractions, so you can push when you're supposed to."

I can't have heard him right.

A wave of nausea swept over me. "Can't you just tell me when to push? Like you did with Lacey?"

"I'm afraid not. The baby's just too big. I need you to be fully alert. Okay?" He patted my leg and left the room, and my heart sank. Everything we'd discussed and agreed on was suddenly obsolete. Dr. Phelps had never let on—until this moment—that the baby's size set us on a different course completely.

Mike saw the panic on my face and took my hand. "We'll get through this, okay? You can do it. I know you can."

Yet reality fully sank in a couple of hours later, when I doubled over in pain from contractions wrenching my front and across my lower back. Soon, the pain gripped me altogether, and I reached desperately for every breath.

"I feel like I'm going to break in two," I cried, squeezing Mike's hand. He called the doctor in again. "Please," I begged, "I can't... Can you please up the epidural? I can't take this."

Dr. Phelps shook his head. "I understand it's bad, Juanima, but I'm afraid we can't increase the epidural at this point. You're only dilated to three centimeters, and if we increase the epidural it'll slow down your progress even more. We can bring you some warm towels and blankets, or a heating pad for your back. That should help." A tear fell from my eye, and he patted my leg again. "I'll have the nurse come in. Okay?"

He left the room, and I heaved my belly over to face my husband. *He completely dismissed me.* The next contraction came and gripped my lower back like a vise. I squeezed the blankets in my fists and moaned, just as the nurse entered with a heating pad; she pressed it up against my back, tucking the blankets around me so it wouldn't slip. The heat seeped like liquid across my back, but relief didn't come. Only when a contraction ended did I have just a few minutes before it began again, and I was never ready. Never prepared for the violent surges and paralyzing waves across my midsection, bringing with it blankets of fear and hopelessness.

Hours passed. I could see the helplessness in Mike's eyes. "I'm sorry, Baby," he said, wiping tears from his eyes.

Family arrived, supportive and excited about the baby's coming. Mike did most of the talking. In between contractions I tried my best to smile, even join in conversation with my parents and siblings, but I couldn't mask my misery when the pain hit. *Be stronger. You're tough. You can do this.*

I tried to connect and meld with the pain. To get above it. I believed I could, just as I had when I was nineteen years old. I had endometriosis, a condition where the lining of a woman's uterus sheds backwards through the fallopian tubes and settles on ovaries and other pelvic organs. If the endometrial tissue lodges itself on nerve endings, the result is usually excruciating, stabbing pain during menstruation. For a year and a half before the diagnosis, I endured these painful periods, where blows to my lower abdomen felt swift and sharp, like a knife plunging into my gut. I thought I was tough, but there is a delicate line between tenacity and just plain stupidity. My stupidity ended one afternoon while working as a receptionist in an insurance firm. I stood up from my desk to sign for a package when the pain shot through my lower abdomen like a bullet.

The delivery boy stood there with an astonished look on his face as I went to my knees, gasping for air, clutching my gut, moaning. I heard him say, "I think she needs help," to someone walking by, and I blacked out just as a fellow secretary put her arm around my shoulders. In the hospital, I met Dr. Phelps, and he told me I had endometriosis.

He scheduled surgery post haste, and afterwards, Dr. Phelps shared some grave results: "The endometriosis had spread to most of your pelvic region. I'm afraid you may never be able to get pregnant, Juanima. I'm very sorry."

But I did get pregnant, not once, but three times. Lacey came first, and Dr. Phelps called her our miracle baby. We dreamed of having kids two years apart, and like clockwork, I became pregnant again. When the baby was only twelve weeks old, I laid on an exam table for a routine ultrasound, only to hear empty silence coming through the speaker. The absence of a heartbeat. "We rarely know the reason why," Dr. Phelps consoled over my tears, "but it's usually because the fetus isn't developing properly." That didn't make me feel any better.

Still, Lacey was my first miracle, and perhaps that's why Dr. Phelps made her delivery so easy for me. He catered to me, taking me gently and protectively through each phase of the pregnancy and birth.

But now, the second time around, with baby pressing hard against my ribs and pelvis, contractions gripping and crushing my lower back, Dr. Phelps did not cater to me. The staff did not protect me, and I was no match for the swells and tidal waves of pain now pulling me under. I needed help. I needed to be saved. I wanted the sweet reality of Lacey's birth to be my reality now, but no matter how desperately I wished it, my hope lay bare. Nobody would change the course of this birth, and no amount of pleading would alter the doctor's plan. I was a helpless bystander in the birth of my own child.

Mid-afternoon, a nurse came in to check my progress. From somewhere far away, a voice said I was dilated enough, and we could head to delivery. I don't remember rejoicing. I was fading away.

As I neared the delivery room, a contraction came again, and I cried out. The back labor pains had become so intense that I could no longer feel the frontal contractions—the ones that mattered to the doctor. I heard a voice tell me, "Get ready to push, Juanima!

Baby's just about here!" I couldn't think of pushing. My body writhed in pain. My knuckles shone ghostly white, grasping the cold, steel bars of my bed. I couldn't bear it. Not another moment. Mike tolerated the fierce crushing of my other hand and kept up with my bed as the delivery crew wheeled it down the bright white hallway. I held intense eye contact with him until another contraction came and swept me away into the undertow of dark waters; but his hand... his hand always pulled me back out, and I emerged from the dark to find him there. He kept saving me. *Don't let go...* I pleaded with swollen, tear-filled eyes. *Please don't let go.*

In the room, I became aware of the beehive of activity around me: people setting up for delivery, hooking me up to various contraptions, water running, lights glaring all around me. The smell of ammonia and rubbing alcohol. So many voices. So much noise and chaos. I had a new anesthesiologist: a petite woman with rigid, brown curls, a pointy nose, and a tight mouth that appeared in my face and spouted orders at me. I couldn't listen to her voice, muffled by the thick wall of dissociation between us. I held onto Mike's gaze, and tried to hold onto my sanity, but felt it slipping away as another contraction flooded over me.

"What's going on, Juanima?" A voice beckoned at me. "Are you with us?"

I wasn't. The voice came from far away, from a distant darkness, while I sobbed. They wanted me to push, but I couldn't. "My... back." I gasped from the fetal position. They tried turning me over onto my back, but it was like rolling onto a tray of nails. "Aaaaah!" I screamed.

Doesn't anybody hear me?

"It's time to push, Juanima," a stern voice commanded. But it was useless. I was drowning, enveloped in a sea of torment, and nobody brought me out. *I hear voices... but I don't know who they're talking to. It can't be me, because if any decent human could see me, surely they would see me going under. Surely, they would stop everything to save me.* "Juanima, I need you to push, okay? Juanima?"

"I can't! Oh—God..." I wailed, twisting forward from the pain. "Aaaaah," came another deep moan. I curled up and tried to turn, but there was no position that eased the pain.

Dr. Phelps approached me, yielding, "Okay, Juanima, I'm going to give you something to take the edge off, okay? But I can't do more than that. I need your participation here. I need you with us, okay?"

The edge... Didn't he know? Couldn't they see? I had already fallen off the cliff, and now plunged helplessly into a black canyon of desolation. But I held onto Mike. He alone kept me there.

Someone pushed a syringe of fluid into the epidural tube, bringing insignificant relief. The surging pain in my body still kept me prisoner.

I gazed tearfully at my husband, his eyes full of grief. I wanted to disappear. *Please let me disappear...* The activity around me became hectic. More nurses flooded in and crowded around my bed. Voices yelled at me to push. I gripped Mike's hand. Then three nurses came to my bedside and severed my only thread of promise. Suddenly, Mike was gone. They had pushed him out of the circle. *No, wait! Please! Please let him come back!* I couldn't get the words out. Just the despairing moans of pain from the contractions that consumed me. Those sweet, brief moments of recovery were no more. I could barely see my husband back against the wall, standing helpless by the window, not knowing if he should intervene or stay out of the way and let them do their jobs. He didn't know what to do, but he couldn't come to me. My one source of comfort and love was out of my reach. They'd taken my lifeline.

I cried out for him, but the stern face of the waspish anesthesiologist blocked my view. She *made* me look at her. "Hey, Juanima. You need to buck up and push this baby out, or there's gonna be a problem. Do you understand me? You need to deal with the pain and push this baby out *now.*"

She continued yelling in my face like a Marine sergeant, and I wanted to choke her. Choke the life right out of her. Wrap my hands around those tight, brown curls in her hair and rip them right out of her head; but my hands were frozen, grip-locked to the steel bars.

Instead, I took the rage and focused it on my belly. That baby inside needed to come out.

I pushed, even as the pain permeated my back. I didn't know if I pushed correctly. I "bore down" as my doctor kept demanding me to do. A hot flood of tears blanketed my face, and I pushed the rage down into my entire pelvic area. *Get—out! Get out of me!* I didn't care anymore. Not about anything. I had vowed I would never have a C-section birth, detesting the idea of the scar that came with it; but as the hurricane of emotions pressed against the walls of my mind, I just wanted out. I wanted to die. I asked God to take me away and let me fall into the darkness that beckoned me. I wanted to scream at them, "Just cut the baby out! Just get it out of me!" The fight was gone.

I opened my mouth to speak and heard Dr. Phelps say, "There's the head! She's coming out! You did it, Juanima! Keep going! Keep pushing! Again! Now!"

So I did it again, but my link to reality had already been severed. My body responded with another push, but I had disappeared emotionally and mentally. As the baby emerged into the world, I was emptied. There were no cries from the baby, but I did not listen for them. Dr. Phelps spoke about the cord being wrapped around the baby's neck... baby being squeezed... the doctor's reassuring words not to panic, as he hastily unraveled the cord. More concerns... no cries from the baby. Then, the raspy squawk of the infant filled the air. Voices cheered around the room, then cheered again that it was a girl. I lay there, still, numb, a void. They finally let Mike return to me, and he took my hand, but I was depleted. They had taken the life right out of me.

A nurse swaddled the baby in a blanket and brought her to me, and I reeled away from her. "No!" I groaned. "No, I can't." I couldn't believe the words came out of my mouth. I sobbed, wrapped my arms around myself, and pressed my face into the pillow already soaked from my tears and sweat. I wanted so badly to curl into a ball and disappear, but Dr. Phelps still sat hunched over me at the foot of the bed, alarmed that my bleeding wouldn't stop. Again, he assured me that I would be fine as soon as he stopped the bleeding. I didn't care. *Just let me go.*

Mike held the baby girl while Dr. Phelps poked and prodded at me. "We need to get the placenta out," he said. A nurse approached my belly and started pushing down. Hard. I cried out, but she just kept pushing, kneading my belly like a ball of bread dough. Her impersonal hands pushed and tweaked and rolled over me, all business, and I was a nothing. An object. The tears poured as the pain of her kneading surged across my midsection. More damage... more disappearing.

Dr. Phelps stopped the bleeding, and the frosty nurse left. Another nurse approached me. She introduced herself as Allegra, and asked if I wanted to hold the baby. I shook my head, no, and the tears flowed again. She took my hand and knelt down beside me, looking me straight in the eyes. "Listen," she said, "It's okay. Alright? After what you just went through, it's totally normal to feel what you're feeling right now. It's going to be okay, I promise. You'll want to hold her, and you will, when you're ready. But don't rush yourself, okay? Juanima? She's not going anywhere, and she's getting plenty of love right now." She laughed. I looked through my swollen eyes into hers and believed her. I held onto her words, absorbing them like they were new life for me. "I promise," she said again, "It's gonna be okay." I cried more.

Allegra continued to hold my hand while Dr. Phelps stitched me up. He said I had torn completely open. *So... You noticed.* I don't remember the words he spoke to me after that, but I'm sure they were cheerful and congratulatory.

When Dr. Phelps finished, my family poured into the room, but I don't remember the words they said as I lay there in my grief and guilt of not wanting to hold my newborn baby. I knew she was being passed around, being gazed at and goggled with delightful glee from grandmothers and grandfathers, aunts and uncles. The smiles abounded, and the cheers and sounds of congratulations filled the air. The room swelled with the utter joy and amazement at the beautiful girl I had produced, yet my family was oblivious to the fact that there on the bed was the shell of the person she had left behind.

My husband touched me, and I sobbed. How could I feel this way? So indifferent to this new child. I hated myself, and closed my eyes as intense emotions battled inside my mind. *No... She's my life. I made her. She grew inside me. She is part of me. It wasn't her fault.* But I hid my face from her, and turned away from the love that surrounded me.

I don't remember being wheeled into the recovery room, nor any visits from my family or friends that day. But I do remember taking the baby girl into my arms for the first time, crying as I held her, and Mike leaning in close and touching my face with gentle hands. I remember the overwhelming shame as I tried to force feelings for this baby I cradled, and the utter dismay that they didn't exist. But I held her. I gazed at her. I needed to try to feel. Deep inside I *had* to love her. I had a responsibility as a mother to this baby. *She needed me.* The baby squawked with hunger, and I had a choice to make.

A nurse walked in to check on us and asked if I wanted to try to nurse the baby. Despite my fear and uncertainty, I nodded. "Would you like me to assist you?" she asked.

"No." My voice wavered. "I've done this before." I trembled under her appraising gaze. I didn't want anyone watching me. I didn't want anyone in the room at all, except Mike, but I couldn't say that. So I fumbled nervously under her watch, trying to get the baby attached, but she fussed and squirmed in my arms. She refused me, and a wave of tears came over me again. Allegra entered then, and rushed to my side when she saw my struggle.

"Oh honey, aren't you hungry?" Allegra soothed the baby's fussing. With my permission, she assisted me in attaching her correctly. After a couple attempts, the baby finally nursed. "There she goes," Allegra smiled, and then she and the other nurse left us alone. I couldn't believe I had any more tears left in me, but they continued to flow.

Tears of shame. I fought to keep my head up. The events of the day had drained my strength. My hope dwindled, but my arms held the little girl, and I stared at her, reaching, grasping for a connection.

Her searching, blue eyes looked up towards my face.

"Hello," I whispered. She continued nursing, and held my gaze. I glanced over at Mike, who smiled, his body emanating exhaustion. "Hi, Baby," I grinned, leaning my head back against the wall.

"Hi, Baby," he returned, "We made it through, huh?"

"I guess we did," I smiled, but I wondered. I wanted to go home. I needed to be out of this place. Away from this nightmare.

A male staff member came in with some paperwork, and asked us if we'd decided on a name for the baby. We hadn't. We had our list of names, but when we looked at this baby girl, none of the names fit. Mike and I looked at each other. "Jordan," we said in unison, and laughed, because that was the one name we'd taken off the list when neither of us thought it would be right. But it was the only right one. We named her Jordan Kathleen Hiatt.

Oh, Jordan... my love. Only God knew this day would be the catalyst of a much greater, more desperate challenge still. A journey that would push us all into a wake of upheaval and defy the ironclad walls of love that held our family together so firmly. Only God knew this day would begin a shattering of souls, a fight for peace, a fight for self... my fight for life.

~

The days and weeks following Jordan's birth teemed with hazy, sleepless nights typical with a newborn baby, but there was something else. The moments of sleep I did get became filled with nightmares about Jordan's birth: lying on the hospital bed being tortured with physician's tools, writhing in pain alone, or suffocating beneath an invisible weight. Each time, skirting death in my dream, I'd burst awake in a frantic state, heart racing, covered in sweat, hyperventilating.

A darkness was falling over me, and I couldn't shake it. The nightmares came nightly, and if I wasn't jolted awake by the graphic violence, Jordan's frequent cries of hunger pulled me out. Always in a panic, for several moments I wavered on the edge of reality until I realized I was home, her cries were real, and Jordan needed to be fed. *Now.* Mike often rose to bring her to me; other times, I stumbled to her in an alternate state, lifted her from the bassinet, and returned to the bed to nurse her. I'd lay there, still trembling from my dream, while Jordan fed to her heart's content.

Jordan's tolerance of my anxious state in those early years still amazes me. It seems now like an act of God's mercy that she didn't reject me or show more distressed behavior. I didn't realize then that babies can *feel* the emotions of their parents—hidden or not—from eight inches away, and will generally mimic those emotions. I think that somehow, she held onto the love that was there in my heart for her. Or God's amazing grace cradled our hearts together. Though the sadness inside me grew to an alarming depth, I mustered up as much strength as possible to hide it. I smiled at her, and spoke to her sweetly. I held her, but desperately wished someone would hold me. I gazed at her, now completely adoring this beautiful new child, but longed for the deep bond that had never taken place.

Many visitors came those first few weeks, and each interaction took courage I didn't have. I wanted to be left alone. But I couldn't turn away my friends and family. Of course, they had to see Jordan, and the joy I had for this precious new bundle. I had no capacity to try to explain the storm of emotions raging inside me or the confusion and shame that suppressed my spirit. So I told them what they wanted to hear. I said the words they expected: "It's amazing!"

It wasn't a complete lie. My heart had always been an overflowing cup of unconditional love. I believe God instills gifts in all of us, and one of mine is love. My dad told me that as a toddler I would randomly go up to strangers and hug their legs. I had love to give and wanted to spread it around.

I saw the world through eyes of grace, and as loving arms passed my new child from lap to lap, I smiled at the people who loved me; but I gave no grace to myself. I brooded and loathed myself for the indifference in my heart. As my sister-in-law, Becky, cooed and teeter-tottered Jordan in her arms trying to arouse a first smile, I smiled too, masking the incessant despair in my soul. I wanted so badly to be happy. I *wanted* to push this tiresome sadness away. The horrible birth experience was over. I should be able to put it behind me and welcome the exuberant joy new mothers are supposed to feel. I'd put worse horrors behind me from my past. Maybe I just needed a little more time and determination.

I focused on the two girls and summer fun. I brought out the video camera one day and recorded Mike holding Jordan against his shoulder under the cool, shaded porch, while Lacey darted through the sprinkler in the yard, squealing with delight as the streams of water saturated her to the bone. She ran up onto the porch and pushed right up in front of Jordan's blinking eyes and shouted, "Ooga booga!" with a swish of her hips and hands flailing in the air. Then back to the sprinkler, screaming at the shooting streams skirring against her little four-year-old body. I smiled and laughed. Through the camera, I admired my family. This cute little wonder on my husband's shoulder, blinking at the sunlight she was still unaccustomed to. My husband, his large, protective hands almost covering her entire back. I looked at this, knowing this child would always have her daddy's love and protection. He would always have arms ready to hug or hands ready to hold. I gazed at Mike's handsome face, the sparkle of affection in his eyes as he watched our dancing Lacey in the sprinkler's torrents, and I knew I was blessed. But something was horribly wrong.

A sense of panic gnawed at my gut, attached to me like a thistle on a sleeve. Just as a woman is unconscious of the actual conception of a fertile egg inside her, I was unaware a seed had been planted in me the day of Jordan's birth. But this seed planted the beginnings of a horror. Anxiety grew inside me, along with a heaviness in my soul that spread like cancer. The nightmares not only continued at night, but I had intrusive thoughts and memories related to the birth during the day. I waited and hoped to wake up one morning free from it all, and have the stillness I remembered from an earlier time fill me once again.

I didn't realize at the time that Jordan's birth was a "trauma," which is an event either experienced or witnessed that overwhelms one's ability to cope, and causes feelings of hopelessness, power-lessness, helplessness, and fear for one's life. Nobody in my family knew the details of what had happened the day of Jordan's birth. Only in hindsight do I see that the staff treated me so wrongly. I blamed myself for the incomprehensible feelings after Jordan's birth, and shame overwhelmed me. Still, I chalked it up to a really bad experience, and somehow I needed to get over it, and get on with my happy life. It didn't work. My symptoms were sending me in a rapid downward spiral from which I could not recover.

What horrified me beyond measure were the intruding thoughts and memories not related to Jordan's birth. Memories of dark things I had hidden away years ago. They came abruptly, and I'd squeeze my eyes shut and shake my head in an effort to thrust them out; but still they came, and they terrified me. I couldn't understand. For fourteen years, I had rarely thought of the dark events of my childhood, yet now they raced in like a long-lost child. Things I did not want to remember, but I had no choice. The memories haunted me, and with them came the suffocating shame that had eroded my self-love as a child. *Shame...* it filled me now, along with the unwavering resolve to keep these unwanted memories silent. *Nobody can know. Nobody would understand. I will wear this smile and hide the truth... like I did for so many years before.*

Lacey and Jordan ~ December 2003

2

LOSING MYSELF

⟡2003-2004⟡

"We're worried about you," my sister, Cris, said. She and her best friend, Traci, had pulled me outside of the house to sit on our porch steps. "You're not coming out of this depression. It's been two months, and it seems like you're getting worse instead of better. We think you should go see a doctor."

I sighed. First, I was disappointed that what I'd believed was a baby visit turned out to be a guarded act of intervention. Second, the thought of seeing a doctor for depression appalled me. "I don't need help, Cris," I argued. "I'm sure this is just postpartum depression, and will go away soon."

"That's just it," she spoke softly, and chose her words carefully. "We thought this was postpartum, too, but... it wouldn't hurt just to go talk to your doctor and see. You've been really depressed, Nima. I think you should get it checked out."

Cris is just short of two years older than me, and often offered her insight into various happenings in my life, sometimes wanted, sometimes not. This time, it felt invasive. I'd never experienced depression like this, nor had anxiety like this, nor had recurring nightmares, but I was as sure as the sun on a summer's day that it would pass. I didn't need help, and I certainly didn't need anyone telling me what to do. But I avoided arguing like I would a mama bear's den.

"I might go," I said gingerly, "But I do think this will pass. I'm sure I'll be fine."

I wasn't fine. Determined to hide the chaos swarming inside me, I continued to deny it and suppress the memories that haunted me daily. I put a smile on and played my roles as a mom and wife, but it became increasingly difficult. In addition, I began to feel pressure about returning to work.

A week before Jordan's scheduled birth, I left my job with the City of Portland for maternity leave. I took pride in that job, as I'd been chosen out of more than two hundred and fifty applicants, all vying to be an Executive Administrator's Assistant working twenty hours a week on a comfortable salary, in a small department, in the heart of the big city. I developed friendships with my co-workers, and we became a close-knit team. Working only twenty hours allowed me privileged time at home with Lacey, giving me a partial realization to my dream of being a stay-at-home mom. We could not survive on Mike's salary alone, but my part-time salary added enough to give us a comfortable existence. It was the perfect situation for all of us.

Across the span of a year with the City, I proved my abilities for managing large projects, such as overseeing the move of the entire department over the course of four months. I selected and organized movers and office furniture suppliers, designed the new office layout including offices and cubicles, and kept within a tight budget and time constraints. With its success, I won the respect and trust of my supervisor, and our business relationship evolved into a friendship I treasured. I excelled at organizing my time, meeting critical deadlines, and juggling multiple tasks efficiently. I thrived in that fast-paced, pressured, multi-tasking work environment.

After Jordan's birth, I made weekly visits to the office to share her smiles with the staff and catch up on the office buzz. During one visit, my supervisor took me aside.

"I know you're not going to like this, Nima, but there have been some changes in your absence. The Board has decided to make your job a full-time position."

My shoulders slumped. "No... What about the job share, so I could keep my twenty hours?"

"They don't want to go that route," she said, "and twenty hours just isn't enough to compensate for the growth of the job. I'm so sorry."

My perfect plan was crumbling before me, and she knew it, too.

"You have some time to think about it," she said, placing her hand on my shoulder.

I already knew I couldn't accept the full-time position, but I didn't know what that meant for our finances. I would have to find another part-time job, and that crushed me. I knew I'd never find another job like my job with the City.

My visits to the office became less frequent, not because of the strained circumstances with my job, but because the anxiety of making the trip became surprisingly overwhelming. Walking into the office with Jordan and Lacey to say hello, I was soon searching for the closest empty room to catch a breath. I couldn't seem to calm the anxiety, and I got more agitated and unable to tolerate Lacey's questions and Jordan's babbling during those visits. I wondered where my patience had gone, and why, in those moments of kids being kids, my sole need was to flee for the elevator and for home. Eventually, the office visits ceased altogether.

As my maternity leave neared its end, I knew I had to make a solid decision. My voice quivered when I told my boss I wouldn't be returning.

She chuckled. "I kind of knew you wouldn't. I understand, Nima, and I'd like you to know the door is open for you to come back here anytime."

I appreciated her kindness, but feared what lay ahead.

❧

The holidays brought unprecedented anxiety for me. What had never before been stressful now caused dizzying, mind-reeling stress. When Christmas came, it brought an elevated panic that astounded me.

Cris lived just a few blocks from us and had prearranged a family Christmas gathering. My mom and her husband, Art, my dad and his wife, Gail, my brother, Josh, and precious extended family would all be there; but for some reason, the thought of going into a sea of people—even family—seemed disconcerting. I didn't understand. I loved my family. I loved gatherings. They came so infrequently, the party presented a rare opportunity to catch up on life, share stories and laughs, and reconnect. But thinking of this night quickly approaching, I felt a pit in my stomach that gnawed, frightened, and confused me to no end. I talked myself into believing it was just exhaustion. After all, it'd been seven months since Jordan's birth, and I still fought for sleep because of the ongoing nightmares. The nightmares I didn't talk about.

The day of the party, I paced the house like a caged lion. An uneasiness poked and prodded at my innards. I tried to focus on the excitement of Jordan experiencing her first Christmas, and Lacey's four-year-old delirium at the gifts and festive atmosphere that brought out the best in her, but fear kept chasing positive thoughts from my mind. *What did I have to be afraid of? This is my family, for crying out loud.* Yet my overpowering anxiety created senseless obstacles between me and my front door. I needed to fill my water bottle. Get Jordan another blanket—and a toy—just in case. Wait, I have to go to the bathroom one more time.

Then, as I stood in front of the bathroom mirror, my family waiting impatiently by the front door, a panic welled up in me. Hot, at first, in my stomach, then into my chest, where it spread across and tightened everything inside.

Mike hollered that we had to go. *Now.* I stood there, confused and frightened by the pains in my chest.

"Just a minute," I said, struggling for that deep breath that would alleviate the dizziness. I didn't want to go anywhere. The inner chaos rippling through my mind and body tormented and confused me. And I couldn't make it stop.

༃

We arrived at my sister's house twenty minutes late. Standing outside the front door, I disguised my inner turmoil with a smile and gave a loud, enthusiastic greeting as we entered. I bestowed a traveling hug through the crowd, and to my nieces and nephews running through the room. When I reached Cris, she asked to speak to me in private. As we rounded the corner to the kitchen, she let me have it.

"I am sick of you always coming late to family gatherings. This time it's gone too far," she squared me face-on, shrinking my personal space to a mere six inches. "When you are late, you are disrespecting me and everyone else. You are saying that your time is more valuable than everyone else's. I would appreciate it if you could show the respect we all deserve by arriving on time."

Her harsh outburst stunned me. Words cannot explain how much I loathe confrontations. I've never been able to cope with someone's angry words unless they wrapped them in a pretty box and put a shiny ribbon on it. Since that rarely happened, I made it a point never to make anyone angry. Ever.

"Cris," I stammered. "I'm sorry. It was hard getting here with Jordan—"

"No—" she retaliated, "I will not listen to your excuses. You always have excuses! Everyone else has a life, too, but they can be here on time. Show us some respect." And with that she left the room, and I stood frozen, flushed, and feeling the need to vomit. I don't know how long I stood in that kitchen before my mom walked in.

"Are you okay?" she asked, touching my trembling arm.

"Cris got mad at me for being late," I quivered. I felt tears boiling beneath the surface. "I'm okay, Mom," I said, and dashed for the bathroom. I gripped the countertop and began hyperventilating. My head spun as emotions swelled and threatened to break through the dam I had so gruelingly built around them. *No... not here. Not now. It's Christmas. My family is in the other room. You can do this. Think of the girls.*

I looked in the mirror at the painful etchings on my face, and with my hands, ironed them out. I worked hard at a normal face—a neutral face—and took an awkward deep breath. The exhale came loud and forced. I tried again... slower. I forced my tears back and found precious air at the bottom of my lungs. I stopped my quivering chin and forced a smile. *Jordan...* I imagined her squealing and laughing at her first sight of gift-wrapped packages under the tree. I opened the door and went to join the group with a smile, kneeling close to my husband to solicit a sturdy hug.

☞

Severed from my job with the City, I knew I needed to find something part-time, and soon. I wanted to work from home, and shared this desire with my sister, Cris. She offered to pray about it. Then in March of 2004, I received a phone call. Cris had a friend, Paul, who owned his own home maintenance company. He needed a part-time secretary to work for him, *from her own home.* I almost cried. The job offered flexible hours, and half of the responsibilities I'd had working for the City. With my executive-level administrative skills, I knew I'd be able to do an above-average job for Paul, even with my two girls at home with me. It was a win-win opportunity. My confidence soared when he hired me on the spot.

The first few months went well, but to my bewilderment, managing my simple responsibilities grew challenging. My brain wasn't working right. I forgot things, and had trouble concentrating. *Call the client, schedule the crew member, and forward the schedule to Paul at the end of the day. Wait. Where did I put the client list? Dang it—the client is calling me back! Where did I put my notes?*

I got by with faking it for a while, but I couldn't ignore the nagging voice in my head screaming, *What is wrong with you? Get it together! This work isn't hard!* I couldn't explain it, nor could I admit, even to myself, that I had a problem. If forgetting wasn't enough, depression dampened the peppy, sparkling smile in my voice that kept the clients happy.

"Is everything okay?" Paul asked one day over the phone. "I've heard from the guys there's been some hiccups in the scheduling."

My face flushed with embarrassment. I was a competent woman who had a job just one year earlier that was ten times more difficult. "Yes, and I'm so sorry. Everything is fine. I think it's just taking me a little longer to balance working at home with caring for the girls. I promise I'll do better. You can count on me."

I worked harder than ever, knowing it would devastate us if I lost the job; but my stubbornness would be the death of me. I needed to face the truth, but instead, I denied the depression that was pulling me under. I denied the key elements of my job that slipped through the cracks and went neglected. I denied the intrusive thoughts and memories that vexed me, and intercepted my train of thought. I adamantly swore that I just needed to try harder. I sat at my desk disgusted with myself that I could not keep up with an entry-level position. I knew I was capable; I just needed to concentrate better, and keep better notes so I didn't forget things.

But my husband looked me square in the eyes and said, "It's more than forgetting stuff. It's time to get help."

&

On May 13, 2004, I shivered, waiting anxiously in the exam room for the doctor to come in. The nurse, a small, perky thing, had already taken my vitals. She fluttered about, asking me in her bird-like voice, "Isn't this a beautiful day?" and "How are you?"

"Fine," I lied.

She entered the data of my vitals into a computer on a tall, narrow cart. She said all the rooms had one now. They were new. Then she left. I hated being there. In the cold silence of that exam room, I stewed about what the doctor would say. *You're psychotic... you're delusional... you should spend some time in a psych ward.* How could I possibly admit, out loud, that a once-capable, confident, happy, assured woman had lost all control of her mind, couldn't concentrate, and couldn't control this nagging anxiety?

"Talk to me about your anxiety," Dr. Hogan said after a brief introduction. I glanced at her face: pretty, kind, and trustworthy. I imagined her as a runner with her tan skin, long, dark curly hair, athletic, slender build and self-assured demeanor. She seemed friendly, but her strong presence intimidated me. I suddenly became aware of how weak and small I felt.

"It's bad," I shrugged. "Like I can't breathe. I'm edgy all the time." I didn't know how to explain. I'd never had to describe anxiety before.

"What are some events that have happened in your life lately that could cause this?"

I talked about Jordan's difficult birth, and how I'd had nightmares for a while afterwards. I explained I had quit my job with the City and got a new job working from home, but struggled with it. The job shouldn't be difficult for me, but it was getting harder to manage both the job and my kids at home.

"Are you having any other symptoms? Like depression?"

God, how did she know? This was the hardest part. I rarely cried in the past, and it seemed lately I couldn't control the tears. Admitting this to her revealed my most embarrassing character flaw of all, and I believed she'd throw me in that padded room once I said it. She seemed kind and concerned, but I couldn't possibly admit I was falling apart. Could I?

"Yeah... I mean yes. I guess I cry a lot. But I think it's because I'm so tired. I'm not sleeping well. I just... I feel overwhelmed with everything." The tears suddenly trickling down my cheek shamed me. *Not in front of my brand new doctor. Not on my first visit!* For sure, she would think I was a nutcase now.

"Well, you've been through a lot," she reassured. Her words released the tears I'd been holding back. "How long has this been going on?"

"It's gotten worse over time... since Jo was born. It's been almost exactly a year." Five days short to be exact.

Dr. Hogan ordered several lab tests to rule out other ailments, and thus began the long road of medication trials. She handed me some samples of Celexa and wrote the names of a few therapists on a card, recommending I seek some counseling. I sighed, and when I got home, I threw the card away. A doctor, maybe. A therapist, not *even* if hell froze over. Been there done that. Never again.

By August, I was in shambles. The depression began to infect me at the core, and I developed intolerance to crowds and loud noises. The hellish stew of dark attributes had thickened substantially, and I could not keep up with my job any longer. Scheduling of the drivers fell through the cracks, important phone calls didn't get made, drivers showed up to do maintenance calls when the owners weren't home—appointments I'd neglected to reschedule. My efforts to fix things were strong but futile, and I could no longer hide behind excuses and promises to improve. After five months, the shortest job in my history abruptly ended when Paul sat me down at his patio table and let me go.

⁓

I kept my past hidden. I hung up my cloak of darkness for my children. To me, there was no other option. They needed a happy mom, and I refused to let my temporary sadness impede their normal lives. I hid my tears. I ran to my room for hide-and-seek when I couldn't breathe. I ran to my room when anger swelled and I couldn't control the scream. I didn't want to yell at my girls. I couldn't believe I felt the need to yell in the first place. Anger was not in my vocabulary, nor allowed in my color-fan of emotions, and I avoided it at all costs. I hightailed it out of a room where an argument threatened to form. In my relationship with Mike, before Jordan's birth, I ran like a scared puppy from a dispute. At any hint of a disagreement, I withdrew, reducing Mike to talk to a wall. I was a silent, vacant face that offered no hope of resolution to the problem at hand.

Now, I suddenly felt the need to scream at the top of my lungs when one of my children misbehaved or the two of them had a spat.

The pillows in my room muffled my screams. The walls of the room became a punching block for the rage I couldn't seem to control.

But moments of laughter came, and they saved me, and helped me go on. I have to remember the laughter, for it reminds me that my life then was not all abominable. Like Jordan running to my bed every morning, arms straight up in the air squealing, "Hi, Mama!" The smile on her face brought tears to mine, because all the in-between times riddled me with guilt and condemnation of being a horrible mom. Her smile brought forgiveness and reassurance that she still loved me, and that my issues weren't damaging her. With high-reaching arms, she'd climb on top of me and bury her face in the pillow beside me and come up laughing. She saw the world as funny. I thanked God for this. She brought belly laughter to my mornings, when just an hour earlier I warred in the depths of a dark nightmare.

The moments we caught on video are my only link today to the joy of those years. Jordan, almost two years old, sitting on her daddy's lap while I sit beside them video-taping Lacey's kindergarten musical presentation. In between songs, the camera moves to Jordan, whose index finger has disappeared into her nostril, twisting and turning for several seconds. She looks into the camera with a mischievous smile, pulls the finger, and laughing, wipes it on Daddy's cheek. We all laugh, until an annoyed parent nearby hushes us.

Another video of Lacey's first determined effort to get a diaper on Jordan earlier that year. After neatly spreading the diaper out on the floor, she models the correct behavior to Jordan by sitting on the diaper, "Like this, Jordan, like this!" in her squeaky, five-year-old voice.

She reaches for Jordan, but Jordan dodges her saying, "Bath? Bath?" while running naked circles around Lacey.

Lacey doesn't give up, though, and tries coercion next. She grabs a toy she knows Jordan loves, and entices her with it over to the diaper. "I'll give this to you if you sit on the diaper, Jordan!" So Jordan sits down—behind the diaper—and takes the toy from Lacey. Infuriated, Lacey glares at Jordan and demands with great authority and a pointed finger, "Get. The diaper. On. Now!" Then Jordan runs naked to the bathroom, with Lacey chasing her, "Jordan! Jordan!"

Oh, the precious moments I captured on video of giggles, trips to the beach, and what looks like a normal me. Those moments were real; and even if moments of pretending were a legion in comparison, I must always remember and hold onto those bits of laughter that broke through the darkness.

Apart from the laughter, my cloak grew heavier around my soul, and on August 20, 2004, I sat in the doctor's office again. This time, I could not hold back the truth about the intrusive memories and nightmares of my past. As Dr. Hogan pressed for details, I revealed my history of child abuse—multiple rapes and molestations—suicide attempts, and drug and alcohol use.

"Juanima," she said, stern this time. "It is critical that you seek some counseling with these issues. You *need* to talk to someone about your past."

"I am talking to someone," I said. "I have a friend who's been talking with me a lot about these things, and I think I'm healing already. I really don't think I need a therapist."

Dr. Hogan smirked and shook her head. I knew her smirk meant *I just didn't get it.* But I disagreed. She typed something into the computer, and then looked me square in the eyes. "You are showing signs of post-traumatic stress disorder, Juanima. This is serious. It's not something you can deal with on your own. You need to see a professional therapist."

For a moment, she had my full attention. There was actually a name for what I'd been enduring? Maybe she knew a lot about this disorder thing, but she didn't know me. She didn't know what I was capable of overcoming on my own. I stared at the floor and said I would consider seeing a therapist, knowing full well I would not. She handed me a new medication sample since the first one had no effect, and ended our appointment. I ran to the minivan and cried. I had no intention of finding a therapist, but Dr. Hogan's pressuring felt like a threat of some sort. She didn't understand why I simply couldn't. I knew a therapist would make everything worse.

Besides, my talks with Traci truly did help me. She was my sister's best friend, but she showed a genuine interest in me and my pain. Traci wanted to know about my past, and I shared, not because of wanting to, or a sensed obligation to, but because it felt necessary now. The memories banged incessantly against my mind like a stubborn woodpecker on sheet metal. She knew my past troubled me, and she wanted to help.

Our first real talk took place during a late-night drive in her van along some country roads outside of town. As I watched the illuminated blur of weeds through the headlights of the van, Traci asked about my doctor appointments. I confessed that I'd finally told Dr. Hogan about my past, and that's when Traci asked some general, non-threatening questions that at first, didn't seem to bother me much. She asked about the first offense when I was seven. After sharing surface facts, I expected her to change the subject. Instead, she asked, "Is there more? What else happened?" Sharing more brought on a trembling as I revealed details I never had before. If it became too difficult for me, she brought humor back into the conversation and changed the subject.

The late-night drives grew more frequent, and each time I tested the waters of trust and respect. The trembling never stopped, and yet she continued, gently, to draw out my memories. Very slowly I let her in, sharing one or two incidences of abuse; but most things I knew I could never speak of. Not to anyone. I would never speak of the violence, and never, ever feelings. I always stopped when it became too real; when she meddled with the edge of my emotions related to the abuse, because that was forbidden.

While speaking about the past felt right at the time, neither of us realized the massive inferno we ignited. Voicing the memories mesmerized and empowered my spirit, but what begins as a small, controllable flicker can quickly become an untamable, destructive monstrosity, much too powerful to handle alone.

I didn't think there was danger in telling. Sharing the memories that invaded my mind felt necessary and healing. The memories terrified me, too, but having Traci there to gently aid in bringing them out helped diminish that fear in some way. Still, I could not understand why they attacked my consciousness in the first place. What was post-traumatic stress disorder anyway? And why was my past coming back to me now after fourteen years of peace?

I know now that there's a reason you don't talk to friends first about repressed trauma. Talking is like opening a door to an attic you haven't visited in years, filled with memories and stuff you've long forgotten about. Remembering brought unexpected pain; not as I told the memories, but after, as they stayed in my mind and simmered like boiling oil.

Alone in my house one day, those boiling memories triggered an attack of a debilitating pain deep inside. Like an explosion of two-edged swords, it cut into my core and into my mind. It submerged my soul, raging like a flood, engulfing my heart, pressing painfully through every limb. Then images of horrible violence flashed through my mind like scenes of a film. People I knew, hurting me. Emotions, foreign and forgotten, roared from deep inside. Feelings I couldn't articulate, but they pierced the protective shell I'd been wearing.

So much terror. I felt a scream building as I sat hunched over on the floor, clutching my stomach against the agony I could not contain or put words to. It was killing me inside. The images wouldn't stop. I cried harder as the pressure inside became unbearable. Desperate, I crawled and stumbled into the bathroom and found a razor blade. With a swift move across my forearm, I released the pressure, and saw the pain I could not articulate or comprehend. Again and again I sliced, until relief came. Until I could breathe.

The shock followed as I stared at what I had done. *My God, what is happening to me?* I had gone to that blade like a habit. Looking down beside the dripping red lines on my arm, I saw the scars of another time. So faded into the landscape of my skin, I had forgotten them. Forgotten their story. Forgotten their pain. The reason for their existence. I stared at them now, horrified that it had come to this. I leaned into the floor and moaned, full of regret.

I did not want to reconnect to those years, nor remember the pain of surviving. I just wanted my life back. I wanted to be happy —a feeling I'd never had to long for until now. I did not want to remember the past. For fourteen years, I thought I had put it all behind me. But what I had really done was compartmentalize it. I stored it away into a room of its own, far from my reach, and easy to forget. I lived for fourteen years ignoring that room, while it leaked poison into my life. Now, the contents of that room were spilling out, bringing with it an indescribable misery.

Bandaging my arm, shame and disgust overcame me; but had I not done that, I reasoned, I would have died. The pain would have killed me. I had never felt pain like that before—so sharp, and so deep. So engulfing. I pulled down my sleeve, and promised that no one would know what I had done. No one could ever see. They would never understand it was something I had to do.

A memory of a party swept in. I was sixteen, at a friend's house with several theater buddies from school. I've lost all recollection of the event that made me run for the upstairs bathroom in the two-story house. I only remember dashing up those stairs, wanting to get away from someone. I locked the bathroom door behind me and sat on the blue tile floor, rocking as silent tears blanketed my face. Consumed with emotional pain, I found a disposable razor under the counter and removed the blade. I cried as I dug the blade across my left, upper arm, learning in that moment how to release my pain, and cope with the things that kept happening to me. The things I couldn't tell anyone about. My best friend, Darcy, tapped on the door, begging me to let her in. I did. When she saw what I had done, she held me, and helped me bandage the wound. The parents came to the door a moment later and knocked, asking if everything was all right. I could not respond.

"Just a moment!" Darcy hollered, but they knew something was wrong. They yelled through the door that they were going to call someone, which made me instantly shift personas. I couldn't risk parent involvement. I jumped to my feet, wiped my tears, and opened the door.

"Everything's fine." I smiled. "I'm sorry to have worried you. I'm okay now." Darcy and I brushed by them to rejoin the party, and I forgot everything bad that had taken place, as I had trained myself to do many times before. Privy to my deception, the parents stood at the bathroom doorway shrugging, wondering if they had misread things. I seemed okay, after all.

Now, deception would once again be my companion. My past invaded my present in full blown time warps. Not as memories of yesterday, but a *reliving* of events, and yet it hurt a lot more than I remembered. As a teenager, I referred to my abuse as "no big deal," but I didn't realize then what I had done to survive it. I didn't know about dissociation—how you separate yourself from reality during trauma so you never *feel* it. By dissociating, I learned to avoid the ruinous feelings. I learned to numb myself. To pretend. To hide the repetitive, painful truths from everyone so I could be perceived as normal. So I would be liked and accepted. So I wouldn't hurt anyone else. I deserved the pain, after all. I had no problem with hurting *me*.

3

HELP IS HARD TO FIND

My doctor, my family, and even Mike pressured me to get help, but the idea nauseated me. Therapy was a scam. I knew that for certain. I also knew that all therapists are alike. I based this on the three or four morons Child Services forced me to chat with as a teenager. I'd walk into their cold offices with their academic plaques on the wall, and bookcases packed with psychology books and encyclopedias, and not be at all impressed. If I'm divulging my darkest secrets to you, you'd better *care about me.* Not treat me like just another name in the appointment book, or another paycheck; and yet, I always felt that way. The first was the worst. He didn't just treat me like a number; he treated me like a guinea pig in a laboratory.

His name was Harold Lynch, PhD. I saw him following the one incident ever to be exposed: the molestation by my stepfather, Ron. Even then, having no experience with therapists, I despised the idea of spilling my guts to a stranger; especially about something as vile as someone touching me where they shouldn't. I'd already been forced to talk once about what my stepfather did the day a mysterious source brought the incident to light. A surviving freshman in high school, I sat in class taking a test when two police officers and a faculty member entered the classroom. They whispered something to the teacher, whose eyes quickly landed on me.

"Juanima? Will you come up here, please?" He spoke in a hushed voice, as if to avoid attention from the class. Right. Two cops walk into a classroom, and the kids just go about their business? I don't think so. The moment they walked in, the kids locked on and looked around, wondering who was busted. Now every eye scrutinized me, and I sat frozen, too terrified to budge. The teacher waved me forward urgently and told me to grab my things. As I inched up the aisle, the whispering among my classmates began.

The men flanking me walked silently through the halls. I held my breath, wondering if I'd done something wrong; clearly I was in trouble, and the last to know about it. When we reached the front office, they led me into a small conference room. There, a group of blank faces stared at me; adults I didn't recognize. One woman asked me to sit down. She introduced everyone around the table—people from child services, police, and others whose business I don't recall. I slid into the one empty chair at the table, plumb scared.

"Juanima," she said, "someone notified the police that you've been sexually abused."

Sexually abused? My lungs froze. The words struck like a slap in the face; my cheeks flamed hot as embers. I averted my eyes to a spot on the table and felt the burning gaze of a dozen adults weighing on me. *How did they know?* I had told only one person about what had happened: my best friend, Amy. Today, I understand the importance of telling; but when you're in the middle of the nightmare, and it's exposed without your knowledge, it feels like betrayal. I thought about the words my stepfather had hissed into my ear, *Keep this a secret or people will get hurt.* Not only was the secret out, but it seemed as though it'd made the front page news, and they may as well have placed me naked under the headline. I shivered in my chair like a frightened rabbit.

The woman broke the silence by saying I needed to tell everyone in the room what had happened.

Every. Single. Detail.

I shrunk down further in my chair. My mouth hung open as I stared at the faces around me, all leaning in, awaiting my account of what had happened. Thoughts raced through my mind: *Why do I need to tell? Couldn't I just tell one person instead of the whole lot of you? I don't know any of you! Why would I tell you anything? How can I possibly say out loud, the shameful things my stepfather did to me?*

As my silence lingered, the woman urged me again saying it was necessary that I share the story with them. Important, so they could help me. *Help me?* Their faces loomed in front of me, intimidating, and judging. All I wanted was someone's hand to hold. Someone I knew, who could stand beside me and tell me everything was okay. Instead, I felt like a cornered mouse with no escape from the sharp-clawed alley cats surrounding me—a very lonely place to be.

The longer I sat there, the more frightened I became of these people, so I told. Painfully, tearfully, every detail, knowing my life was over. I believed Ron would follow through with his threat; but luckily, I didn't have to see him again after that day. I know now that abusers regularly use threats like that to keep the victim silent. Ron didn't go to prison for abusing me, but was put on probation, forbidden to return to the house or see me. I let my guard down, replete with relief, until I learned I would have to see a therapist.

Sitting in front of Dr. Lynch, I watched him flip to a blank page of his legal-sized, yellow tablet, and scribble notes about me. I wondered what he could be writing *already*. I scanned his office, taking everything in. His desk dominated the center of the small room, with the door just four quick steps to my right. For some reason, I felt that was important. Behind him, plaques, diplomas, and pictures checkered the wall, and bookcases stood crammed with psychology titles and encyclopedias. Then I saw the window seat. Against the far left wall of the room, a half-hexagon of three, tall, rectangular windows framed a thick, floral cushion, and donned curtains to match. From that vantage point, three or four stories up, I could see a landscape of plush grass, trees, and people strolling along the sidewalks. It looked peaceful out there. I imagined sitting in that window seat, gazing, getting lost in glorious silence and dreams of a better life. Dr. Lynch cleared his throat, drawing my attention back to him.

"Do you know why you're here?" he asked, pen ready.

Do I know why I'm here? I thought. *Uh—to paint my nails?* It was a stupid question, revealing first off that he considered me an imbecile. Or, perhaps the question merely gauged my mental clarity. In my mind, I groaned loudly. I could think of a thousand places I'd rather be. I so badly wanted to forget the incident ever happened, but I knew I had to cater to this man with a degree.

"I was abused," I said. But of course, he wanted the details. I didn't know this man, and yet he, like the alley cats at the school, expected me to dump out my most sacred, shameful, gut-wrenching secret like a bowl of candy. Didn't they realize that telling means blame, ridicule, and rejection? But Dr. Lynch said he wanted to help me. Funny, I didn't remember anyone *asking* if I needed help. Nobody knew, but I'd been abused before Ron ever laid a hand on me, and I handled those incidents just fine by myself.

Dr. Lynch said we would be meeting several times over the next six months, so it would behoove me to cooperate.

I stared bitterly at his legal pad. I felt like a puppet; but I knew if I wanted this therapeutic nightmare to end, I had no choice but to talk. By the session's end, I was numb from the spilling.

At the second visit, he began prying into a room inside my soul that I locked up as tight as a zoo after hours. A room that even I didn't enter. The room of *feelings*. The floor and walls of that room were unstable, and I never felt safe there. The room bulged with the painful things from my childhood that I could neither articulate nor express. The deadly secret of things unspoken lurked in every corner. But Dr. Lynch knocked at the door now, and begged me to trust him with the contents of that room. I couldn't possibly. No one got in there. Ever. I wavered and manipulated the conversation until the end of the session, but I sensed his relentlessness to get inside. I knew he would try again at the next session, and the session after that. Eventually, his persistence gave me cause to test him.

"Tell me how you felt when Ron molested you," he asked at a subsequent session.

I blinked. I hated that word: *Molest.* And now he wanted to know how I felt about it? The thought overwhelmed and confused me. I'd never tried to scrutinize or vocalize my feelings about being abused. Feelings automatically went into the Feeling Room. So when I actually tried to access it for Dr. Lynch, there wasn't just one feeling, but a dark tornado of them. Maybe I could try to give him just one. I pulled out the single word that felt the strongest.

"Angry," I said. "I felt angry."

He furrowed his brow and leaned back in his chair. Tapping his pencil on his chin, as if I'd said something confusing, he tilted his head and said, "You felt angry?"

"Yes," I said.

"Well… you shouldn't have felt *that* way."

His words stunned me. This quack in front of me, whom I just trusted with sacred feelings, told me in seven words that anger was wrong. That my feelings from the molestation *were wrong.* In seven words, he upset the core of my belief system in regards to feelings when mistreated by others. In seven words, I lost my ability to perceive how abuse should make me feel, and I decided right then that I would never tell anyone again. My ability to trust my own feelings shattered then, and whatever control I had with Dr. Lynch dissolved. He knew everything.

By the end of six months, I had a fierce desire to be done with Dr. Lynch. At our final session, what I thought would be a "Goodbye. I hope you have a good life," turned into something else entirely. As I entered his office, I noticed more chairs than usual. I assumed they were left over from a previous session. As I sat down in the chair closest to the window seat, he asked me how I was. I shrugged, not about to make the mistake of telling him my feelings. No doubt those would be wrong, too.

"Well," he said, "it's been six months, and we're at a crossroads. The courts have said that Ron can move back into the house again, but it's up to you whether or not he comes back. Can you tell me how you would feel about that?"

I stared in shock. I couldn't have heard him right. My brain remained fastened to the words: *Ron can move back in.*

"I—I'm sorry. What did you say? He's coming back?"

Dr. Lynch explained that Ron had served his six months of parole, and would be allowed to move back in if I felt I were no longer in danger, and if I were not afraid of him. I cannot even conceive a legal system that places the burden of that decision on a child's shoulders. Or maybe it was solely the doing of Dr. Lynch. I never had given him my trust, and with scrupulous reason. But what child wouldn't be terrified of their abuser? How could a child determine whether or not the abuser would do it again?

He sighed, annoyed with my silence, but I didn't care. I hadn't once—even for one moment—considered that he would come back to live with us. I thought of my mother. During the six months of Ron's probation, she'd acquired a silent misery. Neither she, nor my siblings, talked with me about the abuse during his absence, so I stuffed the tornado of feelings into the Feeling Room. I perceived my mom's tears and sorrow as missing Ron. I couldn't understand it either, remembering the time I swear I heard him strike her behind their bedroom door. I worried about her, but it seemed not having him there made her unhappy. I didn't want to destroy her chance at happiness.

What I didn't realize was that she was a victim, too. People often carry down the teachings of their parents, and what my mom learned from her family is that you don't talk about abuse. You bury it, move on, and forget it happened. You start telling yourself you're fine, that what happened to you didn't really matter. But it matters. It matters very much. It poisons you and eats away at your self-worth. It enables you to fall into dysfunctional relationships, and the tragedy is that the poison of abuse deceives you into believing you don't deserve better than that. You avoid the feelings of brokenness inside, because you just want to be loved. My mom was unconsciously living out the abuse of her past by taking him back; settling for a version of the love she so desperately wanted. She also believed I *really was* okay. I wore my mask too well.

As Dr. Lynch tapped his fingers, waiting for an answer, I made a decision. I would fix this now. I would make it better for my mom.

"No," I whispered.

"Excuse me? I couldn't quite hear you." He leaned forward.

I shuddered saying the words. "No, I'm not afraid, and I don't think he'll do it again. He can move back in." Oh, how I wanted to escape from the room and fast-forward my life to the possibility of some sense of normal. I couldn't stand this. I could hardly contain the chaos inside me, but I needed to maintain the outer neutral façade a little longer.

He repeated my answer aloud, just to clarify, and then stood from his desk. "Okay, then," he said, and walked around the desk to the door. "Just sit tight."

I didn't know why he left the room, but I didn't like it. As I sat alone, the pit in my stomach grew. When he walked through that door again, he had behind him my sister, my mom, and Ron. I gasped, suddenly ripped apart at the shock of seeing my abuser without warning. I had not seen him since the day, six months earlier, when the police pulled me from my classroom; and here, he walked right in and sat down in the chair next to me. I shook my head at Dr. Lynch because I had no words. I thought, surely he'll see the fear on my face. The expression that so clearly states, *Get him away from me! Get me the hell out of here! I am so not okay with this!* But he didn't. He folded his hands and looked at me.

"Okay, Juanima," he smiled. *Did he enjoy this?* "Please repeat to your family what you said to me earlier."

I looked at my mom and sister, who smiled at me tenderly, and then returned my stare to Dr. Lynch. "What?" I asked in disbelief.

He sighed. "What you just said to me before your family came in. I just need you to repeat that to your family here for the record. Just say it out loud."

He had no idea what he was asking. It had been easy to lie to the therapist, but repeating that to the face of my own abuser was like telling a pathological liar you believed he would never lie again. How could I tell the man who had damaged me, ruined me, inflicted pain and shame on me, that I felt he was okay anyway? Why would I deny my right to a happy life without the terror of his presence in it? I honestly believed that the words I had said to Dr. Lynch would not lead to him actually coming back, because I didn't think my mom would allow it. But here we sat in this stifling office, and I could not lie now. His very presence in the room made me want to vomit. His large frame and cold, deceptive eyes terrified me.

"I—I can't," I trembled uncontrollably.

Dr. Lynch shook his head. "You just told me—Just repeat the words you said, Juanima."

My mom looked sympathetically at me and said, "Just say the words, honey."

Cris followed right behind her, "Just say it, Nima. You can say it. It's okay."

Now I understand they didn't know *what* I had said to Dr. Lynch. They wanted me to tell the truth—my truth—whatever that was. But at the time, I felt they were siding with the therapist, telling me to "just say it." *Just say the words!* For the first time, I glanced at Ron. He couldn't look me in the eye, but I didn't want him to. He stared down at his hands, folded in his lap. The butterflies in my stomach transformed into raging elephants, barreling up to my chest. Sweat formed on my brow and palms. Both my mom and Cris continued urging me to "say it, just say it," and I blew.

"No!" I screamed. "I can't!" I bolted from my chair to the window seat, leaping onto the cushion like a caged animal. I pounded at the windows, desperate to jump out. Oh God, I wanted out. I groped for a latch, but when I could not open the window, I curled into a ball and rocked, sobbing, on the pillow. Then I disappeared, as I had learned to do many times before when things got to be too much.

Ron moved back in, and though he didn't hurt me again, he ignored me. I felt invisible in my own house. He made sure of that.

I learned many things from Dr. Lynch. I learned therapists could not be trusted. I learned I needed to lie and finagle in order to get the result I wanted. I learned they didn't actually care about me as a human being with pain and hurts; they just wanted to get in my head and manipulate my thoughts and beliefs. I would not let that happen ever again. The ensuing therapists I had to see marched into my life like soldiers of a psychological brigade, all uniform in function. They gave the same textbook answers and asked the same questions. I could read every one of them like the book they quizzed me from. They didn't care about me. Not really. They tried to get the truth, but they cared so little, they never once questioned my lies. I became skilled at lying, just to get out.

"Do you ever think about suicide?" Some would ask.

"Geez, no. Look—what he did was awful, but I'm over it. I really just want to get on with my life. I'm fourteen. I have things to do."

"Okay then. You seem fine to me."

I deceived them all too easily. Every therapist asked about feelings, and if I had symptoms of depression, but my adeptness at smiling and donning "the mask" fooled them all into believing the abuse didn't affect me all that much. And yet, it did affect me. Deeply. Thoughts of suicide tiptoed in and took residence in my everyday thoughts, but I couldn't tell them that. I brimmed with anger, hatred, and feelings of betrayal, but I never trusted them with that information. I spent hours in the night crying the pain out, but revealing that would mean more time with *them*. No way. I resolved that I would never see a shrink again; not if I could help it. They were all frauds, and a barrier between me and a peaceful life. A life of my choosing. A life of forgetting the past.

Now, despite the pressure from Mike and those around me, I purposed to delay therapy as long as possible, convinced I could fix myself as I had in the past. But things started happening. Physical things that caught me off guard and frightened me.

My first panic attack came in September of 2004. The sharp pain in my chest, accompanying a suffocating grip on my airways, and a rapid flush of sweat and dizzying threat of unconsciousness. *I'm having a heart attack!* I thought. I couldn't catch my breath. I thought I was going to die, but when I didn't, I went to see Dr.

Hogan. Waiting in the exam room, my preoccupation with my panic symptoms made me forget about the cuts on my arms as the nurse raised my sleeve to take my blood pressure. A gasp escaped both of our mouths simultaneously, but neither of us said a word, nor made eye contact. She left the room, and when Dr. Hogan entered moments later, I feared the worst again: *a padded room.*

"What you had was an acute panic attack, Juanima," she said as she settled onto the dark gray upholstered stool. "It's very common for someone with post-traumatic stress disorder." She went on to describe the symptoms of panic attacks and warned that I may experience them more frequently if my PTSD symptoms worsened. I nodded, thinking I might actually get away with not discussing my self-imposed injuries. No such luck.

"Do you want to tell me about your arms?" her expression was impersonal. She was not my friend. I didn't want to talk about cutting with *anyone*—especially someone who couldn't care less. No one understood this painful, private act. A deep humiliation rushed in.

"It helps me deal with the pain of everything," I said. "The flashbacks, nightmares, and memories. I did it as a teenager to cope, but I know it's not a healthy thing to do. Don't worry. I'll stop."

She typed something into the computer, and I tried, unsuccessfully, to see it. After a long volley of her questions and my evasive answers, she shrugged and asked to see me again in two weeks. She needed to know how the new medication affected me, wanted to be certain I stayed loyal to therapy visits—the therapy which I had not actually started—and had I followed through with seeing a psychiatrist? I explained I hadn't found one yet, but I was looking. While she spoke, the computer screen went into sleep mode, and she left without shutting down my records. Once alone, I quickly brought the computer to life and read through her notes and the long list of diagnoses.

"Anxiety; depression; post-traumatic stress disorder; self-mutilation; panic attack, acute; borderline personality disorder." At first, I was shocked by the long list, and then my eyes narrowed on the last diagnosis: borderline personality disorder. I had no idea what it was, so I went straight home to learn.

I've had a love for research ever since my middle-school years, when my dad let me assist him on his jobs as a real estate appraiser. I learned the ins and outs of finding facts; and now, if I wanted answers, I knew how to find them. However, I never anticipated getting my fill with PTSD, and now borderline personality disorder. If a doctor diagnosed me with something, I wanted to make sure it was correct. I spent the rest of the day, and the day following, researching every single issue my new doctor said I had. All of them seemed blatantly correct except borderline personality disorder. That didn't seem to fit at all. She had taken the one correlating symptom—self-mutilation—and plastered a scarlet letter to my chest with it. The list without it distressed me enough. I certainly didn't need a label-happy doctor.

๛

Despite my determination to stay clear of therapists, it become frighteningly obvious to me that I would have to see one sooner or later. The symptoms I faced with PTSD brought fear and overwhelming feelings of shame I just couldn't bear to admit. I hated seeing a doctor every two weeks to discuss those symptoms, but I certainly didn't want to rehash the past with a desk-bound robot that didn't care about me. More than anything, I just wanted to deal with this alone, as I always had. But even I couldn't deny that things were different this time. The pain I felt during the years I actually lived through the trauma paled in comparison to the pain I experienced now. PTSD felt like an entity all its own, intent on killing me slowly with terror, threatening to throw the door of the Feelings Room wide open. It took a growing effort to keep that door closed, and it weakened me. As much as I loathed admitting it, I needed help. PTSD was bigger than me.

I found a directory of therapists in my area, and highlighted a few that seemed to match my needs. I chose which one to call based on the portrait by their listing, whether they looked caring or not.

The first therapist wasn't taking any new patients. I told the second one my story, my symptoms, and with great trepidation, admitted my self-harm. She said she was sorry, but couldn't help me. *Wait—what? You don't even know me*, I thought. *And it's your job to help people!* I stared at the photo of the third therapist I had chosen, feeling resistance to dial. What if she said the same thing? Telling my story and admitting my self-harm once exhausted me. I didn't have the energy to do it again. I dialed anyway and left a message on her voicemail. I was startled when my phone rang back so quickly.

After she introduced herself, I took a deep breath and started from the beginning. My voice quivered as I answered her questions, but a ray of promise came through the phone when she validated my fear and the difficult time I must be having. That broke the gate of tears. I'd needed to hear those words. In her empathy, I felt hope and a connection, and felt willing to give her a chance. It was not to be.

"I know you are struggling with so much, Juanima, and if you keep looking, you'll find someone who can give you the guidance and counseling you deserve. I'm just afraid it's not me." She went on to explain I needed a therapist with expertise in trauma and PTSD, but I heard nothing more. I wept and could not respond to her soft-spoken rejection. I heard the underlying message loud and clear: *You're not normal. You're out of my league. Your issues are too much for me to handle. You're defective. You're not worth helping.*

I didn't call any more therapists, and I wept again when Mike came home from work, reliving the rejection as I told him what had happened.

❧

When my dad asked about my search, I became irate. "There is no search anymore, Dad. They all rejected me. I don't want to go through that anymore."

He tried to encourage me not to give up. "You gotta kiss a few frogs before you get your prince, or… you know what I mean. Your therapist." He chuckled at his own joke. Then he got an idea. He had been seeing a psychiatrist, Dr. Kirkland, over the years for attention deficit disorder, and he thought highly of him. He would call him and get back to me. Maybe I could see him.

As it turned out, having two patients within the same family made Dr. Kirkland uncomfortable; however, he gave my dad the name of a colleague whom he both respected and admired, Dr. David Peschel. I wrote the name down and taped it on my desk, avoiding it for a full week before making the call. I dreaded that call more than a root canal.

I waited until the house was empty, and brought the phone to the table. The moment I sat down, the tightness crept into my chest, making it difficult to breathe. I thought of not calling, and then thought of the consequences of that. Nobody said this would be easy, but I didn't know it would require relentless courage and determination. I didn't feel I had any of that anyway, but I needed help. I had finally accepted that.

My hands trembled as I dialed the number. I managed to tell the receptionist why I needed an appointment, and that I had been referred by Dr. Kirkland. She scheduled me two weeks out.

On the way to see Dr. Peschel, I belted out songs on the radio to distract me from the panic rising in my chest. I tried to forget about where I was going, or else I feared I wouldn't make it there. The drive lasted a long thirty minutes.

In a small building nestled amidst tall trees and a quiet lot, I waited for my appointment in one of the three wooden chairs by the front door. The ten-foot square lobby, painted in dark oak, held a quaint little console against a wall with enchanting countryside paintings above it. A hallway stretched out in front of me, and a tall staircase at my right. My hands shook, so I shoved them into my coat pockets. My hands had never shaken so much in my life! When I heard footsteps descending the stairs, I knew they were for me. *This is it*, I thought. *Get ready to spill.*

I sat before Dr. Peschel like a small child. I hadn't thought ahead of time what to say, but I needed his help. So I shared every excruciating detail, looking at him only when his eyes averted from me to his legal pad. He seemed amiable, though, and I could tell he listened as I agonized over my story. I told him of years of abuse as a child, including multiple rapes by different people; all of this followed by almost fifteen years of a happy life, a fulfilling marriage and the birth of a daughter. Then came a second daughter, PTSD, nightmares, panic attacks, and cutting—the hardest thing to admit. My stomach knotted with shame, but he didn't shift in his seat, or wince, or grimace. He took notes. I talked for a full hour while he interjected soft-spoken questions.

I asked him about borderline personality disorder, and explained how my doctor had diagnosed me with it. His face went cock-eyed, "No, you don't have that. Some doctors see a patient who cuts and immediately diagnose them with BPD; but you have no other symptoms. You're not borderline. Not even close."

I sighed with relief, but still couldn't help but wait for the words, *I can't help you.*

At the end of our session, he said, "You've been through a lot, Juanima, and I think I can help you. Would you be interested in me handling medications for you as well?"

"Yes!" I perked up immediately. I actually felt excited at his proposal. The medications had been so frustrating for me, and judging by his questions alone, I felt Dr. Peschel knew more than the doctor who had been placing me on one trial after another. A comfort fell over me. Dr. Peschel not only believed me and accepted my story, but he offered me the whole-meal deal. He promised to counsel me and manage my medications, too.

As I left his office, I felt hope for the first time. He had validated me, listened to me, and never belittled or judged me. Perhaps all therapists were not alike.

౼

The next week, I received a letter from Dr. Peschel in the mail. It stated that he could *not* help me and that I might be better served at The Anxiety Clinic in Tigard, Oregon. The letter fell from my hands. In a panic, I picked up the phone and called his secretary asking to speak with him. He was with a patient. I asked the secretary about the letter, knowing she had typed it, and said there must be some mistake. In his office, he had offered to continue seeing me and manage my medications. She said no, that he had decided later that he was not suitable for me. He would not be seeing me again, and then she hung up without saying goodbye.

I gripped the phone in my hand even after I heard the dial tone. I couldn't believe what had just happened. I felt betrayed, shunned, and rejected once again, but I knew I had to get back on the horse immediately or I'd give up.

It took an immense amount of courage to call The Anxiety Clinic, but I did. At least Dr. Peschel had referred me somewhere. I gulped my pride and once again spilled my story and symptoms to a therapist on the phone. I ended with the self-harm, and that is what seemed to separate me from a "normal" person with "normal" anxiety. The line went silent, and then she said, "I'm afraid I can't help you with those issues, dear. But I can transfer you to someone who might."

She put me on hold and transferred me to another therapist in the clinic, and again, I had to repeat my story, my symptoms, and the self-harm. I could not hold it back, as much as I wanted to, because if I was going to brave seeing another therapist, I had to lay it all out on the table. The second therapist went silent, too, and repeated almost verbatim what the first had said, "I'm sorry, honey. I just can't help you with those issues, but... I have someone else here who I think can."

Oh my God... are you kidding me? I can't do this again! I can't tell my story again! The tears were like stones in my throat, making it difficult to speak. "Can you please tell her what I told you? I've already spoken to one other person before you. This is really hard."

"I'm so sorry, hun," she said. "I can just transfer you to her line."

The stones in my throat burned with the threat of a tidal wave. *I can't do this. I can't tell my story one more time. Just hang up*, I thought. But then I imagined my girls, and remembered I was doing this for them, too. Tears of exhaustion crept up and spilled out. I didn't have the strength to continue, and I couldn't take any more rejection. My thumb hovered over the OFF button when I heard her voice on the other end.

"Yes, Mrs. Hiatt, how can I help you today?" I dropped my head and brought the phone back to my ear, but I hung on the brink of emotional collapse. "Hello?" She said.

"Yes... I'm here." I choked down the tears.

"It's okay, honey, just tell me what's going on." She heard the pain in my voice, and tried to be comforting.

"I'm sorry," I quivered. "It's just that I've talked to two other people there already, and nobody seems to be able to help me. I don't think you can either."

"Why don't you give it a try, dear?" Her soothing voice made me hang on.

But I couldn't breathe, and the panic had already numbed my face and hands.

"Can you give it a try, dear?"

I shook my head, trying so hard not to crumble into pieces right then; but the great "what if" dangled like a carrot in front of me. *What if she was the one?* Through staggered breaths, stifled tears and a numb face, I told my story again. I talked about my symptoms. I mentioned the self-harm.

"Oh, I see," she said. I could hear a pen tapping on the desk. She stammered and paused, and I knew what that meant. "I'm so sorry, sweetie. I really am. But I'm afraid your issues are just too heavy for this clinic. But listen, let me give you—"

Click.

The dam gave way, and emotions exploded. Sobbing at the table, I held my stomach as it jarred with intense feelings of worthlessness and shame. All these people, sitting behind their desk with the job of helping people like me, and yet I was too much for all of them. *I am too bad, too messed up, beyond helping. I'm a lost cause.* Dissenting thoughts raced through my mind. *I really am as bad as my abusers said. I am so bad I cannot be helped. I am not normal.*

My case belonged in the "extreme" category, among the unfit and unworthy. I could not understand these professionals who were supposed to help. Being "out of their league" deeply contrasted my belief that my abuse was insignificant. I had minimized it drastically to survive it, but the horrors I relived day to day now seemed too horrible for anyone to help me with. I didn't understand, and I decided I wouldn't be calling anyone else.

ॐ

Back in Dr. Hogan's exam room, I broke into tears when she questioned me about therapy. I told her about my visit with Dr. Peschel and his subsequent letter. I told her of my fruitless and rejecting calls to The Anxiety Clinic. I said apparently, my case is too difficult for anyone to handle.

"That is unacceptable!" Dr. Hogan shouted and pointed her finger. "I'm going to call him and find out what the story is, and then I'm going to get you another appointment." She huffed as she left the room.

I didn't want another appointment. I would only feel embarrassed to sit in front of him again. But maybe she was right, and I appreciated her marching to my defense. Dr. Hogan returned several minutes later saying she'd left a message with the secretary, and for me to sit tight. Dr. Peschel was with a client but would return the call shortly. I had my doubts.

After waiting for a full hour unattended in the exam room for that return call, I rushed out of the clinic without saying goodbye. The piling of rejection on my spirit was too much to take.

Dr. Hogan refused to remove the BPD diagnosis unless I had a letter from Dr. Peschel stating I did not have it. Dr. Peschel would not write the letter unless I came in for a visit, but he refused to see me again. I received no letter, and no removal of the diagnosis, so I left Dr. Hogan, too. I was tired of getting jerked around.

In the bitter cold of December 2004, I relented to make another go of it alone.

4

DENIAL, LOSS
AND DISCOVERY

I can count on one hand the friends who have truly known me in my life. Friends like Claire. She was the wife of my husband's best friend, Tim, a solid friendship of twenty-five years when I met Mike in 1994 and fell in love. A year and a half later, Mike asked for my hand in marriage, mentioning several times that Tim and Claire were "part of the package." Meaning, I'd better accept them or else there would be no us. I'm not sure if the threat was real, but it didn't matter. I adored Claire. In a short period of time, she became my best friend.

For my twenty-fifth birthday, she treated me like royalty for an entire day. During the quiet morning at her house, she gave me one gift after another either wrapped with a bow, or through some act of love. I eyed her suspiciously, however, when I opened a shimmery box that contained a stunning sheath dress in a deep, rich burgundy—my favorite color.

She smiled. "It's for something special later. Today you're getting pampered."

I'd never before experienced Claire's idea of pampering. She made us both a brunch of ham sandwiches and wine, and afterwards, gave me a manicure and massaged my hands and arms—a heavenly treat. Other than feeding myself my own lunch, Claire didn't allow me to lift a finger.

I must've looked like a little kid in her jet-powered Jacuzzi tub, with mountains of stiff, peach-fragranced bubbles heaped around my face and body, but soaking in that healing steam for an hour made every tension in my body drain away. I had nodded off into blissful dreams when she peeked into the bathroom and said, "Time to get dolled up!"

My legs weak from the heat of the bath, I fumbled humorously into the dress. It fit perfectly, though, and that's saying a lot, considering I usually had to try on a dozen dresses before I found one that fit my curves just right.

When I showed Claire, she smiled, but then frowned. "Something's missing," she said, tapping her chin with her index finger. She went to her dresser and returned with something in her hands. Turning me around, she draped a cream pearl necklace around my neck, and then fastened a matching bracelet around my wrist. She took me into the bathroom to see.

The light reflected against it, giving each pearl a sheen like a rich, custard ocean. Claire sat me in front of the mirror and brushed my hair next. With smooth finesse, she swept up my chestnut-brown, shoulder-length hair into a glamorous updo of waves and cascading tousles. She airbrushed shimmering, neutral tones to my cheeks and eyes. I smiled broadly in the mirror, and looked at her with the gratitude I just couldn't put words to. She stood behind me and placed her hands on my shoulders, nodding, pleased with her handiwork.

I had no idea what was still in store for me when the doorbell rang. A flash of excitement spread across Claire's face. "It's time!"

She went before me down the stairs to answer the door, and of course, she wanted me to wait to come down, as *I* was also a surprise to someone else. As she pulled open the door, there stood Mike. The butterflies darted madly across my stomach at how striking he looked. His layered, sandy-blonde hair and brilliant blue eyes like a summer sky. His genuine smile that weakened my knees. Claire's waving hand caught my attention. I had been too enamored with

Mike to remember to come down the stairs! I giggled, making a less than elegant descent.

"Wow..." He exhaled, eyes poring over me. My face flushed at the attention. I felt like the newest addition to an upscale store window. Then I noticed Tim standing behind Mike, and he leaned out to the side and flashed a wide grin. Tim was dear to my heart as well. Every fall, Mike, Tim and I went elk hunting along the West Coast, and we grew close, sharing the relaxing atmosphere of nature, and time spent together joking and laughing. At the end of a day of hunting, we'd settle back at the cabin and change into comfy clothes. For dinner, I'd bring out a hot batch of my dad's famous beef goulash—a favorite from my childhood years—and we'd kick back by a cozy fire, reminisce of our adventure that day, and plan for the next.

Now, Tim clearly enjoyed being a part of a secret plan. Mike's eyes sparkled as he extended his hand, offering me a delicate, beautiful wrist corsage and a kiss on the cheek. My cheeks were already sore from the grin that seemed to be glued to my face.

"Time to go," Claire chimed.

She wouldn't tell me where, but already, I was beaming from every angle. I glanced appreciatively at Claire. *This was all for me*, I thought. I'd never experienced such doting. They kept our destination a secret until it became obvious. As we drove towards Mt. Hood, passing snow-covered peaks and forests, I squealed when we turned towards the Timberline Ski Lodge. There, Tim and Claire treated Mike and me to an amazing dinner, followed by pictures on a high deck overlooking magnificent landscapes of snow-covered mountains and lush, green forests. We stayed until late evening, and stargazed across the black sky that sparkled like rhinestone-covered velvet. Swirly-white waves of the Milky Way stretched across the darkness, making a breathtaking tapestry. I savored every moment, so grateful for this small group of friends who gave me a friendship I'd never known. Claire was indeed remarkable, always turning everyday events into lifetime memories.

Throughout our relationship, I shared some of my past with Claire, but I didn't just volunteer it. I felt no reason to. I believed I had dealt with it, and left it in the past. I realize now, however, that I shared things without emotional attachment. Real emotions were *never* part of telling. I remember a conversation I once had with a distressed coworker who shared that a friend of hers had just been raped. I was nineteen years old at the time—just one year after the abuse had ended for me. I remember nodding and empathizing, sharing with her that I had been raped, too. She was shocked. "You were? But you seem so normal!"

At the time, I believed I seemed normal because I had healed from the abuse. In reality, I was and always had been disconnected from it emotionally. As a child, I didn't know a name existed for what I did every time a man took my control away from me; when I disappeared from the conscious world and imagined I existed in a safer place, detaching from the pain, terror, and feelings of what was happening. Dissociation kept me alive during those years. It also allowed me to minimize the effects of the abuse. Throughout my life, I didn't believe I had endured any trauma. I could acknowledge the abuse to almost anyone, but the details—the feelings—they remained locked behind a door in the far outreaches of my mind. Putting them there was automatic; an unconscious habit.

I loved Claire. She brought an elegant flair to everything she touched, and I trusted her with my heart. I assumed we'd still be bonding as old ladies, sitting in our rocking chairs sipping raspberry iced tea. But I didn't expect PTSD, and it exploded my past and present wide open. It wasn't just a hard time—it was a living hell—and I did not *choose* who would catch me when I fell into the fire. I didn't know it wouldn't be Claire; but instead, someone I barely knew.

I met Traci just one month before Jordan's birth. She spoke at the annual women's retreat through my church, which I attended at Cris's urging. In previous years, I'd purposely stayed away from women's retreats, never imagining I would find any comfort or sense of belonging in a group of blubbering, vulnerable, whiny women. I felt uncomfortable in that type of environment, and had no plans to be part of it. I had no intention of allowing myself to be vulnerable. Not with anyone. Not ever. Nor did I want to talk about my past or other emotional issues, let alone hang out with one hundred other women doing it. One-on-one, sure. I'm an excellent listener and have loads of compassion for people in pain. But one hundred at a time? Not for me. Not when I knew I would be pressured to follow suit.

I don't know how she talked me into going. I joked that she tricked me somehow; but the truth is, I liked a lot of those women from the church, and Cris painted the retreat as "a fun break from the craziness of life, and relaxation with good friends." *Okay*, I thought. That didn't sound too bad. Once there, though my walls were up, I gradually began doubting the stigma I had placed on retreats. I actually had fun, and couldn't stay away from the gym cabin. I spent hours playing volleyball—the favorite game of my youth—despite being eight months pregnant and donned in massive overalls to accommodate my protruding belly. I still had my "killer serve," as my teammates affectionately called it.

I also found that sitting in those dreaded small groups listening to other gals share the deep scars of their lives actually captivated me. By the end of the retreat, I can unashamedly say I was one of those blubbering, vulnerable, whiny women. Though I never peeled more than the top layer, it impacted me to reveal even a little bit of my insecurities and still be accepted and loved. I thanked Cris profusely for getting me to go.

I connected with Traci immediately, inspired by the presentations she gave that seemed to hook and lure me in to the love of Christ for broken people, reminding me how much I needed Him in my life. She further moved me when, in private, she revealed her own insecurities about speaking that weekend, and her deep desire to minister to the women there. I admired her genuine and humble heart, and assured her that she had indeed touched many women, me included.

I believe strongly that attending the retreat that weekend was part of God's plan all along, because only God knew the dark and terrifying battle coming my way, and that I would never be able to survive it alone. He also knew that Mike loved me immensely, but he would not have the capacity to walk with me through my past. At the time, neither Traci nor I understood the unprecedented relationship we would have with each other; I simply felt appreciative to have a new friend.

Later, when Jordan's birth thrust me into the merciless claws of PTSD, Traci proactively tried to understand the dark forces infringing upon my world. In the early stages—the first two years, specifically—changes in me were drastic; after all, I had suddenly found myself in the face of trauma. I relived moments of rape and abuse almost on a daily basis, except I could no longer use the gift of dissociation to block it out. PTSD forced me to *see it and feel it.* Forced me to re-experience every unspeakable moment. Forced me to feel the pain that even my body remembered.

Sometimes when the flashbacks came, I reeled from surges of pain through my pelvis, feeling ripped apart, and feeling my spirit disappear as my innocence was stolen... again. And inside, reliving those moments reminded me that I was merely an object for someone else's pleasure. A nothing. An unlovable *thing.* A worthless but pretty tool for the evils of men.

It saddens me now to know those beliefs about myself had always been there, just below the surface. They are the beliefs that many women and men who have suffered from childhood sexual abuse carry deep in their soul, while denying their existence. But when PTSD shattered the protective shield I had held up for nearly fifteen years, those beliefs came rushing to the surface like a bobber released underwater.

The sparkly girl who laughed, who was strong, who found solace and fulfillment in the outdoors and loved the company of friends had become a small, meaningless stone buried at the bottom of a deep cavern, and there I wanted to remain. *Keep me in the dark... let me hide... let me be. Please, leave me alone.* Fear consumed me. I couldn't bear to leave the walls of my home because the world outside offered only angst and uncertainty. Voices, sounds, smells, touch—I could never anticipate what trigger would send me spiraling, running and hiding from the flashbacks that came. A car door slamming, the tone of a voice, the words, the smell of alcohol, of smoke, of a certain kind of soap, of other things I couldn't pinpoint but they would summon the horrors over and over. Like walking through an unfamiliar forest after dark, I existed in a state of fear, afraid of every noise, startled into panic at sudden movements or sounds around me. I avoided turning a corner for fear of whom or what I might walk into. I was never safe. Not even in my own skin.

One particular day, while Mike was away at work, Traci offered to take my girls to her son's baseball game. There would be many little kids there my girls knew. Traci knew they'd have a blast. She also invited me, thinking it would be good for me to get out of the house for a while. Panic struck me instantly in the chest as I imagined the noise... the crowd... the pull for attention from my girls and other kids. Tears burned in my eyes from the idea alone. Despite my inner scream of *"Hell no!"* at the invitation, I struggled with my innate insistence on being polite. I tried to convince myself everything would be okay, but I knew better. My whimpering must have clued Traci in to my struggle, because she let me off the hook. "It's okay, Nima. Maybe next time. Please just take care of yourself." She always understood.

Traci took my girls to the game anyway to give me the gift of solitude and silence, the greatest gift I could hope for. In the stillness of our small house, I grieved. I couldn't wrap my mind around what was happening to me. In the years I had denied my past, I was a happy person, and tried to have a positive outlook on life at all times. I focused on the blessings in my life, and believed in my own power to overcome whatever challenges came my way. But I'd never faced PTSD before.

After Traci left with the girls, I sat on the couch in my living room with the curtains drawn, arms wrapped tight around my knees, and rocked back and forth in the realization that I had no power now. Whatever this was consuming me, crushing my spirit, and feeding me spoonfuls of terror and fear every time I turned around... this dominated me completely. Exhausted, and in the pit of it, I felt alone and ashamed. And like the child enduring the abuse, I couldn't comprehend sharing the truth with anyone. How could I utter the words about being raped, or describe being molested? These were not like the days when I had separated myself from the trauma and could say without emotional attachment that I'd been raped. These mirrored the days I lived the abuse, and in my silent suffering, I felt it. The shame enveloped me.

Not only was I saturated with the repulsion of the memories of the acts themselves, I could not even begin to touch the guilt I felt for my inability to *stop this*. My behavior appalled even me. I hid the pain as much as possible from my two girls, but there were times I failed. PTSD didn't allow me to just "think positive" and get on with my wonderful life. I couldn't shake it off, or just be happy. I had no choice but to succumb to it, and it became my prison. As the months went on, my family grew more concerned for me, and my husband remained in a perpetual state of confusion over what had happened to the woman he married. Dismayed by this new persona I had taken on of fear, emotional numbness, frequent bouts of tears, depression and yelling, isolation and withdrawal, he stood back, not having a clue about what to make of it, or how to relate to me. Nobody understood the hurricane that had sucked me in, and nobody accepted my withdrawal because of it. It just wasn't comprehensible.

In the throes of this darkness, I could not explain my actions. I did not have the words or the energy to explain anything. Yet I had to try. Everyone who knew me and had a relationship with me expected me to answer the questions: "Why do you want to disappear? Why won't you talk to me about this? Why won't you let me in? Tell me what the hell is wrong with you! Why are you shutting me out?" How could I explain something that I didn't even understand myself? I was plagued with things I couldn't put into words. Pain I couldn't articulate. Pain that nobody could fix or take away anyway. I grieved at all the hurt I caused those around me, but I had no ability to make it better. Their quest for explanations always came back empty. There were no explanations. At least, not yet. I wondered if anyone would be around in my life in five years. I believed in the depths of my broken heart that I just wasn't that lovable anymore. I hurt everyone too much. *Guilt... worthlessness... loneliness... rupturing heart.*

I was so grateful that Traci took my girls to the game that day. I needed time to let the pain be real. It was a heinous mass of emotional knives piercing into me from the inside, and it had a hold on me that day as I sat on the couch listening to the sounds outside my window. The neighbor kids played in the summer sun on the street in front of my house, as they often did. I prayed they wouldn't come knocking on my door looking for Lacey and Jordan. The pain was too intense, even to force a smile for them. I listened for a while, and then decided to peek out. I got to my knees, leaned over the back of the couch, and reached for the curtain. Cupping it in my hand, I pulled it to the side, ever so slightly, when *WHAM!* A fist came right at me, slamming violently into my face. I flew backwards off the couch onto the rug and screamed, crawling into the corner of the sectional on the floor, shrinking as small as I could away... away... screaming for the man to leave me alone.

But I had no injury because there was no fist, and there was no man. But the man existed eighteen years before. When I would not cooperate with his assault on me, he slammed his fist into my face to show he was in charge. Eighteen years before, I was a runaway in Reno, Nevada, hiding in a dirty motel room from the danger he said awaited us right outside. Damon, a proclaimed member of the Italian Mafia, had sworn to protect my friend and me. But he frightened me to the core, and in desperation to leave the room, I pulled the curtain of the window to the side, ever so slightly, to see the danger for myself. And that was the trigger. Pulling the curtain back to see those kids outside triggered a flashback of a horror I had endured eighteen years before, but as concrete and violent as if it were happening in present day.

I buckled on the floor, holding my face, screaming from the intensely real pain and fear. The voice of the man whispered in my ear, "You gonna shut that mouth of yours now, bitch?"

My hands clawed wildly through the air. He was right there, but I couldn't make contact. Against the couch, my body shook and trembled uncontrollably. I sobbed, doubled over onto the floor, moaning in a devouring terror. The iron grip on my chest tightened, and I gasped for air as the panic threatened to pull me into a deep abyss. I had nowhere to hide. The room became a tornado around me, spinning, and my mind reached desperately for someplace safe. *I found it.* My consciousness shifted into a cloudy void, where voices dissipated and anger subsided, and silence became the most beautiful sound. I never wanted to leave that place.

The day disappeared. I don't remember Traci's phone call saying the game had ended, or the hours she kept the girls afterwards. I don't remember the girls coming home; yet by the time they did, I know I had lifted up my mask so they wouldn't think their mother was a freak. I refused to let them see the real me. The monster me.

The powerlessness that accompanied PTSD brought deep despair and frustration. For the first time in my life, I had no control over my mind or the thoughts that resided there. Intrusive memories of trauma did not knock first. They threw the door down and invaded with such force, such a domineering presence, I had no time to prepare for the battle. Like a swift ambush, they swept across my consciousness and seized my control, just as every perpetrator had done while abusing me. I just couldn't take it. My soul screamed desperately for control, and I would do anything to get it back.

In the fall of 2004, I began a desperate fight to produce something in my life that I *could* control. I knew if I didn't, I would deteriorate down to an unrecoverable place. I believed that if I took on a project of some kind, I could beat this thing threatening to destroy me. I had quickly grown to hate PTSD, and became determined to find a distraction. I rationalized that if I immersed myself in something productive, I would survive, and the terrors would go away. I also wanted to prove to the people in my life that I was normal, in hopes that they would relax their efforts to penetrate my world "out of love." So in my desperate plight for stability, I started a jewelry business.

It didn't seem that far-fetched to me. As a creative individual, I discovered that I enjoyed making jewelry, and realized I could do it for others. I could build a website and sell the jewelry online, as well as in local gift shops. I needed to start earning an income to help the family, and a jewelry business seemed like a great idea. The dream unfolded in my mind like a red carpet.

෪

Crafting elegant, colorful jewelry out of Swarovski crystal beads became my headstrong mission to freedom. I believed if I could just saturate myself with the business and commit my whole heart to it, I would be free. Then I could gain control over the fear that gripped my body and mind. *I could gain control again....*

For weeks, I worked around the clock and created a storefront website for my jewelry. I produced over twenty sparkling designs, for most of which I had a bride in mind, weaving clear and aurora borealis crystals alone, or together with white or cream pearls. I also created complementary sets for bridesmaids, available in any color imaginable. The website had professional appeal and eye-catching detail. I poured myself into it, fervently denying the swarm of terrors that still plagued me at night and in moments of silence. The determination within me grew to push it all aside. To push it down.

My husband praised my accomplishments, grateful to see me *living,* and pursuing the healthy task of growing a business for myself. And I was happy! I needed everyone to see I was happy. *The deception, though, above all, was to myself.* I created a webpage on my site titled "About Me," and on it, I wanted to post happy pictures of myself. The only pictures I had like that were pictures that Traci's husband, Sam, had taken of her and me while we sat at their kitchen table in a flurry of childish roughhousing. She tried to make me laugh that day because, at the time, my spirit emanated gloom unless there were cocktails involved. So we indulged in margaritas, which promoted carefree playfulness, smiles, and stomach-jabbing giggles. I posted those pictures on the web page, and beside them, wrote captions of friendship and how important it was to me.

Claire, my dearest and best friend, was not on my mind when I made that website. I had accomplished my goal of making everyone proud of me once again, and though I cherished my new friendship with Traci, it was not the motive for making that page on my website. That page, "About Me," had become a subconscious *front*, so everyone would see me as a "normal, happy, fun person." From the depths of my heart, that was all I wanted to be. I used to be that girl, and I grieved on a daily basis for her, as she slipped away more and more.

I thought I held up my front well, until I received an email from Claire just days after uploading my site. She was crushed over the content of that webpage, and it caught me off guard. Since the page was not really about "friends," I hadn't considered the impact it would have on Claire if she saw it. The content shocked her, as she saw the joy and apparent regard I gave to Traci, while I neglected her and our friendship. Regrettably, she was right, but there was so much more to it... oh, so much more. I *had* neglected her; but sadly, I had aggressively distanced and neglected everyone else in my life as well. This was not intentional, but inevitable, as my mind and soul became increasingly enveloped with emotional numbness, constant fear, dissociation, hopelessness, and overwhelming shame. Nobody could see the invisible storm raging inside me, nor could I open up enough to let them. Consequently, I unwittingly sent many hurtful messages that were far from my truth: I simply had nothing to give. I was falling deep within myself, once again suffering the shackles of abuse.

I could not articulate any of that. How could I, when prior to PTSD my heart always had more room to love and give. Compassion was embedded in my soul, and I looked upon those in relationship with me, and the world, through those eyes. I understood Claire's viewpoint, but how could I make her understand mine? I was not the same person I'd been before. When a cup is full, you cannot build up the cup to make more room. You make more room by pouring the contents out, but I couldn't do that. I would not be able to pour anything out until I could sit down with a therapist and decipher the trauma I had endured as a child; but that knowledge wasn't there yet, and I wanted to address the past like I wanted another hole in my head.

It's nearly impossible to adequately put into words what PTSD feels like, and the impact it has on the mind; so no one close to me understood my desperate battle to cover up the symptoms I endured, and disguise them from the rest of the world. To put on a face that says, "I'm normal." I couldn't simply explain the madness dwelling inside me, or the level of destruction to my heart and soul. I could not escape my pain, but I would have done anything to pretend it didn't exist. I wanted the acceptance and approval from others as a "normal human being"—to be seen as the person I was before PTSD, as opposed to the fragile flower everyone perceived me as. In reality, of course, I *was* fragile. Living in denial did not weaken the symptoms; it merely worked to convince others I was better than I truly was, and it became an obstacle to meaningful relationships and communication.

Happy pictures on a website page were just a front, when inside, the despair eroded my mind, spirit, and body. Though I made attempts to explain my behavior to Claire, and sought understanding, her own sea of confusion continued to swell and boil, and she continued to feel hurt by my choices.

When Halloween drew near, we decided to stay in town with Traci and her family instead of driving the hour to share it with Claire and Tim, as we had always done in the past. I felt the sting from her voice when she expressed her deep disappointment over the phone. In her eyes, it was a personal decision of choosing one over the other, but it had everything to do with the nightmare I lived in. Lacey said she wanted to stay in town that year and trick-or-treat with Traci's kids, which made my decision much easier.

The heart of my travel choices after the onset of PTSD was never based on my friendships. I went where I felt *safe*. Living in a constant state of fear, hypervigilance, and panic, I rarely left the house. I had few places of safety, but I felt understood in those places, and could exist without fear of judgment. I could disappear into the shadows for a while without being questioned or worried about. It wasn't Claire's fault that I didn't feel that with her, but the physical distance between us had become an issue for me. I struggled driving anywhere, or seeing anyone. And the fact that Traci lived less than five minutes away would prove to save my life on more than one occasion.

I hurt Claire by not reaching out to her; but truthfully, I couldn't reach out to anyone, including Traci. I had lost my capacity to reach out. Traci just came. A flower in the ground cannot water itself. In a season of drought, the flower wilts, helpless to the elements inflicted upon it. Unless the gardener comes to it with fresh water and tenderness, it cannot be revived. I barely existed, wilting, struggling to care for myself, let alone my children, my husband, or the household duties. Traci came to me with fresh water, and reminded me that God was working on my behalf, and not to give up. She cleaned my house, and took my girls to do something fun when I could not. She cared for my girls *a lot*. She gave me reminders of God's love by always sending me scriptures that touched my heart and lifted me up. She came in, encouraging me, because during that time I had nothing to give to anyone, *all appearances aside.*

The Perfect Accent, my jewelry business, was simply a means of mental survival. A desperate effort to mask and separate myself from the terrors that resided inside. But for Claire, my unexplained time spent with Traci—and lack of time with her—painted a picture of cruelty and thoughtlessness. She believed Traci was a bad influence in my life, fueling my depression and perpetuating my withdrawal from the world. Others in my life believed this as well. Even Mike, for awhile. I heard things like, "What's happening with you doesn't make sense. This all started right when Traci came into the picture." And, "You're spending a lot of time with Traci, and you're just getting worse and worse."

I endured many confrontations by the people I loved, blaming Traci for my downfall. They asserted that my relationship with her was unhealthy and codependent, that her motives were questionable, and clearly, because of my mental state, I just couldn't *see the truth*.

This enraged me; not only because they were wrong, but when they made unwanted decisions *for* me, they seized my power. Abuse is all about taking power and control from a helpless child—an existence I knew all too well. Now, my friends and family had decided that somehow, my deteriorating mental state was Traci's fault. I explained firmly that PTSD—and the vivid details of my past trauma coursing constantly through my consciousness—caused my depression and withdrawal, but it didn't matter what I said. They felt I was being deceived. They believed Traci drew the memories out of me and made me talk about them, and this resulted in my darkening depression. Traci was an easy scapegoat to explain what nobody else could. It's true that she spent the most time with me. *But she was saving me.* It took time for Mike to see my friendship with Traci kept me above ground, but Claire never saw that.

Neither Mike nor I had ever heard of PTSD, and only later in therapy would I begin to understand the pieces of the puzzle, and make the connection that Jordan's traumatic birth had been the triggering event for the disorder. Early on, nobody knew what had started it, but it coincided with the time that Traci came into my life. The judgment hurt us both, and for a while, I was the only person who saw our friendship as a blessing. She brought understanding, support, and true caring to my devastation. She most certainly was not the cause of it.

In the beginning, Traci took the time to investigate PTSD herself to try to understand what I was going through. She purchased two copies of the book, *The Courage to Heal,* once we realized that the abuse of my past instigated all of my pain. She took one for herself so that she could travel through it with me. She invested herself fully in trying to understand what this disorder was, and why it was causing me to deteriorate.

Over time, I learned a great deal about PTSD. I eventually wrote an email to family members trying to educate them about it, hoping to shed light on my shocking behaviors. I believe it helped some to understand better, but oftentimes when something doesn't organically make sense, it's easier to believe that someone or something tangible is causing the problem. Still, that doesn't change the truth. It didn't change my truth. It simply made it more difficult for me to move forward because of the constant doubts I received from those close to me, and opinions about what I should or shouldn't be doing, and who I should or shouldn't be with.

Then, in November 2004, I received a phone call from Claire. Extremely concerned about my health and my struggle with suicidal thoughts, she believed I should be hospitalized.

"That's not what I need, Claire," I affirmed sternly. "Besides, it's impossible. We don't have the money for something like that, nor do we have the childcare to cover my absence. It's not like Mike could stay home with the girls."

He worked incredibly hard as a self-employed remodeling contractor, but without my income, we had no reserves. We struggled to put food on the table. In addition, I couldn't bear the thought of leaving my family. Despite my emotional concealing and withering spirit, I did whatever it took to protect my girls from my pain. I smiled for them, I hugged them every chance I got, I told them that I loved them, and that Mommy's tears and anxiety were not their fault. I needed them, and they needed me. No, there would be no hospital.

"I hear you, Nima," she replied, "but I think you're wrong. And actually, I've already spoken with your sister about this. She agrees that an intervention is needed. We love you, but we both believe that you cannot make this decision on your own, and we feel it's time to step in."

My anger flared.

"Don't you dare!" I yelled into the phone. "You have no right to step in and do anything! I can make my own decisions!"

"That's just it, Nima," she said in a gentle tone similar to my sister's when she first urged me to see a doctor. "We don't think you can."

My territorial instincts erupted. She not only threatened to commit me somewhere against my will, but I knew it would be for a period of time I would have no control over. No. No! "You will not intervene," I said firmly, "and I will not go to a hospital. I don't need a hospital. I can make my own decisions."

I hung up the phone shaking. Her words planted a deep fear in me that any day, men with a straightjacket would accost me at the front door, and haul me away from my only safe-haven. I thought of my sister, who had threatened the same thing. "It's time to intervene," she'd said. Claire assured me that she just cared about me, and I do believe she loved me and wanted to help. I believe Cris wanted to help, but it seemed to be *their* idea of help... not mine. Not the kind of help I really needed. I needed respect, despite my pain and obvious deterioration. I still needed that, as well as unconditional love and support. Thankfully, the men with a straightjacket never showed.

As time went on, however, the desire to slip away became abundantly real. My thoughts frightened me, and I fantasized about running away to a hospital because I doubted my survival of the constant pain and depression. I loved my children with every fiber of my being, but as I caved beneath the symptoms of PTSD emotionally and mentally, I could not give them what they needed. I simply wasn't capable of it, and the guilt over that consumed me. My vision of hiding within hospital walls was just that: *to hide.* I longed for a place to be alone. I had responsibilities at home that I could not fulfill, reminding me daily of my inadequacies.

Each household task was like being forced to climb a mountain when you're crippled. I did not have the tools or the ability to succeed at it. I'd look at the top of the mountain and it would suddenly stretch out a universe away. The idea of conquering it felt so overwhelming, I would dissociate. It started with my peripheral vision darkening and narrowing in. My chest would tighten, severing my air supply. Numbness would creep across my face, while my vision morphed my surroundings into a distorted haze. The tasks flooded me with panic so intense that I would crumble to the floor in a ball, petrified and frozen, releasing tears of worthlessness.

That mountain was a stack of dishes in the sink, or piles of laundry, straightening up the house, vacuuming the floors, taking a shower, even drying my hair. One simple task was monumental in my trauma-laden mind. If the girls asked me even a basic question like, "Mama, can I play on the computer?" it triggered the same overwhelming anxiety. I lost all capacity to make decisions. Simple, daily living required more of me than I had to give. But I didn't want Mike to leave me—I feared that every day— or become so frustrated that he'd give up on me. So I climbed that mountain, and I tried to answer those questions, but it became more and more difficult.

At that point, I dreamed of being in a hospital. The freedom to feel, and not constantly have to hide my real pain. The isolation, so I could be me, exactly where I was in that moment, and not worry about disappointing anybody, or scaring anybody, or making anybody uncomfortable. To not have to live up to anyone's expectations, which I failed at miserably every day. Yes... the hospital seemed as appealing as a tropical island getaway. I knew it *wouldn't* be a getaway, yet the fact remained that if I were to go, it would be on *my* terms, and no one else's.

The idea of someone "intervening," out of love or not, made my brain scream out in resistance: *Hell no!* I won't let it happen. It'll be a cold day in hell before I let anyone tell me what to do or try to run my life for me. This is *my life!* I'm still here, and if I have enough gumption to keep going through this hell day after day, and stay alive, then I should be allowed to keep going on my own efforts. I'm still alive! I'm still here! Let me fight my fight, and you stay the hell out of it! Everyone just stay the hell out of it!

But I was crumbling into pieces, trying desperately to pick up each piece that fell. I became a marionette whose strings were manipulated by my blazing desire for normalcy and escape from the nightmare I was living. So I fought it, pressing more and more into my jewelry business. Traci and I decided to take an enormous leap and rent a booth at the Portland Bridal Show in January of the following year, 2005. Pushing with an impetuous determination, I submersed myself in creating enough jewelry for the show with Traci's help. I ordered supplies on credit, and Traci gave generously of her time and finances to get us there.

She graciously allowed me to "set up shop" in the spare room of their house, and for the next month, we labored countless hours together designing and producing dozens of jewelry sets. She became my partner, and we dreamed of the success our booth would bring. Thousands of brides-to-be, traipsing along our tables, imagining my sparkling jewelry sets already around their necks, and dangling on their ears and wrists. We visualized the lucent necklaces draped neatly over black velvet easel displays, shimmering under the convention lights with the reflective qualities of Swarovski crystals and pearls. Then the ladies would supply a business lead by entering our contest for a free bridal jewelry set. I couldn't wait.

Yet as I pressed on, a dark turmoil festered and boiled within me. Despite my excitement for the bridal show, the terrors still came galloping across my mind. Flashbacks of violence that seized every nerve, making touch impossible. Visual onslaughts so vivid, they swept me into another reality where pain raged, and sounds around me escalated into screams. The episodes frightened me to the core; and still, I fiercely denied their presence. Instead of sharing my torment with Traci, I put on a smile and said, "This show is going to be amazing." I believed the show would save me, as if I was running a race against PTSD. I thought that once I won that race, PTSD would be the loser, and it would depart from me forever. I had not yet grasped that it was a part of me. There was no race to be won. PTSD had literally altered my brain, changing me forever. I would not be able to depart from it, but over time, I was told, I would learn to face it. To cope with its sinking teeth, and its predictable patterns of destruction. But I wasn't there *yet*.

When the bridal show arrived, Traci and I gushed with vitality. Everyone in my family supported us—especially my husband. I shared breathlessly with him my passion and dream for the business. I had no doubts it would be a success. Traci and I rented a hotel room directly next to the Convention Center, and together, built our booth with breathtaking elegance and regal display. We arranged three rectangular tables in a "U" shape with deep red, satin tablecloths draping to the floor. A white vinyl sign that read, "The Perfect Accent," in a stylish, italicized black font, stretched across the back of our booth. And along the tabletops, dozens of jewelry sets adorned black, velvet easel displays, designed and handcrafted by Traci and myself. The booth beamed like an open crystal cave, bursting with the twinkling reflections of aurora borealis crystals, and mirrors that duplicated and magnified them.

The first day of the show, I stood in the booth wearing a glittering burgundy and black formal gown; accented, of course, with matching crystal jewelry I had designed and crafted myself. I also created a set for Traci to match her stunning gown in midnight blue and black hues. I felt like a star on the red carpet, and Traci dazzled, beaming like a beauty queen.

When the show started, however, I was unprepared both for the enormous crowd, and the impact it had on me. The air around me buzzed loudly like I'd stuck my head in a wasp's nest. The bright lights of the building, though I had appreciated their purpose initially, now pierced my skull and tortured my eyes. The crowd overwhelmed my senses, and though panic crept in, I pushed it down because I absolutely *had* to be on top of this. I *had* to be professional. I *had* to sell jewelry and gain a clientele for my future success. There was no room for PTSD or for weakening.

With everything I had, I pushed through the day. I focused on each individual lady that approached our booth, and with the friendliness and happiness of my yesterdays, attended to each one of them. They always left with a smile, thrilled at the possibility of winning a gorgeous set of bridal jewelry made by The Perfect Accent. Traci and I shared frequent glances of excitement and pride at what we had accomplished. That night in the hotel room, the screams echoed in my head, but I denied the misery that painfully prodded at my spirit, as if I needed to be reminded of its existence. *Thank you very much, but you can disappear now.* I washed it away with several glasses of wine, until I was able to laugh freely and continue to dream of the success of the next day.

But the second day blurred like a faded memory. I slipped through it in a numb state, putting on the face I had mastered. The face that smiled and glowed, that greeted dozens of brides basking in excitement and anticipation of one of the most pivotal moments of their lives; and I could mirror it with my own understanding of what goes into a wedding day, and how The Perfect Accent jewelry would truly make their event memorable and eternal. Somehow, I pressed through again, despite the suffocating crowds, the noise, and hundreds of question-answer sessions that occurred.

When we arrived home, we opened the large, shiny white wooden entry box my husband had lovingly crafted for me, and we pulled out hundreds of entries for the contest. In that moment, fanning the small pieces of paper in my fingers, I felt proud of what we had accomplished. But something dark and foreboding stirred inside, and I felt it rise like bile in my throat.

We did not choose a winner. Nor did I send postcards to all the hundreds of women who didn't win, inviting them to our website store to browse. I didn't make it that far. As stubborn as I am, I know I can't outrun a tsunami. The dark feelings, the fears, the memories and the rage—every symptom of PTSD that I had angrily and resentfully pushed down during the convention came forth in a rush, crushing me like a herd of raging bulls.

I sat alone on my living room floor with the white box in front of me when my control began to crumble. Panic numbed my arms and face and slowly enveloped me like a cocoon, terror rising within me. My chest tightened, I gasped for air, and the beautiful white box changed before my eyes into a hazy white blob disconnected from reality. Everything… disconnected.

"Noooo…" I moaned. The PTSD I emphatically denied filtered out through my pores, stating in its presence that it was not a force to be reckoned with or ignored. My heart pounded painfully against the walls of my chest, and the room spun like a vortex around me. A seemingly unprovoked fear gripped my entire being, but it was the real toll that building The Perfect Accent had had on me, and it came upon me with a vengeance. The storm of emotional pain I'd worked so hard to suppress emerged and engulfed me instead. In agony, I clutched my chest and my stomach as a deep, guttural moan emerged from my mouth, and the wailing followed. I could no longer suppress the intrusive thoughts and memories. They raged across my mind, flashing rapid scenes of horror, and I could do nothing but emotionally and mentally crumble beneath the weight of it. I screamed into the floor, feeling overcome, feeling so frightened, and so terribly alone.

Something changed in me that day. There was so much loss. I fell helplessly from the womb of security I had built for myself, and the brilliance of The Perfect Accent faded quickly from view. In those moments of agony, I realized I could not control PTSD. I could not live in denial, and I could not run from the things that haunted me. But the excruciating pain came in accepting the fact that I was now incapable of things that were previously second nature. *Incapable...* I felt worthless as a human being. Never before had I been unable to conquer fear. Now it ruled me.

The next time I received a request from a family member for a custom pair of earrings, I wanted to make them so badly. I thought, *maybe I can...* But when I sat down in the office chair with the tools, my hands began to tremble. I looked down at the wires, the beads, the crimps and wire spread out before me, and suddenly felt a gripping pressure in my chest. *Not again...* I couldn't breath, and the room began to spin as panic consumed me. *I can't do this again...* With cold, shaky hands I quickly corralled the materials off the table and into a drawer, and rushed out of the room. When I got home, I ran to the computer and disabled the website. Then I finished the job, placing the entries we'd received at the bridal show into a drawer, and shoving files away into the filing cabinet. And then I cried. The deep, agonizing, doubled-over-on-the-floor kind of crying.

All that time and effort, and no matter how hard I'd tried, I could not force it to work. I hated myself. I hated what was happening to me, and I hated what I was doing to my family. I hated what I was doing to Claire; and unknowingly, I was about to be hurled forward into the most difficult part yet of my journey. The symptoms that ravaged me forced me to give up The Perfect Accent, and at that moment, I also started to give up on myself. I knew I had deeply disappointed Traci as well, for she could not carry The Perfect Accent alone. I fell into a sea of emotional numbness, losing whatever hope and belief in myself I had.

Three months later, I received a bitter letter from Claire ending our friendship. Her son, the same age as Lacey, and her close friend since birth, had a birthday party coming up. Claire stated plainly in her letter: "Mike is invited to bring Lacey, but clearly there is no reason for you to come until my heart is in a better place." Her heart never reached a better place where I was concerned. I crumbled in tears when I read the letter. I didn't want this. I didn't know how to let Claire in, and she'd seen and misunderstood too many "cover-up behaviors" for me to try to explain.

In an email to her, I poured out the truth: things were not as they appeared. My apparent joy—and even The Perfect Accent—was an effort to mask the pain. I didn't want her to go. But my effort returned void, and then I couldn't reach out anymore. I had built too many walls around me as I literally existed day-to-day in a frozen state of trauma. My family stood on the sidelines, confused and angry about being shut out, and Claire stood among them. But I couldn't reach out. I just needed to survive. That's all I could do. I did not have the capacity to put everyone around me at ease while my spirit shrunk away; while I died inside, trying to come to terms with the disorder that seemed intent on destroying me.

And now, in the worst of ways, I felt misunderstood, as I had so frequently throughout my life. Another incident where the best of intentions—or in this case, self-preservation—produced disastrous results, and trying to explain didn't change a thing. To this day I feel incredible sadness over that broken friendship; and for months after receiving Claire's email, I wondered if I could have done something different to produce a different outcome. But I know my heart. I know I did the best I could at the time, but there was no ability to reach out, or meet expectations, or please anyone. I could not, when the constant stampede of intrusive thoughts, memories, and flashbacks of rape and abuse had me pinned down. The focus of each moment became a fight to survive, but the will to do even that was fading.

I needed help. I needed a miracle.

5

SILENT SCREAMS

Dr. Linda Cross will always be a hero to me. She was the first to listen, and not glance at the clock every three minutes during our appointments. She asked questions, and treated me with gentle, quiet respect and compassion. During our visits, the tears often fell as I began to feel safe with her and trust her with my pain. My appointments frequently ran overtime, and I could always anticipate the easy knocking on the door reminding her she had other patients waiting. Then her deep apology came, the assurance that we would be meeting again soon, and to take care of myself and call if I needed anything. I should especially call if I thought of harming myself. That, she said, was not okay to do. I needed to stop doing that.

She put me on a trial of Wellbutrin, and it turned out to be the first—and only—medication that helped ease my depression. For the first time since PTSD had started, the edge of the darkness began to lift.

During one visit, Dr. Cross handed me a printout of psychologists and psychiatrists she believed could help me. I sighed as I took it in my hands. I explained that I'd had really bad luck with therapists, and I didn't know if I could risk that kind of rejection again.

"You can't give up, Juanima," she said. "The help you get for yourself now will determine the future you're going to have. This is too much for you to deal with alone. Please. Make some phone calls. If you keep at it, you'll find the right one."

I wanted to cry, but I did as she told me, and after making a couple phone calls, I found Dr. Kali Miller. Kali, as she preferred to be called (or Miss Kali to little children), occupied a small, two-story office space an hour away from home in Gresham, Oregon. The drive was difficult because, for one thing, the busy traffic muddled me; and secondly, I had no hope for therapists. After she led me into her office for the first time, I sat down on the couch in front of her, stiff and resistant. I answered her introductory sentences with short, quick answers, offering no more information than I felt she needed to know. When she turned the focus on herself, however, and told me about her therapy dog, Sarafina, who sat obediently on the floor at her feet, I found myself relax a little. She had a tender voice, and her soft, kind facial features had a way of making me feel comfortable, like she was a friend. When she spoke of Sarafina, or sometimes Sara, her face lit up with an endearing smile. I struggled to uphold my wall.

Kali figured out quickly that behind my unyielding, stubborn front, I was fragile. I didn't want her to know. I didn't want her to see the hurting me, but all it took was the mention of the abuse. When she said the word, I froze, and the rebellious wall I'd placed between us melted. In a moment I transformed into a terrified child, balled up in the corner of the sofa, making myself as small as I could. She had infiltrated forbidden territory, and she knew it. I sat aware that my façade had crumbled, and that she now had the upper hand. The chill spreading across my chest wasn't just from the mention of the abuse, but fear of what she would do now.

"I can see I've stepped into a very sensitive area for you, Juanima, and it's okay." Her pleasantness hushed my fear like a mom would a child. "We don't need to talk about that yet. We can take our time, okay? We'll do this at your pace. Only when you're ready."

I felt too disconnected and frightened to respond, but it was my sense of safety with her that terrified me most. Now that I had found someone I might be able to trust, I knew at some point I would have to speak. I would have to be real, and eventually, talk about my reason for being there: the abuse. I just couldn't fathom it. I didn't trust her *yet*. I resented her silence, waiting for my response, and I judged her harshly in my mind. *See?* I thought. *She's trying to get into my head right now. She's studying me. Trying to figure out how she can take away my control.*

"Can I tell you something I see, Juanima?"

I looked up at her, clutching the brown, velvet couch pillow protectively against my chest.

"You've locked these memories away for a very long time. For years. Now imagine, if you will, a little black bag. And every time you were abused as a child, you put the incident away in that little black bag, and kept it locked away somewhere deep in your mind. You have functioned well in your life, up until now, without ever having to open that bag. And while we don't know yet what happened to release it, the fact is, it's come to the surface. And you are terrified to open it." She paused, and I was glued to her words. "What will happen, Juanima, if you open that bag?"

My chin quivered. Tears stung my eyes, and I tried my best to push them back. The answer burned truth without question. "It will kill me," I said. "The pain will kill me."

I waited for her to laugh. She didn't.

"I can see how feeling that way would scare you. So listen, we're going to take this very slow, okay? I will never push you to do something you're not ready to do. You're leading me. And when you're ready to open that black bag, we'll do it very carefully. Very slowly. A little bit at a time, so you feel safe and not overwhelmed. So, you stay in control at all times. Okay?"

I desperately wished I'd never have to open up that stupid black bag. It wasn't fair. Until Kali described that black bag, I thought I'd simply put the past behind me. Now I understood it differently. Even though I hated the idea of the black bag, hated its existence, I knew Kali was right, and opening it was inevitable. I could deal with Kali's plan, but time would tell if she would keep her word, and really let the pace be mine. For now, I believed her. I believed she was on my side.

⮞

My hesitance to deal with the black bag reminds me of a family trip to Six Flags in California as a teenager. I loved the rush of a good roller-coaster ride, but when my mom pointed to a ride called Freefall, I could already feel the adrenaline begin to surge. It promised a thrill like no other. As we stood in the long, curvy line of vibrating participants anticipating their turn, I craned my neck upwards to see the top of the ride, one hundred and thirty feet up. My mouth fell open as I watched a car *click-click-click* up an elevator-like shaft, thirteen stories up to the top of the tower. It jarred to a stop, creaking as it advanced forward—away from the track—and then suddenly dropped like a cherry bomb to the curved track ninety-six feet below. The fall lasted all of two seconds, and abruptly ended with the car on its back, and a frazzled rider peeled from the inside. It looked terrifying and exhilarating at the same time. The ride manager finally let us through the gate, but as my mom, siblings, and I approached the first car, he said there wasn't enough room for me. I would have to ride in the next car. I turned around to see an old couple in their late seventies climbing inside it. *No. Way.* My older brother, John, yelled, "C'mon Nima!" urging me to hurry up and go. I had no choice but to get in.

The old lady tried talking to me on the way up the track, giggling at what a young thing I was to be going on a ride like this. I looked at her and laughed nervously. *Are you kidding me?* I thought. It was *her* I was worried about. As we clicked up higher, I watched as the people on the ground turned to a scattering of ants on a dirt patch. I'd never been so high in the air before, and I admit the fear gnawed at my stomach and chest. I gasped in surprise when the car suddenly slammed to a halt. Now I was scared! My breathing quickened and my heart seemed to grow five times its size as it crushed my chest wall. *Chink. Chink.* The car moved from the security of the track into an open square frame, and I panicked. *Oh my God... I want off. I want off!*

Clang! The mechanism released the car, and we fell through that square frame faster than you could drop a bouncy ball. I screamed. The old lady screamed beside me and I yelled at her, "PLEASE don't have a heart attack! Oh my God I want out!" And then it ended. The car slid to a stop at the curved track below, and I was too petrified to move. The old couple laughed with delight, and I thought they were crazy. Then I came out, weak-kneed and trembling. I never, ever wanted to go on a ride like that again.

Now, I experienced those same feelings in a different light. As I became settled in with Kali and developed a trust for her, the contents of the black bag began seeping out. Whether I wanted them to or not, whether I was ready or not, the memories began to claw their way out. Kali did not push me to talk about it—I couldn't yet. But the longer I avoided it, the more intense the flashbacks became. Fear imprisoned me, leaving me no windows for light. And like the Freefall, I plummeted into darkness so thick, so suffocating, it swallowed me like quicksand.

I went to see Kali on a weekly basis, but it became dangerous to drive myself. Knowing I was going, knowing I would be opening that black bag a bit more, I would shift into a panic-filled, dissociated state. I physically could not drive. Numbness crawled up my arms like snakes, across my chest, and spread across my face and eyes. Like tingling pins and needles across my body, it stole my physical strength and severed my awareness to the real world around me. That's when Traci stepped in to drive me to my appointments, and graciously honored the silence I desperately required.

The fear of going to those appointments consumed me so strongly on the drive there, I could not consciously connect to thoughts or voice, and often felt separated from reality altogether. So Traci would hold my hand, or let me lay my head on her lap; anything for comfort. Everything inside me resisted the contents of the black bag, but still I went. My reasons at the time were not heroic, but out of fear of the alternative. The consequences of denying the black bag were far too oppressive: the darkness would never end.

Mike already dwindled in patience and hope for ever getting back the woman he married. The girls knew their Mama was not okay. I couldn't hide the pain any longer, and I couldn't ignore my edginess and the instability of my thinking. I *had* to keep seeing Kali. I had to keep moving forward somehow; even if it destroyed me, and I began to think it was.

❧

On the night of August 20, 2005, Traci hosted a party to celebrate my sister's birthday, and I needed to be there. Cris was my sister, after all, but I didn't know how to survive the party. I had a pit in my stomach about the whole thing. Social events, family or not, made me sick to my stomach. The noise, the questions, all in a happy environment, when I wavered on the brink of despair. I felt as out of place as a maimed bird in the center of a crocodile mob—and just as scared. I wondered if I'd be able to fake it this time, for Cris's party, and if I could put on that smile long enough to fool the guests. Traci assured me I could always go to her bedroom and hide if I needed to. I figured I would probably spend most of the evening there, but at least my sister would know I showed up.

I insisted on arriving before anyone else. Walking into a crowded room, where the action stops and all eyes land on me, thrusts me into an intense, irreversible panic state. One I cannot hide. So Traci and I enjoyed some quiet time before the guests arrived, during which I slammed margaritas until I felt the numbing buzz of the alcohol take effect. Just one more, and I felt I would be able to handle things. When my sister arrived, I greeted her with a smile and embraced her, hoping she wouldn't smell the liquor on my breath. If she did, she didn't mention it. Cris didn't drink at all, and neither did her church-going friends, so I kept the drinking to myself. For a while I mingled, laughed, talked, and actually felt normal. That was the gift of alcohol.

As the party lingered, though, my cover faded. Alcohol worked like a cloak to the feelings and the pain. When the effect of the alcohol wore off, the uneasiness and anxiety crept in, and so did the feelings I'd been working so hard to stifle. The Feelings Room threatened to break open, and if that happened, I knew I would unwittingly draw negative attention. I couldn't allow that. I couldn't let anyone know I was hurting. I had to keep up the façade.

I looked down at the soda in my glass. It was *just* soda. I needed it mixed. As the gang stood around the kitchen devouring cake and ice cream amid light-hearted conversation, I looked for an opportunity to sneak into the garage for the bottle of vodka I'd hidden there. I smiled and moved past the crowd down the hall, aware of the panic seeping in. I transformed like a monster with a timed disguise, and time had run out. I had to get the potion to keep my disguise. My hands grew numb as I turned the handle to the garage door. I was feeling, and it hurt. In the garage behind closed doors, with the vodka bottle in my hands, I shook, suddenly filled with shame. I hated the fact that I needed this. I couldn't even enjoy a birthday party. I wanted to stay in that garage and never come out.

Journal Entry—August 21, 2005

The morning brings a new day. I see things differently. I am slightly more clear-headed about reality and the world around me, and how much I am needed. At night—tonight—I am so vulnerable. I feel. I hurt. I am so tired. I lie on the couch and feel this pain in my chest—a sort of agony about tomorrow coming. And a thought crosses my mind. I just want to sleep tonight and not wake up. I don't want to ever wake up. I don't want to face another day of hurt, of covering up, of hiding, of being stronger than I am for my little girls or anyone else. I don't want to meet anyone's needs tomorrow. I don't want to meet my own. I don't think I can.

☙

I was not always a good friend to Traci. Our relationship scale tipped mostly in my favor, as she gave so much, and received very little from me in return. In another time, I imagine it so differently; but living in fear, and being bombarded with flashbacks almost daily, it was difficult to see beyond my trauma. Like being trapped in a room with a one-way mirror, everyone could see me just fine, but I could not see them. I saw my walls, and I felt alone there.

Yet, I didn't want help. It went against everything in my personality. As a teenager, and especially after the chaotic aftermath of my stepfather molesting me, I kept the other incidents of abuse a secret. They were the most painful secrets to keep. I became hardened to the pain and subdued it by pushing it down.

It was no different now. The more I saw Kali, the more that black bag leaked out memories and flashbacks of the trauma I endured. Like an old habit, I wanted to deal with it alone, but Traci wouldn't let me. I resented the intrusion, but she could see right through the shield I held so stiffly between us—the shield that protected me from everyone, even my own family. Traci saw the pain seeping from my pores and just wanted to hold me, but so often my body became rigid in her arms, not wanting the touch or comfort. I couldn't handle comfort. Reliving the trauma reawakened the belief that I couldn't let anyone in. As long as I kept everyone at arm's length, I wouldn't be hurt, and I wouldn't hurt anyone else. A hug meant acknowledging the pain, and if I did that, I knew I would fall apart. And if I fell apart, I knew I'd never come back together again. And yet, at the same time, deep down, I was so desperate to be held, understood and comforted. The little girl in me still screamed for love. But she would have to wait. I wasn't ready to allow that yet.

I didn't just detest the affection. I now hated the talking, too. Over time, as I relived more and more of the violence and abuse of my past, the onslaught of traumatic feelings became overwhelming. Shame, abandonment, rage, hatred, and loneliness filled my cup. Traci begged me to share feelings—she could see they ate me alive on the inside like a disease—but I couldn't. They swarmed and confused me, far too numerous to isolate and identify. She wanted me to talk about my flashbacks; I couldn't do that either. They brought so much terror, putting them into words made them even more real.

My rigidness became the expected response to her touch; but rather than give up, she'd laugh and hug me anyway. Traci knew that beyond the wall, beyond the stubborn pride of her friend, beyond the words that told her angrily to back off, there existed a broken, fragile child, desperate for touch, and desperate for acceptance. Traci believed that if she didn't give up, that one day, her hug would break through the barriers and reach that little child, terrified and alone in the dark, and she would reach back. So despite my pulling, and pushing her away, Traci remained. It became her mission to see me through.

Her perseverance of my heart made her my safe place. But poor Traci… our relationship reminded me of the lyrics to the song by Lorrie Morgan: "Go away, no wait a minute; I want out then I want in it; I'm all confused but I admit it; go away, no wait a minute." And the more pain that came, the more I pushed her away. But I also needed her more than anything.

Journal Entry—Tuesday, August 24, 2005

Wind blowing across my face. The rustle of trees nearby. The wind comes again my way. I hear it travel through trees behind me—a wind chime plays its song. A little girl screams in a house across the street. I strain to listen. My heart stops as I wait. She screams again, and I think it's only play. Now she is silent. A man across the field rolls his brown can of yard debris down his driveway. He stops and looks at me. After a moment he walks back into his house. I lie alone in the middle of the field next to a playground, half shaded by the cluster of trees behind me. A group of kids in their twenties sit at a covered table nearby celebrating a friend's birthday. They laugh… tell stories. My jeans are damp from the grass.

A black man with his three children plays at the playground. What a good father, loving his children this way. I hear them laughing but I don't turn to look. Time moves at the speed of sound. The wind chime quiets. The voices of the group of friends have faded. And I am so tired. I walked here—eight blocks from home. I don't know why I came. I don't know why I rested here. Did I intend to keep going? I think of running away. But it didn't work when I was sixteen. My drink is strong. Already, I try to forget. And now, the thoughts just come. This world is so big around me and I feel so insignificant. God has billions of people in this world to fill His home—why would He need me, too?

Thoughts and feelings flood my mind. Some are lies, some are fears, some are bits of knowledge in my head, but not in my heart. Tears lay waiting... they want to come and my face succumbs to them. I want to disappear... just fade away. I don't care anymore... do I? I can't fight anymore. I focus on this page but hear so many sounds around me. I know I can refuse to see them with my eyes but they still exist. I can't ignore the memories. I can't refuse to see them.

Traci... it is so unfair for me to keep the walls up. I have dropped them down and admitted I needed help, but I can't scream enough. Why can't I say I need help? I need the people I love to reach out for me because I can't reach out for them. I need them to pursue me because I have no courage to ask for help. In my mind I'm crying out—I'm screaming—please see me. Please see that even though I'm pushing you away I need you to fight. I need you to not go. I need you to not leave me. I want you to stop at the door and turn and say, "I'm not going. You can push me away but I know you really need me here." And then I can crumble to the floor but I won't be alone.

I don't really want to cry alone. I need someone I don't have to lie to. For once, to not have to say, "I'm okay." I don't want to pretend. I don't want to hide. I don't want to be tough anymore. Read my mind. Or wait in the silence until the words can come alive.

But it's a dream. The truth is, this is what I have. Me. Silence. Alone. My pain. My face numbs. My fingers, too. Panic. It always creeps in to join the pain. It comes unwelcomed. My drink is gone. Would anyone notice if I just slipped away? I don't want to go back, and I need to get away from here. Whatever peaceful sounds surrounded me before have transposed to obnoxious voices, cell *phones, yelling kids, dude this and dude that. I need to start walking again, but don't know where to go. I am lost....*

&

I can't speak, so I cut. A constant hurricane roars inside me that I can't release in words. I have no ability. But I have a rage so strong that if it existed outside of me it would rip limbs from the trees like blades of grass. But it's inside, and it won't stop. It envelops my mind with twisting confusion, hopelessness, and pain I cannot describe. It does not ebb and flow at the edge of my soul—it smashes across it mercilessly. And nobody knows. I cannot speak of it. I cannot explain it to anyone. And I cannot scream enough, so I cut. As the blade digs across the flesh of my arms, the pain thaws into the bright red teardrops that fall. They make me feel real. They tell me I am alive. But I am numb. I do not feel the pain, but I see it. Thank God I see it. I am saved for another moment. I will not die from this invisible storm raging inside me.

&

I forgot to take my Wellbutrin one day, and the looming sorrow it protected me from oozed in and across my mind like a poison. I fell deeper into a chasm of hopelessness as the day wore on, and it did not cross my mind to take my pill. I had not realized I'd forgotten it. The day blurred into night, and I existed in a black closet, feeling separated from reality and the people around me. My children laughed and played around me, oblivious to my despair. I asked Mike to please bring pizza home. I just couldn't cook. That night, I cried myself to sleep.

The next morning came and went, and I forgot to take my pill again. In the small and barren corner of the sofa, emotional pain barreled through me like a reckless train. My world darkened and cloaked me with a sadness so profound, so painful, my thoughts centered on self-destruction and harm. I imagined standing on the roof of a tall building, feeling the bitter wind across my face, and feeling empty. I imagined the best thing for me was to step off, and let the rushing wind carry me to a place where the pain rescinded. I knew I needed to call Traci for help, but in my stubbornness, I didn't even attempt to dial the phone. I didn't call anyone. Instead, I grabbed a razor blade, and gave voice to the pain that overwhelmed me. I wept as I created cut after cut, but it felt like no amount of red could bring relief. The blackness covered me, and I felt myself shrinking beneath its weight. It seemed to have come out of nowhere. I didn't think of the two forgotten pills that lay waiting in the bottle.

Traci called then and asked if I wanted to come over. I didn't, but I did. In my sweats and baseball cap, I made the short drive and spent the afternoon with her. I did not admit the sad events of that day. I fixed myself drinks, which perked me up some, but by the end of the evening, my grief covered my face in tears. It was midnight. Traci had called Mike earlier to let him know of my struggle, and he'd said not to worry. He would take care of the girls. Now I stood at Traci's door to leave, and as she hugged me in the doorway, I fell weak in her arms.

"I feel like I'm hanging on a rope, and everyone—you, my family—are hanging onto the other end trying to pull me up. But you can't pull me up," I said, sobbing quietly in her arms. "You can't pull me up, so I just want to tell you to let go. To just let me go." I couldn't say anymore.

I squeezed her tight, a goodbye for me, and somehow drove home through my convulsive wailing and tears. Sneaking into my house, careful not to wake anyone up, I held my breath. The tears wouldn't stop. I plunged onto the sofa, and in the deafening silence of our small home, I gave up. I gave up freedom. I gave up life. I gave up fighting. I gave up on myself and my ability to hold on. I couldn't do it anymore.

Through tear-filled eyes, I went to my desk and grabbed the bottle of sleeping pills Dr. Cross had prescribed for me. The pills that had gone unused since I'd filled it because though they allowed me precious sleep, I woke up feeling like I had fifty extra pounds of weight across my limbs and the fog of an entire meadow in autumn in my brain. I couldn't function, so I didn't take them. Now, I held the full bottle of the tiny green things clenched in my fist. Dr. Cross had warned me gravely against these pills, refusing to prescribe them if I was even the slightest bit suicidal. I assured her at the time I was not. She'd looked me square in the eyes and said, "Juanima, these will not give you an upset stomach if you overdose. These will kill you. It is a guaranteed fatality." Again, I assured her I would handle them with extreme caution.

That meant nothing now. I wanted to sleep, but I wanted to end the battle permanently. I thought of my girls, and sobbed harder. The thoughts that went through my mind were so real to me, and made so much sense. I could not be a mom to them. I could not give them what they needed. The hugs were not enough. The forced smiles were not enough. In my grave state, I did not remember the numerous, pure moments of love and laughter across the days. The moments of realness, of belly laughing, of light. I could not remember or see anything for dark. Empty of hope, I felt God had abandoned me, too. So worthless, even God had turned away, disgusted with His failed creation. I thought of Mike. *He'll find someone new*, I thought. It will hurt the girls for awhile, but they'll recover. They'll like their new Mommy, and Mike will be glad to have a woman without pain. Without baggage. I looked to the future, and saw a tunnel with no light. No end to its dark passage.

I tiptoed into the girls' bedroom, and my heart shattered into pieces, embracing me in failure. I wept over Lacey and Jordan in their beds, and kissed them goodbye. I wept over words of love and sorrow, and asked them to please forgive me for not being strong enough. I ran from the room and fell onto the sofa in complete abandon. I poured the little green pills into the palm of my hand. "I'm so sorry, Baby," I sobbed. I had failed my husband, too. I looked at the blurry mound in my trembling hand, and in the instant before launching them into the back of my throat, my cell phone rang.

Jolted from my suicidal trance, the pills flew across the sofa cushions. I grabbed frantically for the phone to stop the ring that was sure to wake the house. It was Traci. She was ruining everything!

"What are you doing!" I scolded in a harsh whisper.

"What are *you* doing?" she countered. I replied with a stunned silence. I could not say.

"Nothing... I didn't know you cared," I teased amid the tears streaming down my face.

"If I didn't care, would I be parked outside your house at one o'clock in the morning?"

My heart slammed against my chest. "What?"

"Can I come in for awhile?"

I peeked through the curtains, and sure enough, there she sat in her white minivan, peering through the rain-streaked windows. "Yeah," I said. "Come in."

I quickly swept up the pills with my hands and got them back to my desk before letting her in. I did not speak of what I had almost done. We did not speak at all. She hugged me long and steady, standing on the floor of my living room before she motioned to my blankets on the couch. Without question, I crawled under them, and then she sat behind me and lifted my head onto her lap. As I succumbed to my exhaustion, she brushed my hair with tender fingers.

"You're safe," she whispered.

"What made you come?"

"Something in your hug scared me," she said. "I told Sam, and he said, 'You need to go to her, Trace.' So here I am."

Here you are... Exhaustion enveloped my weary mind then and I slept, and no evil came into my dreams that night.

In the morning, Traci asked me if I'd remembered to take my Wellbutrin.

The realization spread across my brain like rippling water. I didn't tell her about the missed doses, but I immediately swallowed one. I vowed silently to work harder at remembering.

6

A WAKE-UP CALL

⌒2005⌒

I sat in Kali's office while Traci read a book in the waiting room. This time, I didn't try to hold back the tears. They gushed out as fast as the words from my mouth. "I can't do this. I can't be a mom. I can't clean the house. I can't keep up with everything. I can't cook. I can barely get myself into the shower or get dressed. The flashbacks are so horrible. I just can't do it. I'm yelling at my children, Kali. That's not okay with me!"

It devastated me. I never lost my cool. Not the old Nima, anyway. I was always a patient person, but not anymore. I lived on the edge of rage, where the slightest provocation triggered its release. And in those moments of eruption, I hated myself.

I explained to Kali how Lacey and Jordan, normal inquisitive kids, came at me daily with questions, arguments, or whining. I shared the story of one afternoon, when they both ran to me, squabbling about what the other had done. They were two and six years old. Within seconds I felt trapped, cornered like a threatened animal, and needing to escape. My hands flew up in a protective stance and before I could stop it, the yell blurted out. That particular day, I screeched with such desperation and anger, my little girls jolted in fear. They burst into tears, which flared my anxiety even more because I couldn't stop it. Any of it. I couldn't think of *how*.

Instead, my mind swarmed with panic and confusion, and I ran. I sprinted to my bedroom, slammed the door, and screamed into the pillow. But that was not enough. Hearing the girls crying outside my door, I paced frantically, tormented with guilt and shame for yelling at them. The rage inside me still screamed to get out, but I refused to let them see it. I don't know why I thought hiding behind a closed door protected them, when they could just as easily hear.

They heard me pound the wall with my fist, over and over, until my hand turned numb and purple, throbbing with a stiffening pain that prevented me from closing it. The painful emotions bubbled rapidly, building up a pressure against my skin so intense, I feared I would erupt. I couldn't control the tears, but I had to pull myself together somehow. I opened the bedroom door and scooped my two little broken-hearted girls into my arms, squeezing them with love and deep regret. I looked them in the eyes and said, "I'm so sorry. Mommy's crying and yelling is not your fault, and I'm so, so sorry. Please forgive me."

I hugged them until they laughed, thanking God for their resiliency and grace.

"I'm not okay with this anger dance with my children, Kali," I cried. "It devastates me to think I could ever be capable of scaring them like that."

Kali nodded. "You can't continue this, Nima. You need to take a break. Is there someplace you can stay for a couple of weeks so we can work on this stuff without you having to be a mom, and clean the house, and cook, and do the laundry? Would Mike support you to do that for awhile?"

No way, I thought. How could I possibly leave Mike to handle everything on his own? What would the girls think if I wasn't around? They needed me.

"I don't see how," I said. "I think I just need to try harder to hold it in."

"Nima!" she scolded. "This is the time when you need to take care of *you.* Clearly, you are not physically or mentally capable of handling all of the tasks you're trying to take on, and you need to let yourself off the hook. It's okay. It's really okay to put yourself and your needs first right now."

I sobbed. I didn't know how to put myself first. To me, it felt wrong. I had always felt responsible for everyone else's happiness, and sadly, never learned to love and respect myself. It seemed easier to just act happy and make sure everyone around me was happy. Keep the peace. Now, Kali suggested I disrupt my home by leaving my children without their mom, and my husband to do all the work. Impossible.

"Nima..." Kali whispered, leaning her elbows on her knees and getting as comfortably close as I would allow. "What do you see happening if you don't go? If you don't take care of yourself right now? Will your girls have a happy mom?"

In my heart, I knew they would not.

"If you want your girls to have a happy mom, you need to do this for yourself. Your expectations of yourself are too, too high, my dear. After a couple weeks, you can start visiting them, but it will be to do something positive. Play games, read them books, watch a family movie together. By taking this time away from the responsibilities at home, you will be able to breathe. You will get more out of your sessions with me, and you'll be a better mommy to your girls. To function at home you must be able to switch the feelings off that arise from our time together, but you're not able to do that yet. So you're trying to do all these things at home, and perform, but meanwhile you're going crazy."

"Story of my life," I joked.

Kali smiled, but with all seriousness, she sent me home to discuss the plan with Mike, Traci, and her husband, Sam.

To my astonishment, they unanimously agreed to Kali's suggestion. "But how will you manage all the cleaning and taking care of the girls?" I argued with Mike. "What will you say when they ask where I am? I can't just leave them! How will you keep up with all the laundry and dishes and the—"

"Hey," he said coolly. "The girls will be fine. I'll figure that out, and I'll tell them you're taking a Mommy vacation at Traci's house.

And the rest, well, you'll just have a lot of cleaning to do when you come back."

I laughed. Mike always had a way of adding humor to the direst situation. But right now, I stood alone fighting the decision, and the three of them looked at me with raised eyebrows awaiting my agreement. I gave in.

❧

The first night brought a level of pain so excruciating, I questioned my decision. Alone in Sam and Traci's spare bedroom, I thought of the girls at home, wondering about me. Were they sad that I wasn't there? I missed them terribly, and felt guilty for being in this position. A battle warred in my mind—the same battle that took place daily. The fight, the hating of PTSD, the anger that I had lost the life I'd had, and lost the person I used to be. The rage, that I could not control the many destructive arms of this disorder. I could not control the pain, or the memories, or the flashbacks, or the nightmares, or the fear that I wore like a second skin. I couldn't make it go away. I couldn't calm the storm, and the only release I felt from it was either a numbing, alcohol-induced state, or taking the blade to my skin. Almost daily, I chose the blade because I couldn't—and I didn't want—to be drunk all day. I refused to let my girls ever see me in that condition, so I controlled my intake fervently. Never drunk... just enough to be free, to laugh, and to play.

It brought overwhelming anxiety to be home, trying to be a mom and wife, while incessantly fighting the raging storm inside me. Yet, I felt so lost at Traci's without my family near me. Like being out in a raft at sea amid tossing, thrashing waves. The waves bring terror, but I'd rather feel the terror with those I love, than cast myself away to deal with the waves in a meager donut-shaped life preserver alone. And sitting on a mattress in the spare bedroom at Traci's house, I felt more isolated than ever. I had no distractions from the pain, and it dropped on top of me like a huge boulder.

As Traci peeked in and smiled a goodnight, and the lights went off from room to room, I trembled in the dark silence. I hated the silence now. It did not bring me comfort. But sleep terrorized me even more. I delayed it as long as possible, dreading the vivid, gruesome nightmares that always came. But tonight, as I lay awake, I saw shadows that didn't exist, and heard noises that weren't real. I heard footsteps of no one there. My heart raced at the imagined sounds in my head as once again, the emotional pain I'd pressed down sprang back up, swallowing me whole. I buried my face in the blanket and sobbed; so forcefully, I was sure I would wake Sam or Traci up in the next room. But they never stirred, and I cried through the night.

The next morning, I sat huddled beneath a blanket on the mattress, saddened at the thought of Mike and the girls running around without me there. Did they wonder about me? Or miss me? That day I existed on a numb, isolated island. My mind had checked out, and I avoided Traci's kids and the company that came by that morning. The darkness covered my eyes to the bright world right outside her window. When I made an appearance, I stared, empty, into Traci's eyes as she tried to carry on conversations about life. She spoke through my dismal silence, smiling at me as a cheerful participant in her conversation; and I appreciated it, since I didn't have the capacity to even smile at the appropriate cues. She did not ask if I was okay, or what was bothering me, or what I was feeling. I think that somehow, she understood I didn't have the strength to speak anyway. An empty shell, I sat in her presence weak and depleted of everything that made me human.

It seemed the months of sleepless nights not only caught up with me; they devoured me. I left Traci to go lie down on the mattress again, but instead of sleeping, I wept, and I did not emerge from those walls. I did not shower. I did not change my clothes. In the small room, I looked around at the pictures, the memorabilia of a family life, the happy, tropical colors that Sam and Traci loved so much, and the reality of my dark existence slapped me across the face. I saw not even a keyhole of hope. More than two agonizing years brought a solid streak of pain that only sharpened and deepened like a knife in my soul, and I saw no signs of it getting better. I saw no signs of freedom, and I did not have the strength to keep fighting.

As night fell and the house quieted for the night, I lay in my bed until 3:00 A.M., nursing the gloominess until I could stand it no more. I emerged from the room and sluggishly, silently, went to the kitchen to find a method to end my life again. Pills, anything. I found nothing, and shuffled defeated into the living room. In the dark, I reached down to the TV and turned it on. There, on the screen, looking right at me—yelling at me—was a woman I'd never laid eyes on before. In the lower left hand corner of the screen I read the name of the show, *Enjoying Everyday Life*. But in those first sentences that came from her mouth, I felt she knew me. The weight of her words pulled me to the floor, but I quickly rose to find paper—anything—to write on. I found an index card with crayon markings on it from Traci's young daughter, a pencil, and rushed to the screen again. I scribbled madly as she spoke. As the camera closed tighter on her face, she looked right into me.

"I can say God loves me, not because I'm lovable, but because He decides to love me. And I can say I like myself—not because I'm likable or lovable—but because Jesus *died* for me. So if He died for me, I ought to have the decency to like myself! Jesus died for *you*— do you know how much He suffered on that cross? I mean unbelievable agonies that we cannot even imagine. And He didn't do it out of some obligation; He did it *for us* because He loves us that much. And if He could do that for us, how insulting is it for us to hate ourselves and reject ourselves and be against ourselves, and only think about everything that's wrong with us all the time? There's not one of you that would like your children to feel like that."

With those last words I stopped writing, and shrunk with shame. My mind suddenly widened with an awareness of the consequences of my near suicide attempt. My God, if I had followed through. I thought of my daughters, Lacey and Jordan, sleeping in their beds at home. I pictured Mike and the two of them, alone, with the permanent absence of me, and I saw devastation—not relief. I saw all of them darkened by the selfishness of my suicide. I saw day-to-day existing with the heaviness of the knowledge that their Mama had given up. And what would that teach them? That giving up is the answer. That life is not worth fighting for. That *they* were not worth fighting for.

I saw them in the future, living with that belief, and living with the empty spaces I had left behind. And a profound realization crept in that if I gave up, the chain of abuse would remain unbroken. I know well that abuse passes down from generation to generation until *someone* digs their feet into the harrowing muck and pays the price of healing. If I didn't do it, it may be one of them. The thought of Lacey or Jordan enduring even one act of abuse, or the destructive PTSD that I now lived with... this choked the breath out of me, and a fresh pain plunged through me. Deep and familiar, the pain that came daily moved like a double-edged sword, slicing away the hope, faith, and anything optimistic inside of me. I wouldn't wish it on my worst enemy. The thought of my daughters ever feeling it broke me apart.

As I cradled myself against the tidal wave of grief-driven tears, I grasped hold of the anger that gushed up in my soul. Like the rage of a mama bear defending the life of her cubs, it pushed me to my knees, and I begged God for all the courage and strength He would give. Begging, in that moment, to never let me give up. No matter what happened, no matter how painful healing became, I could never give up. My girls could never know this pain. Never!

The realization enveloped me slowly like a cocoon: Only one person could end the cycle of abuse. One person could take on the ironhanded burden of healing and save my daughters from a potentially dark life of abuse, shame and torment. A life like mine. A life of secrets. And the one person who could change the course and set them on a good path of strength, courage and self-love? *Me.*

And if it was up to me to teach them self-love, strength and courage, I needed to first learn it myself. The only way to that meadow of freedom was to press through the hostile entrapment of the swamp, the thick fog of confusion that laid a constant hold on my mind, and the fear that plagued my spirit. And I didn't know how, nor did I have the means in that moment; but somehow, I would find a way to press through, and I would do it so my daughters wouldn't have to.

꙳

My new mission unfolded in my mind, and from the moment of its inception, it rooted itself as deeply as a century-old oak tree. I knew that if I felt like giving up, I would only have to think of my girls feeling even an ounce of the pain I'd felt, and it would send me forward—if only an inch.

With my new determination came the acceptance that in order to heal, I would need to face the abuse head-on. I had no choice in this. Though it terrified me, and I wanted nothing more than to live in denial for the rest of my life, and though I knew it would be the absolute hardest thing I'd ever done—it *had* to be done. I couldn't run from the terror anymore. My kids depended on me to fight.

The first time I visited the girls, per Kali's instructions, I embraced them with the determined spirit of a brand new mom. We enjoyed dinner together that night as a family, and then watched a movie and stuffed ourselves with bag after bag of microwave popcorn. After a couple private, quick, stiff drinks in the kitchen, I relaxed and laughed with the girls. I felt no guilt for the liquid assistance, seeing my daughters' faces light up and their eyes dance because their Mama was home and smiling. I saw the knowledge on their faces that I loved them so much and enjoyed spending this time with them. That part was all real.

I didn't quite make it two weeks at Traci's house. One night, the grief and emotional pain was so intense I slept on the floor beside Sam and Traci's bed, and Traci held my hand through the night. I was hurting, but *I wanted to be with my family.* While Kali didn't approve, I moved back home. If I was going to integrate myself back into my roles as a wife and mom, and embark on my new mission of healing, I didn't see any reason to delay it.

꙳

By late August 2005, I had shared some incidences of abuse with Kali. The surface facts I could share, but not the details. Not the feelings. I couldn't do that. But in one session with her, I told the basics of the incidences with my uncle at age seven, eleven and thirteen, and then the incident with my stepfather at fourteen. I told her that later that year, my first real boyfriend raped me, after which my spirit plummeted. My grades fell from straight-As to Ds and Fs. I couldn't concentrate in my classes anymore, or focus, or care. My teachers urged me to try harder, but you can't try harder if you don't *want to.* I turned to drugs, alcohol, lying, and shoplifting, until my mother kicked me out—not because of those things; she didn't know about those things—but because of my rebellious attitude. She forced me to go live with my dad.

I told Kali that even then, in a new environment, abuse followed me. A man raped me at a party when I was fifteen, and I attempted suicide shortly thereafter. For some reason, I couldn't get the suicide thing right. A close friend and I made one more plan—one that would surely work—but at the last minute I decided I didn't *really* want to die. I just wanted the pain to end. So she and I fled to Reno, Nevada, with no plans of returning.

"A lot of bad things happened there," I said. "Things I can't talk about. I think I'll just stop for now."

Kali shook her head. "I know I had told you that we would need to process your trauma, but I want to reassure you that we won't have to process each and every incident."

I exhaled with relief, shoving my trembling hands deep in my lap.

"You see, your trauma is like a rope with several knots in it, and those knots represent those incidences that affect you the most. The ones that stick out more than the others. Can you think of a few of those?"

Immediately, I thought of my stepfather. I thought of Damon in Reno. The emotional ties... the things that he required of me. I shuddered.

"Yes, those," she pointed at my face when she saw the disgust and fear of those memories. "Those are the ones we must process;

and then one-by-one, those knots will unravel. Processing one really bad one will alleviate the pressure of the others, and pretty soon you'll find they have lost their hold on you. Does that make sense?"

It did, but I shrunk back at the thought of addressing those two events. "I'd rather process the little ones, though. Can't we process those instead?"

She apologetically said it wouldn't work that way. Those two events came to the forefront of my mind because they had the most power over me. Reno, most of all, but I felt I absolutely could not address it ever. Reno carried far too much terror for me. I classify it as one event, but it was really a cluster of horrific events wrapped up tight into a stiff-leathered pouch and tossed deep, deep into the bottom of the black bag in my mind. Farther back than all the rest.

When the realization sunk in that I would need to bring it out of the black bag and spill the contents, I felt sick to my stomach. The ever-recognizable panic crept into my chest, my arms and hands. My face. Shallow, quick breathing was leading to complete dissociation. *It's too much...*

"Nima? Listen, honey, we won't do this today. This is down the road; when you're ready. We'll lead up to it slowly, okay?"

How about...never. Terror was taking hold of me. Thinking of Reno for even a moment, and what happened to me there, brought the violent images forth. My hands rushed defensively to my eyes, but nothing could stop the images. Nothing could stop the movie that played.

"What's happening now, Nima?" Kali could see my struggle, and leaned in to help.

"Nothing," I lied. "I just don't want to talk about Reno." My inability to control my mind embarrassed me, despite the fact that Kali had explained it was part of the PTSD; part of the control of the trauma, and that my brain was frozen in a state of it. It wasn't my fault. Still, I hid it.

"Okay," she whispered. "Forget about Reno right now. We won't even go there. We'll start small, and work our way up. You'll know when you're strong enough to confront it, Nima. You'll know when it's time. Clearly, it's not now. And that's okay."

"When…" I demanded nervously. I needed a timeline. "Tell me when."

"That's not something I can tell you," she said. "This process really is up to you. We'll take as long as you need."

I looked in her eyes and saw that she meant it. *Good,* I thought. *I like the idea of never.*

☞

As it turned out, starting small in Kali's mind still amounted to paralyzing fear for me. As the contents of the black bag spilled out more and more, I struggled to stay human. The terror I felt on a daily basis made me crazy. Additionally, my numerous medication trials had brutal effects on me. It seemed that any medication I took for anxiety had an opposite effect on me. A rage burned inside me, gushing up like a geyser at the slightest trigger, and I couldn't withhold it.

One morning, alone in my house, my hair dryer caused a circuit to short and the house abruptly went dark. I screamed as if a thousand screams had been imprisoned for a thousand years and were finally being released. I let loose, pounding my fists against the wall with the rage of a charging elephant. It frightened me to the core. I'd never felt so out of control. And when I realized it was a part of me, I worked overtime to conceal it in an airtight container inside my mind. I managed to hide it from everyone around me. Except one time.

On a chilly, drizzly autumn afternoon in our pocket-sized rental house, Mike and I argued quietly about household duties while Jordan snuggled him on the couch watching her favorite TV show. I stood on the other side of the room at the kitchen table, searching through multiple cookbook binders for a recipe I'd misplaced. I wanted to try to cook that night, a task that had become overwhelming. At first, Mike was sensitive about the topic; he knew I hated confrontations. But I know he hurt, too, in all of this mess. He still had little understanding about the effects of PTSD, and he didn't understand why I couldn't clean more, or do dishes more. He didn't understand that I was barely alive. I kept the depth of my hurt to myself—an act that nearly destroyed me and every relationship I cared about. As Mike asked question after question, looking for explanations, I had not a satisfying word. Everything that came out of my mouth about "what the PTSD was doing" sounded like a lame excuse, even to me. I was still fighting to accept it all myself.

His voice escalated, "I'm working my ass off! The least you can do is help out around here. I mean, how long is this thing supposed to last? When are you gonna start getting better?"

"I don't know!" I cried. "I'm working on it, okay? I'm trying to get better but I'm just now starting to talk about things!" The anxiety was building. My face grew numb. Voices amplified.

"Well, while you're working on it, everything is falling to shit. I can't do it all by myself!"

My tears flowed, falling to the recipe pages as I turned from one to the next, but I no longer registered the content of the pages. In my grief I closed the book and began stacking them to put them all away.

"Hello?" he was loud now, exasperated. "Are you there?"

The pressure, the noise, the fighting. The rage won. I picked up the binder in both hands and raised it up over my head. The rage pressed through my arms, through my hands, and out my mouth as I screamed, "I'm doing the best I can!" and slammed the books to the floor with an explosive crash.

The reaction of both Jordan and Mike were instantaneous. Jordan wailed in his arms, and Mike jumped to his feet and charged at me, shouting, "Get the fuck out of my house! *Now!*"

I screamed in sheer terror and ran from him, through the kitchen, frantically turning the knob to get inside the garage. I slammed the door behind me, still screaming. The single-car garage was like a packed storage unit. I scrambled wildly and clumsily over the mountains of Rubbermaids and boxes to get to the sliding door, falling several times from the tears that blurred my sight. Lifting the heavy door in one, forceful swoop, I darted from the house and sprinted down the street as if Mike was still at my heels. I ran, not looking back. I ran, as the rain pelted against my face and chest.

Street blocks coursed beneath my feet like a hi-speed treadmill, until I reached the bordering forest of a park near Traci's house. In a small, private clearing, I knelt on the dirt ground beside a boulder, buried my face in my arms and screamed again.

Never. Never in the ten years that Mike and I had been together had I raised my voice like that. I'd certainly never screamed, or thrown a book to the floor in a rage, or had a tantrum. Not to Mike, not to anyone. Ever. The horror of my actions shocked me to the core, and I bent against the boulder, grabbed hold of my stomach in painful disgust and wailed. *My God... who am I? What have I become? I'm a fucking monster!*

I had fled the house with no coat, and the deluge now soaked my skin. Too terrified to go home, I clung to myself by the boulder and cried the tears of bitter anger I'd suppressed. Tears of hatred for the confusion and helplessness I felt. Tears of guilt for having PTSD, and for scaring little Jordan on that couch. Deep, longing tears of guilt to take back that moment. I knew I couldn't, so I prayed she would forget. They were tears of terror at the six-foot four-inch man who had charged me like a wild animal. My husband, who had never raised his voice at me, and always treated me with loving-kindness, had just screamed at me to get the fuck out of his house. That alone was difficult to wrap my mind around. I'd never seen him turn mean. I believed his fatherly protection of Jordan sprung into action the moment I made her cry. That, and paper-thin patience. We both snapped.

The tears flowed until dark, when I could no longer sit shivering under the trees. I thought of Traci's house, a ten-minute walk away, and decided that's where I would go. I felt I had no other choice.

Drenched, I knocked on the white door of their home. Sam opened the door, and I could tell by the look on his face that he had spoken with Mike. Sam stepped back, opening a path for me to walk through. "Come in, Nima," he said, hugging me as I walked by. Four hours had passed since I ran from home.

Traci embraced me, and then led me back to her bedroom. We sat on the bed, and she handed me the phone. I honestly don't remember any words that Traci and I spoke to one another, but when I called Mike, he was the Mike I remembered.

"Come home, Baby," he chuckled, as if he'd just seen the stupidest show ever.

"I didn't think you'd want me to come home," I cried.

He laughed again. "Of course I want you home. I just—I just reacted in the moment because you scared Jordan. Of course I want you here."

Traci drove me home, and Mike took me in his arms at the front door. "I'm sorry," we said in unison. I didn't know a body could hold so many tears, but I seemed to shed enough for all of us.

As time slipped by, it became clear to Kali that our current method of processing fell short of her expectations. Symptoms—and life—overwhelmed me, leaving me unable to function at home. The contents of the black bag overpowered all natural thinking, and I couldn't close it up as she had trained me to do. Ideally, I opened the black bag during our sessions—a safe environment—and then closed it up before I went home; however, I was never able to close the black bag. The trembling terror began when I stepped foot in Traci's car to go see Kali, and it continued through the sessions, along the trip home, and through my daily life. I lived in constant fear.

At a subsequent session, Kali revealed her ultimate solution, "I believe it's time for you to consider an inpatient treatment center."

"What's that?" I asked, emotionally detached.

"There are many programs out there that help individuals process trauma. And for one or two months, you would spend dedicated time in one-on-one sessions, group therapy sessions, and also have plenty of down time to process things and journal. You could let things happen naturally without having any responsibilities other than to take care of yourself and make it through one day to the next. Because... this just isn't working for you, Nima. Coming here, and working with me one day a week, and then going home and trying to function...."

She spoke the truth. Therapy once a week only sent me spiraling further downward, as I continuously released trauma that I couldn't put back in the black bag. But did I hear her right? One or two *months*?

"How could I possibly leave my family for that long?" I balked. "What about Mike and the girls?"

"Do you have family that could help out? Help with the girls?"

I thought of my dad and stepmom who lived in town, as did my sister and her family. Traci lived close by, too, and had already been helping so much with the girls. My sister, Cris, had taken the girls several times for me as well. I was sure my mom would drive the forty minutes to help if I needed her. Still, it seemed impossible. And again, my guilt shrunk me down and I shook my head. "No way," I said. "It's just too much to ask."

"Are you saying you're not worth it?" Kali asked point-blank.

"I—" I stumbled. Her question struck too deep.

"I want you to speak with your family," Kali countered. "I want you to be real with them and tell them what you need. If you need to bring them all in here so I can explain things to them, I would be more than happy to do that. But it's *time*."

She talked more about the inpatient treatment programs and what I would need to tell my family. I couldn't believe it had come to this, but it had.

My first point of surprise came when I sat Mike down to discuss the idea with him. Afraid, oscillating with a nervous stomach, I relayed the information that Kali had shared. I waited for him to start yelling again, fed up with the fact I was driving us further under. Financially, for starters, as an inpatient program would cost around thirty thousand dollars. Insurance wouldn't pay for it all, and Mike and I were broke. We would have to petition our families. Secondly, how would he maintain his work hours and manage the girls, too?

"I think it's a good idea," he said. "I think we should figure out how to make it work."

I stared, speechless. "You do? We should? But—"

"No, Kali's right. It's time. We gotta do it. Or I don't know if we'll survive."

He placed his hand on mine, and I leaned into his shoulder. "Okay," I said. "Okay." It was time to lean on God completely.

7

STEPPING INTO THE FIRE

Journal Entry — Tuesday, September 13, 2005

So much of what I feel I can't even express. It just comes out in tears. My eyes are burning. So many decisions to make that will affect the rest of my life and those around me. Mike, my little girls. My heart is broken by the sadness Lacey feels. Maybe Jordan feels it in some way, too. She knows her Mama is sad. She knows her Mama cries. She catches a glimpse of a Band-Aid beneath my sleeve and insists on kissing the owies better. But when she smiles it's as though her world is okay. But oh, sweet, sweet Lacey. My little Lacey. I am so sorry for my sadness, for the pain I've caused. Too much for her child heart to bear or understand. Will she be okay? Will Jordan be okay? Will Mike? My friends? Will I survive this? I feel weak. I am tired of fighting. So many lives will be changed because of the decisions I'm about to make. And in those decisions lie so much pain and fear and agony and sadness. It is hard to see how going away will bring light back to our lives when it's over. It's hard to see any light at all right now.

The pressure to do what's right for me right now engulfs me. I'm so tired of fighting. I thought by now I would feel stronger. Strong enough to make decisions without falling into pieces. Where is God? Will He come through with strength for me? I wish I could feel Him carry me right now. Oh, to be cradled in His big, strong arms and for once feel secure. To feel the warmth of His touch and His love consume me. To know for sure that everything is going to be okay. To see things clearly. I want to smile and have it be real. I want to be healed and whole. God, how I want to be on the other side of all this. It seems the pain has barely begun.

࿊

I knew nothing about an inpatient treatment program, or how it could possibly benefit me. In my mind, the negative impact it would have on the girls if I left far outweighed any level of help I might receive. I could think of a thousand reasons why I shouldn't go; but really, I needed to focus on the one reason that I *should*: My girls. My absence for a short time would hurt them far less than a lifetime with a hurting mom. I needed to take a step of faith, even if I walked blindly.

So I made the commitment to myself. I made it for my family.

What I thought would be an easy process of finding the right place turned into an exhausting and tearful frenzy of repeat disappointments. After numerous calls, I realized I would not be accepted into a treatment center to process trauma. Person after person revealed to me that no one would help me process trauma until I was stabilized—meaning, until I stopped cutting. This devastated me, even though I understood. Processing trauma is an intense journey, and unless I'm stable and can cope with the intensity in healthy ways, I would be too much of a risk to myself.

Kali confirmed her deep suspicions that I needed help in this area, and steered me to other inpatient programs that would help me get stabilized. I agonized over this, because to me, it emphasized my desperation, and how deep in the muck I stood. I had hoped for a thirty-day trip to process trauma and return home a brand new woman. My reality? I wouldn't be processing anytime in the near future, and I knew our families couldn't assist us financially twice. They emptied their pockets for me for *this* trip.

I buckled down and began a new search for a treatment center that would help me get stabilized. Making those initial calls chafed my pride, and I trudged through them like I was walking knee-deep in a snow drift. I didn't *want* to give up the blade. It was an enemy I loved, and the one thing that helped me survive. I couldn't drink all day. I couldn't drink every time the inner pressure threatened to implode my mind. I couldn't talk to anyone about the pain I endured, or share the storm of feelings I couldn't articulate. I concealed the cutting from everyone, because no one would understand it. Intensely ashamed of it, yet I relied on its relief. Traci knew about it, and for years she tried to help me stop the addiction. But I didn't want to admit how much I needed it, and often kept it hidden, even from her. There were times she dumped my purse out to take them from me, but I just bought more. You have to *want* to quit.

Despite my internal battle of resistance, I continued forward with the search. Sitting with Traci at her kitchen table, we worked together to research and make the calls. Each time, there would be a grueling series of questions that I had to answer truthfully, or else it was a waste of time. An interview would often take an hour to get through, and some days I could only muster a single call. They exhausted me; but after a week, I had found a good fit with Lake Chelan Hospital's Behavioral Program.

The email went out to the family, and their response shocked me. I received more support than I could have imagined. Though not all could provide financially, every one of them offered encouragement and prayer. But the money came in. My brother-in-law, Kevin, also a pastor, called the inpatient treatment center and negotiated a lower price. He and my sister, Cris, my stepsister, Kristen, and her husband, Tom, and Mike's Uncle Jim and Aunt Susan, together provided the finances for the treatment program. I also received assurance from every woman in my family that the girls would be taken care of, and Mike would get the help he needed.

I couldn't believe it, as I saw the reality of an inpatient treatment program unfold in front of me. I cried tears of gratitude, and tears of absolute fear. Yes, the family would step up and help, but was I ready to do my part? Was I ready to step into the fire and do this work? Was I ready to leave my family and take a valiant step out on my own?

Hell no.

⁊

On October 7, 2005, Mike and I made the drive to Lake Chelan, Washington. He attempted to keep the trip light and fun. He talked about hunting, and we both scoured the hillsides searching for deer and elk; but my nerves screeched and grated like a train wreck, and I couldn't calm the floundering knots in my gut. It reminded me of my first trip off the high-dive when I was nine years old. My dad took my siblings and me to the Forest Grove public swimming pool as a treat, and the place was packed like a sardine can. I wasn't even that great a swimmer, but the flexible plank suspended high up in the air intrigued me, as did the unabashed flips and turns the kids performed before they plunged into the water below. They made it look so easy and fun. I enjoyed daredevil stunts back then, but I had no idea what I was in for as I climbed up the steel ladder to the top. As I stood at the back end of the diving board, a sudden fear gripped me like an anaconda around its prey. I felt the blood drain from my face.

I turned back to the ladder in a panic, but it was already clocked up with children waiting anxiously for their turn.

"I need to go back down!" I shrieked, though it sounded more like a dying animal.

"You can't!" the girl at the top snapped. "You gotta jump off!"

"Yeah, go!" the boy beneath her yelled.

Tears stung my eyes. To make matters worse, the piercing shrill of a lifeguard's whistle reverberated and echoed through the air of the entire building. I looked over at him, sitting on his high-tower seat. He was blowing the whistle at *me*.

"You're holding up the line!" he bellowed. "Jump down!"

The girl at the top of the ladder scowled at me, again telling me to go. The lifeguard pointed, arching his arm down to the water as a command for me to do the same. I had no choice but to jump, and I knew I was going to die.

Terror shoved me into a run—not a walk—straight off the diving board. As I dropped like a boulder straight down, my insides rushed straight up, and time seemed to stall for hours before I hit the water with an explosive crash. I had jumped for the sheer purpose of getting to the ground below. No trick. No anticipation. Just purpose, and I would never do it again. I never wanted to return to that pool again, either, because all the kids were angry with me, and called me a sissy and a wimp.

$\approx$

As Mike and I neared Lake Chelan, he said he was proud of me, and that it took a tremendous amount of courage to go through with this.

"You'll come back stronger and healthier," he smiled. I appreciated his encouragement. But me... I was looking at the end of that diving board.

Every nerve on my outer body numbed as I walked through the double doors of the building. They stood waiting for me. They explained there would be a check-in process, and some paperwork to sign. I needed to sign a form saying I had no weapons of any kind, including a razor blade. I signed the form, thinking of the Kleenex-covered razor blade in the front pocket of my sweats. My fear heightened when staff ushered Mike out immediately; there would be no drawn out goodbye. He smiled as he went through the doorway. I panicked. These people got down to business.

A gruff, heavy-set woman guided me into a small room that looked like a doctor's exam room with a narrow, sheeted table, a small sink and a mirror. She closed the door behind her.

"We'll be doing a strip search to make sure you're not hiding anything. We'll look through your clothes and pockets. Go ahead and undress down to your underwear and your socks."

She did not smile. She was not friendly. "Are you going to watch me?" I asked nervously. She made me enormously uncomfortable.

"You'd be amazed at what people try to pull in here," she said flatly. "Yes, I'll be watching you."

Oh...grueling. I slowly lifted my t-shirt over my head and laid it on the table. I was sure they would find my razor blade. But they didn't understand! It was like my security blanket! If I didn't have that, I'd be naked. Zero security. Maybe that's what they wanted. Maybe that was the point of this program; but I wasn't ready for that. No way.

I had my thumbs in the waist of my sweats, about to push them down, when there was a knock on the door. The heavy-set woman turned to open it, and in that split second, I made my move. My hand swiped through the pocket, cupped the razor blade, and held it until she closed the door again. As I slid my sweats down to my ankles, I shoved the razor blade into the back of my sock against the curve between the ankle and the heel. The woman watched me closely as I pulled the sweats off each leg. My heart pounded against my chest; I wondered if she'd noticed what I'd done.

She sat, arms folded across her large bosom, watching as I tossed my clothes on top of the exam bed. I felt horribly exposed in my underwear, and embarrassed about the numerous visible scars along my arms. She stared a little too long at me and my shame; I crossed my arms in front of me and looked away. A second woman entered the room, and she greeted me with a smile and a warm hello.

"I know this is uncomfortable," she voiced with compassion. "I promise it won't take but a minute. I'm Gloria."

Of course she was. Her face was soft, smooth and kind, with a wide, uplifting smile. It fit. She forewarned me of each move before she patted me down, looked around my mouth and under my tongue, even felt through my hair. The heavy-set woman—who had never introduced herself—felt every inch of my clothes, tossing them like a salad on the tabletop, searching through pockets and across seams. Apparently, she was satisfied because she left the room.

Gloria raised her eyebrow at me, sensing my curiosity. "She's had some long days."

I smiled politely.

Gloria pulled a pencil from the dark-brown chignon at the back of her head and giggled, "My own portable pencil holder! You can get dressed now, hun. We're all through." She scribbled on a clipboard and exited the room.

Having a cantankerous nurse assisting newcomers is not helpful. Just walking through the front doors frightened me bad enough. I had made the arduous decision to leave my family and step out on my own to face a fearful and intimidating process of confronting my past, and potentially give up my one coping mechanism that worked. I needed support, not a grumpy woman who made me want to run out and never return. I needed a nurse to take me by the hand and say, "It's good that you're here." Sure, maybe Ms. Grouchy-Pants had some hard days, but being in this place scared me like a small child who'd lost her parents in a busy mall; I did not feel brave. I felt incredibly alone. Maybe I didn't show it, but beneath the skin, a raging storm of sheer terror threatened to dismantle my heart.

I briskly pulled my clothes on, leaving the razor blade snuggled deep in my sock. I couldn't believe I'd pulled it off, and felt a bit of pride at that. When I opened the door, Gloria stood waiting to escort me to my room.

The first few hours after my arrival were inundated with paperwork. One staff member after another brought in a new form to sign, a schedule to keep, and details of what to expect. I began to understand why they recommended coming before 5:00 P.M. A staff member left my room with the last of the paperwork at 11:00 P.M. As I took my first full breath, a young girl's face appeared in my doorway.

"Hi," she whispered. "I'm Joy."

"Hi," I answered with an exhausted breath.

"You just get here?"

I nodded.

"You want a tour? I'll show you around the place. Most everyone's asleep, but I can show you where everything is."

"Sure." I slid off my bed and followed Joy as she pointed out the dining room, the staff station—where someone would be twenty-four-seven—and then the kitchen.

"Penny labels all of her food in the fridge. Don't touch it or you'll never hear the end of it. Plus she'll pound you. If you're late for a meal, you won't get it. So don't be late. Unless you want to starve. There are some girls here who don't eat."

The features of the place reminded me of a small wing of a hospital: a dozen or so patient rooms, the staff center in the middle of the hallway, and a couple larger, open rooms furnished with a TV, coffee tables and upholstered chairs.

"Don't freak when the staff wants to escort you everywhere," she said. "The first couple of days, it's like you're on lockdown. You get no privileges, and you can't go outside—in case you run away, I guess—and you can't even go to the bathroom without someone guarding you. One time, a girl broke the bathroom mirror and sliced her wrists with the glass. They don't take any chances now."

Geez... a prison. Guess it didn't matter that I was there voluntarily. When I parted ways with Joy, I collapsed into my bed and prayed for sleep. I'd had five nights in a row without it, and I was paying the price.

In the morning, my brain felt like tar. I groaned with frustration at another sleepless night. I emerged from my room with my toiletries bag, jolting at the presence of a staff member right in front of me. Jillian was a tall, round African-American woman donned in colorful scrubs and a pleasant smile. Despite her kindness, I detested the rules.

"You're not allowed to take anything in with you except a toothbrush and toothpaste. If you want to shower, take in just what you need, but no razor blades allowed. You'll just have to grow hairy armpits," she chuckled.

I didn't laugh. I hated people looking over my shoulder, and telling me what I could and couldn't do. Then I pictured the razor blade hidden beneath the mattress of my bed, and I realized they made these rules for people like me. "I'm only gonna brush my teeth," I said.

"Okay then, I'll be right here."

I just needed to get through the first two days of the mama birds and strict rules; then I could sift into the background and remain unnoticed, and come and go as I pleased. I forced a smile at Jillian and shut the bathroom door behind me. The small room had a tub and shower combo, a sink and toilet. I looked longingly at the shower, but I knew breakfast was in the near future. I thought of not going. For starters, I had no appetite, and I hated being the new girl. I knew everyone would look at me, wondering about my story, expecting me to talk. But they would have to wait. I didn't plan on spilling my guts anytime soon.

I decided to skip breakfast, and soon after got called in for the first group meeting of the day. The room looked cozy, set with plush sofas, plump chairs and rugs to sit on.

"Sit where you're comfortable," a man said. He introduced himself as Jim; he would be the host of many of the group meetings. I picked a chair where I could easily see everyone, and curled up in it. The first session focused on goal setting.

"Goals are so important as you heal," Jim started. "It's important to define what you have, what you want, what you can do today, and ask yourself if what you're doing is working. There has to be something beyond the pain of the here and now. If you're focused only on that, there is no direction, which leads to feelings of helplessness and hopelessness. If you approach healing with a broader awareness, and set small goals along the way, you'll have a greater sense of accomplishment by seeing those small successes."

There are always "talkers" in every group. I am not one of them. I listen, observe, and study others in the group, and as I did this, I learned for the first time that there are others like me. Before walking into that hospital, I knew no one else with PTSD. No one else who cut. No one else who was healing from a childhood of sexual abuse. Gazing across the room, listening to others talk about their many issues, I realized I was not alone. The muscles in my face, neck and back suddenly relaxed—I didn't realize I had been tensing them the whole time.

Lauren looked to be about twenty years old; a large girl, wearing thick grey sweats and a salmon-pink t-shirt that was too small. She tugged it down over her belly repeatedly, and I wondered why she wore it if it bothered her so much. She leaned into the thick arm of the sofa and talked about her family, holding one hand up to her face, ready to smear away the tears that hovered at the rims of her eyes. She grieved about how they were distancing themselves from her, just so oblivious to what she was going through and the pain she experienced on a daily basis. She sobbed then, tired of feeling so alone, wishing someone would understand her. She leaned forward until her thin, dark hair covered her tear-streaked face like a curtain.

I understand, Lauren.

As the coordinator validated and verbally comforted Lauren, and then continued the discussion, I watched Lauren weep. She sat deeper in the corner of the red sofa, pulling her legs up as tightly as she could. My heart swelled with compassion for her. I understood the loneliness of healing, as well as the frustration of receiving constant criticism that you aren't healing fast enough.

My family wanted to see me heal and get better, but they didn't understand my personal struggle through it. I had trouble externalizing what PTSD did to me. I struggled to vocalize the symptoms I experienced, like the violent flashbacks that came frequently, the painful body memories that swept through my pelvic region and face, or the excruciating "feelings" of the abuse that I could not put names to. PTSD brought a pain so bright, so terrifying, and so consuming, that being present in the real world took extraordinary effort. I fought with all my might to control it and hide it—determined to shield others from it ever since the day I watched Traci's son, Jonas, for a few hours at her house. When Traci returned home, Jonas told her I made him *uncomfortable.*

Those words from a child horrified me and broke my heart, and I purposed never to make anyone uncomfortable again. To do that, I kept much of my journey—and pain—to myself, because I knew nobody would understand. I knew it would make them uncomfortable and speechless. My words would be like a foreign language unless they had suffered it themselves, and no one in my family had. So I fought a silent, lonely battle, keeping my family at arm's length, while they tried earnestly to push themselves in. My sister pushed too hard.

She met with me one day at a local coffee shop for what I believed would be a nice visit, and a break away from my dark pit at home.

As we sat across from each other at the glossy oak table, she reached down and pulled a thick book from her bag and slid it across the table. On the cover, it read, *Healing is a Choice.* I hung my head, infuriated.

I believe Cris cared a great deal about my suffering, but I know now that people don't always know how to approach someone who's hurting so deeply. It's partially my fault, because I hid my pain well. Because of my silent suffering, and the mask I wore portraying normalcy, she didn't *see* me moving forward in my healing. Instead, she believed I was choosing not to heal.

"I'm working very hard at my healing, Cris," I said with gritted teeth, and looked out the window beside me. The streets glistened from an earlier rain, and now the sun bore down on the asphalt, creating pillars of steam. I could feel the heat inside me, and didn't want to get started trying to explain myself.

I never told my family what I went through to get to therapy every week, and the panic attacks that ensued every time I did. I didn't talk about the brutal fight to discuss my past, but that I tried anyway. I didn't complain about how impossible it felt just getting through the day, let alone clean the house, cook a meal, or take care of my two children. I could barely care for myself. I didn't talk about the slow, painful, emotional deterioration of my heart and soul. I knew how hard I fought, but I didn't feel the need to disclose the details to my family. So often, words mean nothing, and actions mean everything. But with childhood sexual abuse and PTSD, healing is agonizingly slow, and often gets much worse before it gets better. Actions can be misinterpreted. *My actions*, as I struggled with PTSD like a drowning victim in a rapid current, were grossly misinterpreted.

As Cris sat there questioning my desire to heal, saying that surely if I really, really wanted to heal, I'd be so much farther along, I wanted to scream at her. I wanted to scream out my reality, and make her see that healing doesn't happen overnight.

I tried to explain that, but my words didn't satisfy her.

For an hour and a half she shared her opinions about my lack of progress, and then brought up my relationship with Traci and how she felt it was dysfunctional and co-dependent. I had hoped our visit would be a peaceful chat about whatever things happy sisters talk about—but instead, I sat across from her in tears. Still, the grilling continued as she tried to get her point across; and inside, my rage boiled, but my voice had frozen. I've never been able to talk back to my sister. Through my teenage years, I had no power in our relationship; and in this stifling coffee shop, I didn't have much fight in me. But rage pushed the words forth.

"I'm doing the best I can," I said, raising my voice enough to draw glances from across the room.

"Hush—" She scolded. "We are in a public place."

My chin dropped. I sat there in shock, tears streaming, nose dripping. For the last thirty minutes, I'd wanted only to run from the coffee shop, run from her, and run to the safety of my home, screaming all the way; but I'd been frozen in my chair. Frozen under her thumb. But panic rose into my throat now, and I couldn't breathe. The room started spinning, the people around us blurred, and the blackness crept across the edges of my peripheral vision. The numbness had begun to spread across my face like butter across bread, and I choked on my tears. I knew I had to run.

I bolted from my chair in desperation and pushed through the double glass doors of the coffee shop. Weakly, I stumbled towards my van, aware of human presence all around me, but too pulled from reality to *see them*. I felt like the sky was falling, and turning pitch black around me. Blindly, I grappled through my purse for my keys, even while my knees threatened to buckle beneath me. I couldn't stand any longer. I knew people stopped to stare. I fell, and Cris's arms braced me. She pulled me up and hugged me, while the rage surged through my skin like a flash flood. I was too weak to speak, or even respond. I sobbed uncontrollably in her arms, but I wanted to scream at her to get away. While Cris thought we bonded in that moment, my reality was that I had just suffered excruciating torture by ruthless hands, bled out without an ounce of concern, and stood humiliated before an audience of dozens without being saved.

෨

Yeah... I understood Lauren and the tears she shed on that red sofa. I understood the hurt feelings and the isolation she described. As the meeting came to a close, I felt compelled to speak.

"You know, I just thought I'd share something I did that seemed to help my family."

"Go right ahead," Jim urged, projecting his hand toward me as if to give me the floor.

"I wrote an email to all of them, trying to explain what I was going through. I'm sure they didn't really get it, but I shared things I never could have shared out loud. I said I realized that PTSD is something they've never seen, and it's uncomfortable for them, and sometimes they don't know what to say, so they remain silent. I included information about PTSD, and gave a couple links for more info online. I also told them about cutting... and that was, of course, the hardest part. But I guess it was my way of trying to let them in. I guess I felt that the more they understand, the less intimidating this will be for them. And *I* needed to realize that every one of us has been shocked by this disorder. My family suffers because I'm suffering. They love me. And I believe your families love each of you, too," I said, sweeping my gaze across the room and pausing at Lauren. "They just might need help understanding."

There were nods all around, and I shortly understood that no one had tried this. I hoped Lauren would.

ॐ

I ditched lunch, hiding alone in my room, but a knock at my door interrupted my silent haven. A man peeked in and introduced himself as Dr. Webb, and said he would be one of my psychiatrists during my stay. As he pulled up the chair in my room, he didn't hesitate to start questioning me. Gently at first, and I did my best to share openly and honestly. I knew my family had emptied their pockets for me so that I could be here; I couldn't let them down by not giving it everything I had. However, my ability to participate in the conversation waned. As he fired question after question, the tightness in my chest squeezed my airways like a vise. He asked detailed questions about medications, and which ones I'd taken. I could only think to say "every one" because that was true, but he wanted details. A history.

I couldn't give it. I couldn't remember. It was like someone was piling bricks inside my brain. The more questions he asked, the more bricks came pounding down, and I grew more and more flustered that I could not remember. The tears welled up.

"This is hard for you, isn't it?" Dr. Webb interjected.

"Yes..." Blackness crept across the edges again. My face numbed.

"Do you want me to change the subject?" he asked.

"It's not the subject," I answered, though at first I didn't realize *what* had triggered the panic. Dr. Webb looked at me, curious. "It's the questions. Just... too many questions."

"What happened for you?" he asked.

"I don't know," I searched for feelings. I hated trying to explain feelings. "They just came too fast. I felt cornered. Confused. I don't know. I'm sorry."

"It's perfectly okay," he smiled. "We'll move on to something else."

ॐ

For hours after, I felt the aftermath of the emotional sprint with Dr. Webb—of dumping out information about my past to be cooperative, not realizing I had cracked open the lid of Pandora's Box. In the quiet isolation of my room later, a horrific flashback thrust me into a dismal grave.

A weight on my chest. Darkness. I can't breath and feel terrified. His haunting eyes pierce into my consciousness; they are above me. They look right into me. Laughter. He has the power, and the swift sweep of his hand over my mouth stifles the scream in my throat. The words "Get off me!" are trapped in my mouth. No one saves me. I fight to get his weight off me, but he is so strong, and he knows it. My chest is going to explode. My God no, not again. I can't breathe. I can't breathe!

I am suddenly kicking in my bed. Kicking the covers away, and I am back under the bright fluorescent light above me. Panting, gasping for air. Forgetting where I am, then remembering... but wanting to forget *him*. Shivering, I pulled the covers over my head and tried to calm the adrenaline surging through my veins.

∾

By the time dinner arrived, my stomach rumbled with hunger. I dragged myself to the dining room and sat at the head of the long, mahogany table in the center of the room. Looking around the room, I noticed cupboards without doors, and all the necessities of a kitchen sitting out on the countertops: a toaster, microwave oven, napkins in vertical holders, and the coffee pot, where three girls stood in hushed conversation, stirring sugar into cups of tea. One looked over at me and smiled, and suddenly the room filled with the other girls of the ward. Close behind them came the four-tiered food cart stacked with covered plates of food; one with my name on it.

"They put your name on it on purpose," one girl said, noticing my bewilderment. "It's so they can keep track of how many meals you skip. If you miss too many, you'll be put on anorexic watch, and you don't want that. So, if you're going to starve, at least be here to take your plate. Then you can dump it if you want."

The girls seemed to have a system to work the system. They'd obviously been here before.

"I'm Angela, by the way," she smiled.

"Nima, nice to meet you."

When all the girls had taken their seats, Angela took the liberty of introducing me around the table. They seemed like a friendly bunch, but I ate my dinner in silence, listening to the monotone conversations around me. They spoke about the upcoming schedules: a nice, laid-back day tomorrow, and then the next day, Monday, "hitting the pavement hard." I didn't feel ready for that.

I really missed home, but I wouldn't be allowed to call until the following night.

I shared pieces of my story throughout the day with nurses and doctors that came in and out of my room during break times, then psychiatrists, psychologists, and psychiatric nurses. Their questions weren't difficult or too deep, but deceptively easy. They served their purpose, unbeknownst to me, of opening the black bag a little more, causing swarms of dizzying terror that crept into my room at night. And that night, it swirled around me like a vortex when I shut my eyes, then jolted to a stop as a face of horror, just inches from my own. A man with jet-black hair, eyes that emanated a foreboding evil, and dark shadows that cast an eerie warning of pain to come. Instantly, the suffocating feelings came. I tried to scream, but nothing emerged. Frightening images flashed before my eyes like a sped-up slide show. I saw the face of a rapist illuminated, like by a flashlight in the dark. I couldn't shut it off. I knew he wanted to hurt me again. Then just as quickly as it began, it ended, and I got off the merry-go-round gasping for breath, clutching my hands over the fierce beating against my inner chest wall, and wiping the sweat that had soaked my hair.

I heard a tap on the small, rectangular window in my door. I looked over and saw Bruce, one of the aids in the ward. Bruce was a large, black man in his early thirties with a smooth, kind face. He smiled as he pushed the door open a couple of inches.

"Everything okay in here?" he whispered.

I didn't realize I'd made any noise. "Yeah... just... rough night, I guess." The embarrassment was lumbering. I still felt like I was the only person these things happened to. I still felt like a freak.

"Hey, it'll be okay," he reassured me. "How about I make you some tea? The girls really seem to appreciate chamomile tea when they have trouble sleeping."

So I wasn't the only one. I agreed to the tea.

"You know, Lewis is a great guy to talk to. He's over at the nurse's station. He's got lots of ideas about getting to sleep. Really... you should talk to him."

It wasn't a feeling or a desire to talk that drew me to the nurse's station; it was desperation for sleep. The terrors haunted me nonstop and wouldn't let me be. But Bruce was right about Lewis. As he heard my plight, he didn't look shocked or disgusted. He listened.

"You're not a freak, Nima," he smiled warmly. "I know this is tough, but what you're experiencing is actually part of the process. When you're talking so openly and deeply about the past, you're bound to stir up the pot. It's normal to have nightmares and flashbacks, but that's why we're here. To talk to, or just listen. Some girls just use us to scream and yell at."

I laughed as Bruce showed up with a steaming cup of tea.

"You think I'm kidding? I'm not!" Lewis laughed in return. "This is not easy stuff you're dealing with! We've seen more pain here than you can imagine."

I could imagine.

"Listen..." he went on."I'm not really supposed to do this because it's only your second night. But you seem like an honest person. I'd be willing to give you a CD player for your room if you promise not to do anything harmful with it."

"With a CD player?" I mocked.

"Hey, you'd be surprised what a desperate person will do."

I thought again of the razor blade still hidden under my mattress. I knew desperation. "Okay. Yeah... I promise."

Lewis walked me to my room with a CD player in hand, and soon the comforting music of Kenny G and his hypnotic soprano saxophone played softly in the background. Sitting upright in bed, sipping my tea with the covers pulled up around my waist, I hugged my pillow and prayed for peaceful sleep. And for the first time in six nights, it came.

On Sunday afternoon, they played the movie *28 Days* with Sandra Bullock. I watched it, curled up in my favorite plush, yellow chair, with some other girls who sat on the red sofa. Trigger after trigger in that movie brought me to tears, which I kept quietly to myself. I probably should have left the room, but I stayed. Sandra plays a fraught alcoholic at her rope's end, and she fights the process of recovery; that is, until a girl in the program commits suicide. I was glued to the scenes of aftermath that followed, and grieved intensely from my own recent near attempt. It was the mother's reaction—the devastation that emanated painfully from her whole body—that struck me so deeply. She didn't cry right away, but you could see the shock, the abysmal sadness and disbelief of her cherished daughter being ripped suddenly and mercilessly out of her world. She'd had no say in it, and she could not reverse it or bring her daughter back. As the mom walked away from the resident home clutching her daughter's belongings, it hit me like a freight train: the monstrosity of what I had almost done.

In that moment, I knew deeply and with certainty that if Traci had not shown up that night, and if I had swallowed my death, that would be the look on their faces. Mike's, Lacey's, and little Jordan's. The memory came back vividly, sitting on my own sofa at home with the fatal dose of green pills in my cupped hand, and I recalled the draconian belief that the world of the people I cared about would be so much better without me in it. Now I knew better. I knew that maybe they wouldn't get over it at all. The devastation I would cause to their world would be unforgivable, and tormenting for the rest of their lives. I wept into the sleeves of my sweatshirt, soaking in the realization of my family's imperfect but incredible love. They may not know how to love me now, but I could suddenly see that they did, indeed, love me a lot. Even my sister.

❧

That evening they allowed me to call Mike for the first time, and I cried into the phone. The pain of missing them burned a hole in my heart. But in his magical way, he lifted me up, made me laugh in my most dire moment of grief, and said the girls were doing just fine. His cheerfulness removed the boulder from my shoulders. He made me believe they would be okay. "Just do your best and take care of you," he said gently. "We're doing just fine here."

I assured him that I would, and would make him proud.

"I am proud of you, you goofball," he chuckled.

I sent my hug through the line.

❧

Journal Entry — Monday, October 10, 2005

Today I met Eva, my new contact person, and an Asian beauty. She moves a mile a minute and so does her mouth. But sharing my beliefs about myself in a matter-of-fact way drew a constant look of shock from her. She finally said, "You are a tough one, girl. I can see you're going to be a tough one to crack."

I don't know what that means. I'm telling my truth; but here, I'm starting to make connections between the trauma in my past and who I am today. I believe I have some great qualities and abilities, but I'm living in my head. When I met with my psychiatrist today and shared my belief of being undeserving of real love, he tried to use the "reversal of positions" technique—trying to make me put myself in someone else's shoes to view me—and I stopped him in his tracks. "Traci always does that to me and you can't. Because I'm different!" I warned.

I. Am. Undeserving. I love to reach out to other people and care for them—especially when I see someone hurting. That's me. But I can't receive it from them. Not as a selfless gift. I receive something and I either believe I now owe them, or I question their motives. But I did realize something while talking with Jim about processing trauma. Before I came here, that was my goal—and Kali's goal—to process the trauma. But now I see the definite value in learning first how to control the flashbacks and memories, rather than them having the power over me. I need to be strong, confident, and ready. Otherwise, I'll have no tools to box up the trauma when I need to. It's different than "stuffing." It's putting the box on a shelf and getting to it later, when I'm ready. I need to learn new coping skills. I don't want to stop cutting, but I know it's not healthy. I know I must quit.

My motto today: "Be willing to try something different!" I haven't been willing. I've wanted to cope the way I'd been coping. Cutting works for me; and yet, it's dysfunctional—I know that—and it only hurts more in the end. Starting the processing will be explosive and will bring up new stuff. I need to be ready to cope—to respond to those memories—without harming myself. Otherwise it will never end.

࿏

On Wednesday, Eva pulled me aside to ask me some questions. She had been pondering the beliefs I shared about myself from the trauma, and wanted to know more. I told her that I'm unlovable, and that I'm ugly and dirty. She leaned into my face.

"Whoa! If your best friend was saying she felt those things about herself, what would you say to her?"

I got mad. "Damn! You guys and your role reversals! I told you, you can't pull that reverse crap on me because the rules don't apply."

"Why not?" she demanded.

"Because I'm different than everyone else!" I shouted in a high-pitched voice. *Why couldn't they get this?* My hands were shaking, and her silence emphasized my labored breathing.

"What makes you so different?" Her face tilted as if she couldn't wait for my reply; like it would reveal the answers of the universe.

I opened my mouth to give her a definitive, undisputable answer, but nothing came out. She had me. Instantly, the tears burned in the backs of my retinas because I knew the answer to that question was in a deep place in my heart where I didn't want to go.

"It's okay," she said, relieving my panic. "I won't make you respond. *Yet.* But I really want you to think about the answer to that."

Eva walked away, abating my discomfort with a gentle grip on my shoulder. I sat alone, suddenly reminded of the secret belief I'd carried all my life about Jesus' love for me. Throughout my teenage years, I told many people about the love of Christ. I believed the Bible, and that God granted mercy and grace to all people, not because they deserved it, but because of His love for them. I prayed the prayer of salvation many times with others, witnessing with utter joy as people gave their hearts to Christ, and I believed without a doubt that their lives would be changed. And yet, in the darkness of night, alone with my heart, I knew the truth. Yes, Jesus died on the cross for everyone... everyone but *me.*

I knew He didn't die for me, because I'm unlovable.

Just as strongly as I believed this, I also believed I was different. I watched, in group after group, as the girls shed their tears, experienced grief, and let their emotions pour out like a jackpot machine in a Las Vegas casino. I just couldn't do it. Only within the safety of the docile walls of my home, alone, would I allow myself to expel the tears and torture of the pain inside, and even propel a scream now and then. But not to anyone else. *Never* would I cry in front of someone else, or show anger, or reveal the anguish burning my inner walls. And yet, these girls seemed to express their fear and emotional burdens so easily; I felt envious that they could do so. How freeing it must be to release that, and to receive the validation I witnessed time and time again for their hurt. But I knew I would not receive that. Somehow... innately... I was not okay. I was not worthy of acceptance.

Then a thought crossed my mind. *What if?* What if I was brave enough? What if I was willing to show emotion?

In a session with Eva, she told me that to be real, my outside must match my insides. I must be willing and unafraid to let down the tough exterior and be real with these girls whom I did not know or even feel safe with. I laughed at the improbability; or more accurately, impossibility.

"They'll totally reject me," I said.

"Well, perhaps it would help to think that they won't be in your life forever, or even after you get out of here. Worst case scenario, they totally reject you, as you fear, but then they're out of your life."

I'd been pondering that ever since that session with Eva. Somehow I knew that I would never change and grow if I couldn't be real and open with the hurt. But I was terrified to go there. Terrified to open the black bag of junk, or reach into the depths of my heart to the places where people don't see. The real stuff behind the mask: the pain, the tears and sorrow, and the unbearable hurt there. Over the last several months before coming to the inpatient treatment program, I had reached that place alone. I allowed it. I felt the pain, and felt like dying because of it. But to show it to someone else? No way.

Why do I feel it's necessary to hide it? Why do I shut off the pain so quickly when someone walks in the room or triggers an emotional gust during a conversation? I immediately switch to the smile that says, "I'm fine! I'm handling things. I'm okay. See my smile?" And then I use humor to deflect whatever concern I see flash in their eyes. Why? Because if they don't ask, I won't need to tell. There is no threat of losing control, which is what would happen if I punctured that black bag of pain. Because then what would people think of that Nima—vulnerable, exposed, and falling to pieces? Would they reject me? Think I'm just a big crybaby? Think I'm weak? And judge me?

If one of these girls asked me that about themselves, I would say, "Of course not! They would think you were courageous and brave, and respect you for being so real and honest. Sharing your heart is what fuels your healing, and makes you stronger and closer to being whole. *You must be real.*"

There I go... playing those reverse roles. Oh, how I wanted to believe that was true of me.

ॐ

In my next meeting I met a new therapist, John Marshall. We discussed my identity and relationships with others, and I realized I've always played the safe route. I adapted easily to peoples' lives— learning their needs, what makes them happy—and then lived in a harmonizing way. A way that constantly keeps the peace in the relationship.

"What happens if you make a mistake?" John asked, leaning forward, elbows to knees.

"Something really bad," I answered sadly. "It's very bad to make mistakes. I can't make anyone angry with me. Ever."

"Or what—" he asked.

"Or I'm out of the picture," I quivered. "If someone gets angry with me, it's over. They won't love me anymore. So I'm a peacemaker. If I do something wrong, I have to make it up to them before they realize what I've done. And I will keep making it up to them until I see that look on their face that says they're okay with me."

John sat back in his chair, astounded by my words, but I had trouble reading him. He looked confused.

"You live your life to please others, rather than putting your own needs first. You live to conform to their lives, their way of life. But doesn't Nima get lost in all of that? You've been doing this all your life—so much so that it's become second nature to you. But don't you lose yourself in the process?"

I was crying when I looked up and said, "John, I don't even know who I am. Not really. I've built my identity around others, and around these distorted beliefs inside. I'm a fraud."

"No," he said. "You've been bruised, and misguided. But you have to start realizing that you are an amazing woman whose needs matter. Whose thoughts matter. *You* matter. You're not a fraud. As a matter of fact, you have a very important place in this world."

"And what's that..." I droned in disbelief.

"Just being you," he whispered, "And that's what will make a difference in the world and in others' lives. You, being real. Just being you. I think somewhere in there, you know who that is."

❧

Journal Entry — Friday, October 14, 2005

I'm so teary today. My usual methods of shutting off the hurts and bad feelings aren't working. I feel bombarded by the things they're teaching. I have been challenged, but today it feels like too much. People are leaving today; people I've grown close to and connected with. The two people staying, I have nothing in common with. One, I don't like her attitude much. The other talks so much I never get a word in edgewise. I don't feel like sharing my feelings anyway—the hurt and abandonment I feel. But it's not just abandonment; it's a longing for me to be the one leaving. I miss my little girls. Jordan is changing every day and I'm missing it. I miss my husband. I need his arms. I need Traci, and one of her hugs. I suddenly feel so overwhelmed with loneliness. I have Jen here for two more days—she's leaving on Sunday. I can't even begin to know how to say goodbye to her. She's been a security for me.

I keep telling myself that there is a reason why I'm here—that I'll be with a brand new group of people who are hurting. I'll be the "old timer" here. It will give me an even bigger opportunity to reach out and offer compassion and kindness. But still I grieve. Yesterday, looking at the pictures I brought of my family made me laugh. I showed Jen and felt this warmth inside because I know I am loved.

Today, I can't even bear to look at them. I need them. I feel so far away.

And I hurt so much from these sessions with John—from all the unexpected realizations. I came here thinking I just needed to learn some new coping skills. But I realize instead there are so many issues that run much deeper than the trauma. I called them "little issues," but John argued, "They are not little things! These were all tragic events that never should have happened to you!"

I pondered that, but had difficulty accepting it. The rapes. The abuse. My belief for so many years was that these events affected me for a short time, but then I had to move on. Sure, the pain would come, but I could lock it away with the turn of a key. Be tough, Nima. Let it go. And so I did, and that became second nature. They were just "little things" that, if I could just push through—or push away—then I would be stronger. My God... I have so far to go before I can even face the abuse of my past.

And now I feel so sad about that. I'm afraid to tap into all the feelings I've locked away all these years. I have been a strong and tough survivor. What will I be then? Who will I be? I don't want to be weak. I don't want to feel those things—but damnit! I know I need to. I know I need to push through it. I'm so afraid to cry. I'm afraid to fall apart. I'm afraid to lose control. I'm afraid of others seeing that.

I'm getting very tired. Tired of the noises. Of all the people talking. Today I had to walk out of group. It was too much. I'm tired of everyone asking me if I'm okay because "I look different today." I say, "I'm fine," with a smile. I don't know how to respond. The feelings—the emotions—are overwhelming. I have to keep up this appearance that I'm calm, and everything is okay. But it's not. The thought of trying to explain the truth to someone overwhelms me. Just the thought of it and a panic attack starts. So I have to lock it away again. It's just too much. There are so many feelings swarming and it scares me. I can't just pick one and talk about it. Some I can't even identify. If I try to grab one they'll all come exploding out, and I won't be able to stop them. They are so much bigger than me.

God, I miss home. I miss being in places where I feel safe. Everyone sheds so many tears here, and I see and feel their pain. But me... I still can't accept that the rapes, the abuse, were traumatic. I was led to believe long, long ago, that being hurt that way was okay. For some reason, it was supposed to happen to me. And somehow, I was supposed to let it. So I would close my eyes—I would leave— and I wouldn't feel a thing. But I felt pain later. The leftover bruises and blood, the leftover shame. I sure felt those. I still feel those....

☙

What makes me so different? Why don't I allow compassion from others? Why can I not stand up to be applauded when I break through a huge barrier? Why can't I play with my daughters? My therapists have all told me it's a lie—that I'm *not* different. I'm trying to believe that. But my abusers made me believe I was different. Somehow, I was marked for abuse, not love.

☙

Journal Entry — Sunday, October 16, 2005
    My barrier is breaking down. The first several days here, I was being my tough, usual self. Not fighting the system so much, but not giving it my all. It's just not that easy, changing everything I've believed to be true for most of my life into something else. It hurts, and it's sad, and it's scary. Sometimes I feel ripped up inside. I feel confused, trying to see myself the way God sees me, but fighting that belief because it's not what I've been taught to believe. How do I believe I am chosen by God when deep inside I feel that I was chosen to be abused? That I was chosen for bad. And I search for the hope of God's promise that He works all things together for the good, and He will avenge me, redeem me, and make me whole. God makes so many promises. I need to believe them. But I've been feeling a lot, and it hurts so much. God... it hurts so much. I want to cut, but I'm fighting it.

Journal Entry — Monday, October 17, 2005

Why can't I stop? I look at these scars and think, for what? Did it bring me any healing? No. Release yes, but not healing. What does it do, besides bring a momentary confirmation that I'm broken and worthless and don't deserve the love that God wants to give me? That is not healing.

I hate these memories. They haunt me. Pressure against my brain, and they play over and over again through my mind and my dreams. I see flashes of horrible images of me cutting—not just my arms—my whole body. And there's blood everywhere, but I can't see my face. I see myself in that bathroom with Damon. But I'm separated, and I hover higher and higher until I can't hear the girl crying anymore. She lies limp. She has been used again in horrible ways for some sick pleasure of a madman. And there is only darkness all around—it's just that bathroom. Just me. Just him. I hover higher until the image is but a flicker of light in this deep darkness. But I know she is lying there... with her arms wrapped tightly around herself. I know she is still crying. And I know she will never stop.

Journal Entry — Tuesday, October 18, 2005

God touched my heart today! For the first time, I feel hope. Today, it is my mission to be kind to and care for myself. I will work on believing that I deserve that. Today, I'm believing that I can achieve healing and wholeness because God loves me. I feel that today. I feel a warmth in my heart, and a soft voice saying it will be okay. Somehow... it will be okay.

჻

On my last day at Lake Chelan, I took the razor blade from beneath my mattress. I held it over the garbage can in my room, then suddenly realized I needed to do something more than just throw it away. Walking out to the nurse's station, I asked to see Gloria, the cheerful woman who had originally checked me into the program. After a short while, I saw her walk around the corner. She smiled when she saw me.

"You did it!" she cheered. "You're going home today?"

"Yes," I replied. I looked down, took her hand, and placed the razor blade in her palm. She looked up at me, shocked. "I managed to get this by you when I checked in. I hid it in my sock. You guys didn't check there. You might want to in the future. I want you to know I didn't use it; and I don't know why I'm giving it to you, but… it just seems like the right thing to do."

"How very brave, Juanima," she said, taking my hand in hers. "It *was* the right thing to do, and shows how very strong you are. *Thank you.*" The last words, she spoke with a deep emphasis that spoke to my heart. A "thank you" that applauded me for taking care of myself. For showing myself love. It was an enormous, crucial step in my healing, and one I would need to practice daily from then on.

❧

As I carried my suitcase out the double doors, I saw the beautiful smile of my best friend running towards me. She tackled me so hard I nearly fell over. Ahh… my first glimpse of home.

The long drive back was nearly unbearable as I thought of my girls and my husband waiting for me. I imagined I would burst through the door and sweep my two girls into my arms, and then twirl them in endless circles until they were consumed with my love for them. I imagined Mike standing back with a proud grin on his face, glad to have me home. I imagined he would give me a smart remark like, "Finally! Now you can help me clean!" But inside, his heart would swell when he saw the change in my eyes and in my smile, and the charge I emitted from my spirit saying, "I'm here to stay, and I'm on my way up. We're gonna make it."

I envisioned something good, and that was a step forward for me.

8

AN ANGEL NAMED SANDY

My heart nearly burst when I saw my family. Tears filled my eyes as I embraced my precious darlings, and then threw my arms around Mike while the girls clung jovially to my legs. I felt rejuvenated, with a new sense of purpose and strength. No doubt the constant support and encouragement I received at Lake Chelan gave me the boost I needed to return to my home life. I had tasted hope there, and the promise of a different future, and I believed I had entered a new chapter of my healing.

How disappointing to discover that as time went on, the renewed confidence I'd gained faded as I warred alone with the trauma once again. With the safety net of counselors and fellow survivors now absent from my life, the hope and promises I clung to became a fragile thread that held me over the deep, foreboding chasm of what was still to come.

The black bag had been punctured at Lake Chelan, and there was no resealing it. As the flashbacks became more frequent and intense, I became desperate for relief. Every moment, I thought of just cutting away the agony that feasted upon my spirit. Dr. Cross recommended I pursue other forms of medication, since conventional medications made my symptoms worse. She wanted me to try antipsychotics, which I reluctantly agreed to do.

She sent me to see Pearl Kidman, a mental health nurse practitioner who offered to guide me through some medication trials. Because of perilous side effects, I refused to even try Geodon, but agreed to a trial of Abilify. On the second day of the trial, however, I drove past the school where Lacey attended and felt a sudden surge of rage so intense, I had to pull over. It consumed me in a way I'd never experienced, like a fiery force thrashed against the inside of my chest, crushing my airways. I clawed at my chest as I struggled to take air into my lungs. A wave of panic seized every nerve in my system, and for a moment I thought of rushing myself to the hospital. But somehow, experience overruled; I knew the drug caused my symptoms, though this was the most intense and terrifying drug experience yet.

Looking out the window, the neighborhood around me blurred and vibrated, clouding over like a fog. And inside me, a burning anger seemed to come from nowhere, wrapping around my brain like a fist, squeezing, gripping, and seizing my thoughts with a dark blanket of rage. I screamed. Loud, and long, and I couldn't stop. I threw myself down across the passenger seat of the van, clutching my chest in a fight against the urge to rip the interior of my car apart. It took thirty minutes for the rage to ebb, and for my vision to return so that I could finish the drive home. With trembling hands on the wheel, I numbly inched my van down the final block, so relieved when I finally pulled into the driveway. My legs shook as I dove for the front door and stumbled inside, still gasping for a breath. That was the last time I took Abilify.

While Pearl couldn't successfully provide medicinal relief, she gave me a much greater gift. It was through her that I met Sandy Neale, a licensed clinical social worker who specialized in trauma. Though I had developed a special relationship and fondness for Kali, the hour-long drives and accompanying panic attacks proved too much to endure. Weekly visits also put a heavy financial burden on my family. I'd been searching for a therapist closer to home when Pearl referred me to Sandy. I hadn't seen Kali in three weeks, and unfortunately, I couldn't see Sandy for another two weeks. I knew this would make that first visit as grueling as my drive to Lake

Chelan. Having a weekly therapy routine helped me stay accountable; stay focused on my progress, and set goals for my next session. Gaps in therapy gave me a needed break, but if they extended too long, fear made it feel impossible to return again. In the absence of therapy, I'd quickly shut down and fall back into my pain and isolation. Before long, I would be resistant to open that black bag again for anyone.

However, I tried not to waste my time alone. In the days waiting to see Sandy, the depression worsened, and I had to fight steadily against the desire to stop healing altogether. But my awareness of the consequences of my near suicide had impacted me so deeply—how it would have destroyed my girls and family—that it became an automatic kick to my backside. Anytime I felt like giving up, I thought of them. I reminded myself that it was up to *me alone* to break the generational chain of abuse. No matter how tormenting the journey, even if all I could do was hang on, I would be okay as long as I didn't let go, or give up. I had to fight for them no matter how painful it got for me.

During this—and all—absences from therapy, I journaled frequently and reflected over therapy notes, and took mental action on things I or Traci had written. For instance, why negative feedback from Mike triggered a fight or flight reaction. I believed it was because of my perfectionism, and my belief that if I'm not perfect, something bad will happen. Or the belief that if I make a mistake, Mike will no longer love me. I know if I actually said that out loud to him, he would say it was the stupidest thing he'd ever heard. But I believed it inside.

I also wrote emails to Traci, and quickly learned that writing was my healing token. I could easily put things on paper that I could never say aloud. The more I wrote, the barriers between me, my past, and sharing it with others broke little by little. Traci rejoiced over every deep piece of writing I sent to her, and the times I shared my pain. Sometimes I felt brave and wrote to others in my family, praying they would understand me better. Traci fought hard to understand what I was going through, and I appreciated the questions she asked in efforts to stand closer to me through the journey. Still, my healing burdened her, too. In the early months and years of PTSD, the emotional weight drained her and her entire family. I have never seen such love, as they selflessly continued to take me in as a friend and nurture me, never judging me, but lifting me up, praying for me, and keeping me afloat. But I did not always meet expectations as a friend with Traci. I could talk to her about my pain, but at times it was so overpowering, so crushing, I couldn't speak at all. The silence sometimes lasted for days, and tormented her to no end. During those days, all I could do to survive the pain was contain it. There were no words to express. Truly, she is the most patient friend I've ever known.

Her encouragement abounded. She so closely walked with me that she, more than anyone else, noticed the small victories. I spent days with her at her house when the girls were in daycare. I knew that with her, I could breathe. I was safe, at times from myself. And I knew it was healthy for me to interact with someone, rather than drown in the isolation of home. God knows I preferred seclusion, my comfortable and welcoming ally. It was a fight to do the things I knew were right—the things that would bring healing—like *talk*.

I loved being with Traci, but on the days I hurt the most, making that drive to her house grated hard against my will. She longed to hear my heart, but finding words for my emotions was like grasping through swampy waters for a lost treasure. When I found words, she celebrated, and each time meant a milestone for me. But expression exhausted me, often rushing me back mentally to a childhood state whenever I reflected on the abuse, and I would fall into her comfort like a needy child. When the time came for me to leave, I felt like a five-year-old being sent out into the bad, bad world alone, and in the pouring rain, no less. On those days, I drudged my way to my car, knowing I had to be a responsible adult and go home, but I was so scared to leave the safety of my friend.

One winter afternoon, I sat in my van, parked in Traci's driveway. I had left her only moments before, but I just couldn't drive away. Inside the van, I trembled. I knew I had to go home. Traci had a large family to take care of. She simply couldn't cater to my dark, emotional state on a constant basis, but it was as hard for her to send me away as it was for me to go. It was titanic, bearing the pain alone. On this day, the fear clutched relentlessly at my chest. Strangely, I didn't even feel old enough to drive the car, which I later learned was a phenomenon called age regression. A trigger had literally sent me back mentally to the age of when the abuse occurred. I suddenly felt like a child: scared, alone, and unable to shift the van into reverse. I sat there for what seemed like a mere few minutes when Traci knocked on my window, sucking me out of my trance. I rolled it down.

"What's going on?" she asked with a hint of frustration.

"I'm going home," I managed to say, weakly.

"You've been sitting out here for over half an hour," she said, realizing I wasn't altogether there. She reached in and hugged me. "Are you gonna be okay?"

I nodded. It was the answer I had to give. It was time for the responsible adult to come forth and push the little scared child down, though it felt impossible. My hands went through the trained motions of putting the van in reverse. I looked back at Traci and waved as the tears began to rise. I stepped on the gas and drove away, straining to see the road through the tears now cascading down my face.

Dissociation happened on a regular basis. When emotional pain overpowered me, I unconsciously slipped away. Hours at a time could be lost, and I would have no recollection of what had occurred. When therapy became routine, and I delved deeper into the black bag, dissociation came hand-in-hand. It's the reason I remember very little about my therapy sessions. Honestly, I cannot recreate many of them for the purposes of this book, save for a few powerful sessions that are permanently imprinted in my brain. My struggle—and the terror I felt—attending a single therapy session was so profound, I often couldn't stay mentally present in the room, let alone respond to questions from the therapist. The scars my past abuse had etched into my soul were so monumentally painful, and shoved so far back into my subconscious, that handling it and bringing it to the surface was more than I could handle. Kali had worked at such a slow pace for me, but it simply didn't take much to make me disappear—to retreat into my safe place, away from the danger and darkness of my past.

೩

In February 2006, my first appointment with Sandy arrived, and I could barely climb into Traci's car. Surely God pressed against my back, pushing me there, because I could not walk on my own two feet. My absence from therapy had stretched so long, I'd closed the black bag up tight. I knew I would have to tell my whole story again, and the thought of that made me sick to my stomach. I didn't think I could bear it, but I knew I would have to try.

Sandy's office was inside a small, vertical building in a large business park. We parked right in front, and sat in the car until the last minute. Traci remained silent, knowing my state of panic was so intense, I barely held myself together. We went to the door of the building, and a small bell rang overhead as she pulled it open for me. Sandy had said her office was at the top of the stairs, which was just inside the door on the right. Taking a deep breath of courage, I climbed slowly up the steep, narrow carpeted staircase with Traci right behind. A few unoccupied offices flanked the top of the stairs, but one immediately next to the staircase had its door closed, and I heard muffled voices on the other side.

"Come in here," Traci whispered as she disappeared into an open room adjacent to Sandy's. The room had a small waiting area, with a dozen chairs backed up against three of the walls, and a short rectangular table near Sandy's second door that held the makings for tea or hot chocolate. I went up to it, hoping for some cocoa, but the hot water carafe was empty. A portable radio sat on the table edge, which I turned on for quiet distraction from the noises in my head. I fought to contain my fear. I could already feel the numbness creeping along the right side of my face and across both hands. I sat down in a chair next to Traci and took a deep breath. She grabbed hold of my hand and smiled. The short waiting period before my therapy sessions scourged my nerves. I'd made a habit of leaving home as late as possible so I could arrive directly on time for the appointment. The waiting reminded me of when I was a child, and if I did something punishable, Mom would say, "Your Dad will deal with you when he gets home."

The hours would pass, and then I would see his car coming up the long, gravel driveway. If I had done something terrible in his mind, I knew I would get multiple lashings of his belt across my backside. So as I waited, the fear grew to trembling heights when he'd get out of the car and head towards the house. I'd hide in my room, which was on the opposite side of the mobile home than my parent's. He would come inside, see me and smile, not knowing what his forthcoming duty was. He would disappear into his bedroom, where Mom waited to tell him what I had done. In those next moments of silence, of whispering, I wanted to hide under my bed and never come out. Never ever! I knew it was coming any minute! I would have much rather taken a whipping from Mom at the time of the act than go through this horrendous waiting. All that time to build up the punishment in my mind of how much it was going to hurt; how bad it was going to feel. I just wanted to run away.

Now, I could tell that Sandy was wrapping up her appointment, and I just wanted to run. The fear gripped my chest and lungs. Just as the room started to spin around me, Sandy opened the door.

"Juanima?" she asked with a smile.

"Yeah," I said, rising weakly from the chair. I forced a smile as I walked into her office, and Traci followed. I had asked her to join me in my sessions to take notes because the dissociating response was so strong, and so prevalent, that after the session I remembered very little of what we had spoken about. The work was being done, but I needed to remember what to do afterwards, the instructions that were given, and key points I had learned that made an impact on me. Traci always seemed to know what those key points were, and wrote them down for me.

As I entered Sandy's office, I took on a different persona. Just as I had with Kali, the Nima who entered the office was a defiant, tough, impenetrable sixteen-year-old, determined to keep her secrets and personal battles locked up tight, protecting herself at all costs. I flopped down in the chair, not immediately realizing the muscles throughout my body stiffening and tightening like a bowstring.

First, we discussed the financial aspects of our visits. Her cost was half of what I had paid for Kali's time. That in itself would help immensely. Then she said those fateful words: "So tell me about yourself."

I had prepared for them. I knew she would ask them. I knew every new therapist asked them, but it never failed to trigger panic, numbness, and dissociating. I took a deep breath, knowing I needed to answer that question, but the rebellious teenager spoke first.

"What do you want to know?" I asked flippantly with a smirk. Traci rolled her eyes.

"Why don't you start by telling me what brought you here?"

I looked at her, studying her, wondering if she was going to be everything Pearl said she would be. I wondered what was behind those glasses-covered eyes. She didn't have the look of a highbrow, arrogant, emotionless shrink who would try to get in my head. In my "teenage" mind, Sandy reminded me of a sweet, petite grandma. A simple woman with a blue sweater, corduroy slacks, and Birkenstocks, who fussed little with her dark brown, short, layered haircut. Sandy seemed like a real person, and she waited patiently for my answer. I knew I could continue my teenage charade of deflecting, and avoid the real reason I was there. But seriously... what a waste of time. I knew I had to man up and get to the point. Get to the *pain*, and give Sandy a chance.

"I've been diagnosed with PTSD, and I heard you could help me. I... was abused as a child. Many times. By different people. I've had some therapy already—out in Gresham—but I haven't really talked about the abuse yet, and I needed to see someone closer to home."

"Okay," she nodded. "Well, I'm glad you're here. Do you want to tell me more about the abuse?"

Just give facts, I thought. No details. I can do that. I averted my gaze to the floor as I told my story. "I was abused by an uncle when I was seven, ten, and thirteen. My stepfather molested me when I was fourteen, and my boyfriend also raped me that year. I was a freshman in high school then... he was a senior. I was a virgin." I took a constricting breath. This never got any easier to say. "We moved that year, and then my sophomore year, I was molested by a twenty-eight-year-old at the apartment complex we lived in. He lured me up to his apartment from the pool. By then, I was doing a lot of drugs... drinking a lot of alcohol. Nobody knew. I stole my sister's car at night to get to parties. I shoplifted. Then my mom kicked me out and made me go live with my dad—they had divorced when I was ten. I hated him at the time... that's another long story. I was raped at a party that first year, and then I tried to kill myself. When that didn't work, I almost tried again, but decided to run away instead. I did... with my friend, Darcy. We lived on the streets in Reno for a week, and I was raped three times. Those... were all really bad. Really bad...."

I was shaking, and the blackness was creeping around my vision.

"Do you need to stop?" she asked, concerned.

"No—" I said firmly. "I need to finish." A few moments passed before I could speak.

"Darcy and I got found out, and the police arrested us. Our parents flew down to get us. I never spoke about what happened to me."

"Did anything happen to Darcy?"

"I don't know." I stared at the floor, out the window; anywhere but Sandy's eyes. "After Reno—when I got home—I kept my dad in the dark about what had happened to me. I told no one. Later, I found out I was failing high school and wouldn't graduate. My dad said he'd help me through summer school, and thought maybe I also needed a break from everything. He had a friend with horses, and I loved horses. This guy had a wife and two children about my age. We spent a long weekend out there, and had a great time until my dad left to do an appraisal. His friend came into the kitchen and stuck his hand up my shirt. I couldn't believe it... I just couldn't... anyway... that's pretty much it. I mean... there's more... but..."

"I'm so *sorry*... for all that's happened to you, Juanima. For all that trauma."

I heard the tremble in Sandy's voice and looked at her for the first time. "It's okay... it really wasn't that traumatic," I replied from a distant place. I figured she must say that to all of her clients.

"*No!*" Her response both shocked and jolted me from my daze. She was the one shaking now, furious, and almost in tears. "It's *not* okay! It's horrible! *Horrible!* None of this should have happened to you, Juanima! You should be angry! Very, very angry at these guys!"

I stared at her, frozen in the words that she had unleashed. My mouth hung open, locked in her genuine compassion, and the anger she so freely displayed. The anger she said I should have. The anger that Dr. Lynch said was so wrong. This woman was gushing with it, and it shocked me. I honestly didn't understand what she was so upset about. But as we talked about the abuse further as a whole, my state-of-mind in relation to my abuse became clearer to her.

"Tell me... when you picture one of these incidents that happened to you, how do you see it?"

"Like it's happening to someone else. Like I'm up in a corner of the room against the ceiling, watching it happen."

Sandy nodded with understanding. "You don't believe it was trauma because you dissociated through it each and every time. When you do that, you have no emotional attachment to it. It's derealization, depersonalization. You mentally leave your body. It's common. It's how many children survive their abuse. But I'm here to tell you, Juanima, that what happened to you was very wrong, and very traumatic, and you didn't deserve any of it."

Yes I did, I thought. But I didn't want her to yell again, so I kept silent.

"I'd really like to keep seeing you, Juanima," Sandy leaned toward me with genuine caring. "Will you come back to see me?"

"Yeah," I nodded. "Yeah... I will." I didn't know what to think of Sandy's outburst, but one thing I did know: that was the first time any therapist had gotten angry about what had happened to me. Sandy showed a tremendous heart of compassion and a true desire for justice for abuse victims, and for *me*. I knew I would be staying with her for a while. I knew my next step of healing would be starting here.

చ

"It's coming..."
"What is coming?"
"My past."
"It makes you uncomfortable?"
"Yes."
"What about it makes you uncomfortable?"
"All of it. It's all uncomfortable."
"What else are you feeling about it?"
"Anxiety. A lot of it."
"What are you afraid of?"
"I don't know. I'm afraid it will kill me. And I'm afraid of confrontation. I'm afraid you'll ask me questions that are going to make me feel cornered, and that I won't be able to get out."

"Okay. Juanima, first you must know that I will never put you in a corner without giving you a way out. I promise. You are in control of these sessions, not me. I'm more like a guide, and when you share something with me, I'll take that information and try to lead you to a better way of thinking, and a better understanding of things. Tell me another time you have felt cornered."

I'm sure Sandy had no idea how difficult this was for me. It wasn't just talking about the abuse that put me in a panic, but all the stuff surrounding it. Feelings triggered a wave of mental hysteria because I couldn't put a name to them; so most of the time, I didn't know what I felt. And since our discussions were all based around the abuse of my past, the frustration of trying to talk about feelings was like someone grilling you for facts about a place you'd never been to. They are so convinced you've been there, and demand answers and descriptions, but you just don't have them. Sandy, however, was being amazingly patient with me.

"I feel cornered when someone confronts me. About anything. I panic. Even with my kids. Especially with my kids, because I'm supposed to be the parent. I'm supposed to be in control, and patient, and always have an answer. Lacey cornered me the other day, and it was horrible." Just thinking about it brought tears to my eyes. "The girls were arguing. Jordan's just three, and Lacey is seven. They fought over a toy, and I couldn't take it. I yelled at them to stop fighting, and Lacey ran to me, crying, and stated her case. Jordan was right behind her, also crying, trying to yell louder. But it's like they're both yelling at me, and then my chest got tight, and I couldn't breathe. And, my God, I'm supposed to be the parent, right? I'm supposed to be able to kneel down beside them and help them solve the problem. But I just froze! I stood there grabbing my hair in my hands and just yelled for them to stop... which, of course, made them cry more.

"It's also when people ask me questions. I can't make decisions. I get confused, and panic. Even Lacey asking me to play on the computer... I panic. Like I'm on a stage in front of thousands of people and someone asks me a question I don't know the answer to. I feel cornered when my sister confronts me about my healing, or anything negative I'm doing. I feel cornered anytime I go to a family function, and someone asks me how I'm doing. Or what I've been up to. What am I supposed to say? 'Oh, I'm great! I'm dying a slow, horrible death while healing from sexual abuse! How are you?' Yeah... right. It's any confrontation at all, basically."

"Wow, Nima," Sandy puffed, leaning back in her chair. "You really are hard on yourself, aren't you?"

My chin quivered with the validation I didn't know I needed. Sandy continued.

"Every time you were abused as a child, you were cornered, and not given any voice power to get out of your situation. You are re-experiencing these feelings now every time you're confronted. It's like a trigger. Were there other times in your childhood when you felt this way?"

"Sure," I said, trying to release the catch in my throat. "My older brother made me feel that way a lot. He picked on me all the time. He'd sit on me and hold my arms and let his spit fall on my face, or he'd thump my chest with his knuckle. I really didn't have a say about that. And many times, if he did something and I'd run home crying, I'd get in trouble for crying. No... I was not a powerful kid."

"What about your sister?"

"I honestly don't remember much of my childhood. I don't remember what things were like with her at all. Not until I was fourteen, when she told me if I wasn't out to the car in two minutes she was going to make me walk to school. It was quite a walk. I went outside after a few minutes, and she was gone. She actually left! I don't know... it's like she thought she was my mother or something. That's how I felt. That's how I still feel. Like she has all the power in our relationship, and I have none."

"So, it's like you're living under everyone else's conditions?"

"Yes... very much like that. I just don't have a voice. I've never found it. I can't stand up for myself at all. I get confronted and freeze like a deer in the headlights." I told her about meeting my sister at Starbucks.

"Okay, so let's take baby steps. You don't feel safe meeting one-on-one with your sister. So, do not meet with your sister alone. Invite a friend to join you. And you decide, from now on, who you're going to meet and for how long. And you say it ahead of time, like you only have an hour, or whatever. When you go to a family function, set up a strategy to protect yourself. You can say, 'Oh, I need to go check on my daughters,' to get out of a conversation if you need to. It's also okay for you to just say, 'You know, I'd really rather not talk about that.' You're in charge. You have a right to have boundaries and not answer every question someone asks you."

"I can't just tell Cris I can only meet for an hour, or that I have to have a friend there. She wouldn't understand, and I'd be confronted again about why."

"Then you say, 'Listen, this is what I can do. Take it or leave it.' You set the boundaries, Nima. It's your right."

"I just hate this so much. My life was fine. For fifteen years, my life was fine."

"It's unfortunate, but it's normal to have PTSD hit after many years. Like you, many children endure the abuse, do whatever they must to survive it, and then they repress it. They shove it away deep into their mind and try to forget about it. But you can't forget about trauma. There will come a time in one's life when something triggers a memory—it can be another traumatic event as an adult, a death in the family—and then *whoosh!* The past trauma comes rushing out of the subconscious, and you must deal with it. It's not fair, especially because people don't understand it. With cancer, or a broken arm, it's easy to see. The evidence is there that they're sick or hurting. Everyone understands and gives compassion. But with PTSD, it's an invisible illness. There's no evidence on the outside, and there is plenty of judgment all around."

"Tell me about it," I huffed.

"Respect your PTSD," Sandy said. "It's here for a purpose, and in the end, you'll be better for the fight you're having now. In the end, you'll be healed. For now, I'm here to help you get through the battle and understand what it is you're dealing with. Just take one day at a time."

"One moment sometimes…"

"Yes. One moment. And I, for one, am so proud of *Nima* for stopping the legacy of abused girls. Your daughters will have a different life because of you. You're incredibly strong, and taking on a task not many have the courage to take on. So you need to be proud of Nima, too."

The tears flowed as I listened to her words. How could I feel proud of myself when the shame and guilt of my past reminded me constantly of my worthlessness? I felt no pride, but I was determined to keep fighting for my girls. To indeed give them a different life than I had. To give them a promising future, maybe not free of heartache, but free of abuse, if I had anything to say about it. Somehow, someday, I believed I would see fruit from the nightmare I was living. Someday, surely, I would see evidence of my fight for freedom.

9

AVOIDANCE

The evidence did not come quickly. I knew therapy was necessary, but I stalled on giving it my all. Instead, my attitude was, "Let's meet on a weekly basis and talk about *why* I need therapy," but avoiding the real issues didn't make therapy any easier for me. The fear of going to those appointments slithered through the inside of me like shocking, electric eels, numbing my nerves, numbing my skin, stealing my voice. Then, once Sandy opened the door to me, and I sheepishly crawled into the chair, I'd realize I was in a box, and the rebellious, angry, cornered teenager would emerge and make it difficult for the angel Sandy to pierce the thick shell. And round and round we went this way for months. I would need a few humbling lessons before I would experience the profound revelation that I was but a child in a grown-up's world.

I still wrestled with the notion that I could get better on my own. That I could somehow beat PTSD like I was some sword-yielding warrior, and PTSD was the helpless adversary whom I could snap in two like a toothpick. How humbling to discover I was the toothpick. The lessons came slowly, and it began with my body. The first lesson happened on a drizzly spring day. A day when my tears were like rain, falling heavily with intermittent breaks of dreary stillness. By noon, the heavy storm of emotions had exhausted me.

Flashbacks came at my mind hard and constant like a hail storm, each one taking me into terrifying, alternate realities of an angry hand smashing across my face, or strong arms pinning me to the ground, hurting me.

Then suddenly, it was time to pick up my children. Emotional storms and flashbacks came almost daily, but life also happened. One did not stop for the other, and oftentimes I needed help getting back to reality. Sandy had given me a "grounding tool" during one of our sessions together. A keychain, handmade with tiny, brilliantly-colored beads, threaded in a circular pattern like a rainbow pinwheel. Touching it during a flashback reminded me that I was safe, that the flashback wasn't really happening; thus, grounding me back to reality. If I ever forgot the keychain, however, I still had a blade in my pocket to bring me back. Though I had purposed at Lake Chelan to end the addiction, I just wasn't ready to. The suggested methods of snapping a rubber band on my wrist or squeezing ice cubes in my fist were no match for the intensive pressure inside. I knew I needed to stop cutting, but I just wasn't determined enough yet. I still relied on it too much.

I had to pick up Lacey first from the grade school. As I pulled my van to the curb, I prayed no one would strike up a conversation with me. I saw the usual groups of children emerging from the building with their teachers, and the awaiting parents crowded around the school's doors. Lacey saw me immediately and flashed a wide grin. She tugged on her teacher's sleeve, pointing to me. I stepped out of the van and waved, and Lacey ran to greet me with that massive smile spreading ear to ear. Oh, how I counted on that smile. I smiled, too, and swept her into my arms, squeezing a gallon of love right into her. Before I even had her buckled in her booster seat, she poured out a one-sided conversation in her squeaky, child voice about all the things she had done that day. I was relieved that she was doing all the talking, as my own words were still stuck in the terror of the violence I had seen—or imagined—just an hour before. I forced an open smile as she spoke and, when appropriate, interjected a timely, "Wow!" or "Really?" To her, I was participating, and that's all that mattered.

She was teaching me a song she'd learned, when she interrupted herself to ask, "Are we picking up Jordan?"

"Yep!" I replied, and then her song continued. That's when the headache started.

I pulled up to the daycare to get Jordan, and Lacey let herself out of the van, prancing behind me up the concrete stairs and stomping through puddles along the way. The daycare was originally built as a two-story home at the end of a cul-de-sac, overlooking a small, swampy field—a haven for frogs, geese, and a large family of ducks. The owners had transformed the lower level into a daycare/preschool, and at the end of the day, they retired to the space upstairs. Lacey enjoyed coming with me to pick up Jordan to not only have an opportunity to taunt the ducks, but also to climb on the multi-featured play structure in the yard. That was the best part. As I opened the front gate, she bolted past me, running straight to the slide with a squeal of delight. For a few precious moments, she would have it all to herself.

"Look, Mama! Watch me, Mama!" I chuckled at her fearlessness as she clambered to the top of the slide and leapt across the structure like a nimble monkey, and then descended down the simulated, slanted rock wall, wet from the earlier rain.

"Careful, Lacey Lou. It's slippery," I warned as I approached the entrance to the daycare.

"I know, Mama!" Her blonde curls bounced with the energy emanating from her. I took a deep breath before walking into the chaos and noise of the room, full of three- and four-year-olds, a scene that normally sent me to the edge of a panic attack. But I always hid this, too, behind a friendly smile and a nod to the providers of love and attention to my little one; because for that, I was truly grateful. But today, the growing headache hindered my ability to fake it. When Jordan saw me, she ran up and hugged my legs. I swept her little body up into my arms and squeezed tight, tuning out the noise around me. My love for her had deepened and broadened down to my core.

Despite the fact I was like a walking pressure cooker, the love and dedication I had found for my children through my hardship was unbreakable because I had tasted the possibility of its nonexistence the night I nearly took my own life. But that event birthed a deep-rooted realization that they needed me. They needed my love, and I would never withhold it from them.

After watching my two little ones splash their way back to the van, and we got back on the road, the sweetest voices I'd ever heard began singing behind me. I smiled with deep adoration, but my headache was growing to unbearable measures. As I drove towards Traci's house for one of my frequent visits, Jordan began telling me about her time at the daycare. I understood her darling three-year-old language, but I suddenly struggled to understand the *meaning* of her words. Lacey piped up and said, "Can we go visit Faithy today?"

Faithy... I knew I was supposed to know that name, but I didn't. "Who?"

"Faithy!" Lacey cocked her head to the side and furrowed her brow like I was some sort of idiot. "*Cousin* Faithy?"

I did not recognize the connection. Not wanting to reveal my alarm to the girls, I smiled and said, "I know that, silly girl!" But tears were forming because I had just lied. Something horrible was happening to me. As I pulled up to Traci's house, the girls immediately jumped out of the van cheering and bolted inside. I sat frozen, as a wave of dizziness swept over me. Traci appeared at my window.

"Something's happening to me," I whispered. My words were starting to slur. "I don't know what's going on. Lacey asked if she could go to Faithy's and I didn't even know who that was."

Traci immediately helped me from the van and walked me inside. The dizziness and sudden fatigue was so overpowering, I stumbled into her room and collapsed on the bed.

"What can I do?" Traci asked, deeply concerned about my condition. "You want some tea? Maybe some chocolate?" She laughed, trying to lighten up the situation.

I cried harder, "I don't know what that is! What the hell is wrong with me?"

"Why don't you sleep," she comforted. "Just sleep awhile. I'll take care of the girls. Don't worry about anything."

I couldn't argue with her. Within seconds, I was out like a light, and slept solidly for two hours. When I awoke, I had no recollection of the day, and Traci called the Emergency Room at the nearest hospital. They said to come in immediately.

Once there, I underwent CAT scans, numerous blood and other diagnostic tests, and dozens of questions about drug and alcohol use. I feared I'd had some sort of stroke, but whatever it was, I knew it couldn't be good. After nearly five hours in the ER, the confusion was gone, and I had regained clarity. As I shared my relief with Traci, a doctor finally came to my bedside, giving his medical conclusion: I'd had a migraine.

"A migraine?" I snapped. "A migraine is a really bad headache. I had them for years. I couldn't remember my own niece's name today. I didn't know what chocolate was. My words slurred as if I was drunk—which I wasn't, by the way—and I couldn't remember anything about my day. You call that a migraine?"

"Yes," he stated simply. "They can happen like that. So, if you'll just sign this release, you're free to go."

I stared at the paperwork. I was relieved at his easy diagnosis, but also felt dissatisfied. I had never experienced something like that before, nor have I since. But it was the precursor to lesson number two.

Weeks later, I was driving through town with Traci riding beside me in the passenger seat. In the midst of a light-hearted conversation, a numbness started sweeping across my face. This, in itself, was nothing new. When my anxiety got especially bad, I could almost always expect a full-blown panic attack, and they started with the numbing of my face. But on this day, I was not having a panic attack. My anxiety was not especially bad when the numbness began spreading at a rapid pace. First my fingers, then my hands. It moved across my body like a sheet, up my arms, and down over my thighs.

"Traci..." I whispered fearfully, "Something's wrong. I think I need you to drive." I pulled over and climbed into the passenger seat, while Traci stretched over me to get behind the wheel.

"What's going on?" she asked, turning the car back towards her house.

"I don't know," I said, slumping down involuntarily into the seat. I wasn't just numb—I was entirely void of strength. I couldn't hold up my hands anymore. Within seconds, the numbness had spread all through my legs. "Oh my God!" I began to cry. I couldn't move anything, suddenly overcome with paralysis. My head fell against the window. Tears burst from my eyes as my body collapsed limply against the door. I'd lost all control.

Traci pulled into her driveway, and I blurted tearfully, "I have to pee, but I can't move. I can't open the door."

She rushed to my side of the car and opened the door, first lifting my legs out of the car, and then hoisting me up to her shoulder. I had no strength to walk, so together we dragged my feet along the pavement to her door. It was beyond embarrassing. When I got to the bathroom, I couldn't unbutton my pants, so Traci had to go through the motions for me, and even help me sit down on the toilet. As always, she got me laughing, but inside I was scared.

I didn't have the fortitude to endure another extensive round of testing in the ER, so I decided to wait it out, hoping the paralysis would fade. It took a little over an hour, but thankfully, my limb functions returned to normal. The next day, I visited my doctor. She told me it must have been a severe panic attack, but she initiated what would become a series of visits to numerous specialists over the next six months of my life, and various scans—including an MRI—to determine the cause of my frequent bouts of numbness.

When the time came to have the MRI, I sat in the lobby filling out the paperwork needed for the procedure. Apparently, I had mentally blocked out the first MRI experience I had after the initial onset of PTSD, because I wasn't scared of undergoing one now; and when the form presented the question as to whether or not I needed anxiety meds before the procedure, I declined. Big. Mistake.

The nurse who inserted my IV was arctic cold and unforgiving with the needle. She didn't glide it in, she shoved it in, and triggered an instant fear to my already apprehensive mind. Still, I tried to breathe deeply and press through. I don't know if I wanted to impress them, or prove to myself that I was capable, but either way, I acted in full idiocy. Two male technicians operated the machine from behind a large window. Unlike the nurse, these men were kind. As one disappeared behind the window, the other, Nick, showed me a small device with a button, which I would hold in my hand during the procedure. "If you need us to stop, just push this button, okay?"

I nodded.

"You okay? You ready?" he smiled.

No! No, I'm not ready! I don't want to do this! I thought. But I nodded anyway. I wished I had asked for that Xanax. I'd be a lot more relaxed right now. My breathing quickened as they pushed me into the metal tube. Already, I couldn't breathe, yet when Nick asked if I was okay, I nodded. I couldn't tell him no. I couldn't ask for help—a problem I'd endured my entire life.

"Here we go," Nick eased. His voice came from a speaker near my head. "If you look up, you'll see a mirror. Can you see us?"

I looked up, and saw the reflection of the techs. Nick smiled and waved. Suddenly, the loud clanking of the machine began. *Clang! Clang! Clang!* Then it quickened, as if someone had tied me down and jack-hammered around my skull. I wasn't literally tied down, but I may as well have been. I remembered the stern warning from the nurse before I went in, shaking her finger at me like I was five. "If you move at all, we'll have to start all over. Understand me?" I hated that nurse. Could she not see the fear in my eyes? Could she not see my trembling?

Already, my mind was screaming. My hands wanted to rush to my face, cover my ears... my whole head. They said the procedure would last about twenty minutes. It had been maybe two when I'd had all I could take, and I fought the impulse to rip the IVs out of my arms and run out of there. I felt the device in my hand. Swept my thumb over the button. I wanted it to stop, but that simply meant going through it a second time.

As the jack-hammer continued, I closed my eyes tight to shield them from the lights moving across my face, taking repeated image "slices" of my brain. I thought I remembered the tech telling me to keep my eyes closed for my protection; but when I did, a flashback started.

Three men stood close to me, their faces blurred. *WHOOSH!* One of them was in my face, clear as day. His eyes, dark and foreboding, pierced terror into mine. His black, greasy hair brushed across his forehead, and he laughed mockingly, jeering, "Hey, bitch!" He pulled back a few inches, and then rushed back in, again and again, because it frightened me, and that empowered him. He pressed a knife to my neck. "You want some of this?" he taunted.

I whimpered. I needed to open my eyes, to ground myself, but I couldn't. *This is not real!* I screamed inside, but the evil face—I knew who it was—he seemed emphatically real. And so did the knife.

"Are you okay, Juanima?" Nick asked.

Tears streamed from my eyes, forming little puddles in my ears. I couldn't do it anymore. "No," I quivered. "No, I'm not." I pushed the button a couple times, just in case he didn't hear me.

When they pulled me out of the machine, I was visibly shaking, though grateful just to open my eyes again and see real people surrounding me. I felt embarrassed for not being stronger.

"What happened?" Nick asked, squatting in front of me.

"I need..." The words wouldn't come. The room and the people in it had taken on a glazed look, the barrier my mind created when I dissociated. I was still half inside my alternate reality when the nurse rushed into the room.

"What's going on?" she barked.

"I need a Xanax," I said, brushing my hands up and down my frigid arms. I felt so traumatized I'd misplaced my manners.

"I can't give you a Xanax," the nurse said briskly. "It's too late. We just need to finish this up."

She had my full attention now. But surely I didn't hear her correctly. How could they not give me a Xanax? I knew how quickly they worked—I'd been on the prescription for two years already. Surely she wouldn't withhold it from me now, but she did. Nick looked helpless—it wasn't his call. I knew by the expression on the nurse's face that not only was I *not* getting a Xanax, but I needed to lie down and get back in the metal torture chamber.

"It won't be much longer," Nick comforted. It was all he could do for me.

I lay down, and they slid me back in.

~

I survived the MRI, though it took days for me to recover from the trauma of it. The neurologist who had ordered the MRI called me in to verbally discuss the results, and I felt both hope and horror when he said they recognized a small shadowed area in the pituitary gland, indicative of a tumor. I felt hope, thinking I had a possible answer to my health dilemmas, but horror because... well... I had a tumor! In my brain!

The amazing part was how so-called specialists all had a different philosophy about that tumor. The nurse who initially discussed the tumor with me said that chronic stress and anxiety could cause a pituitary tumor. She seemed to know what she was talking about. However, the neurologist, and subsequent doctors, each speaking with authority on the topic, had strong and differing opinions, each one proclaiming the others were wrong. I would hear, "It's related in no way to your chronic anxiety," to, "Yes, they can be caused by anxiety." I wasn't going to get a straight and definitive answer unless I got it on my own.

The year following my diagnosis was scary. I spent hours each day researching whether or not I was going to die. My primary doctor urged me to get a second MRI exactly a year after the first one to gauge any change in its size. The neurologist agreed, and said this would determine whether the tumor was benign or malignant.

~

Aside from my emotional terror of enduring another MRI, the financial impact was just as frightening. My insurance covered a mere portion of the cost, leaving us with an instant debt of over seven hundred dollars. Having no credit due to the bankruptcy we were forced to file in 2005, and no savings, we enrolled in the hospital's payment plan. This required a payment we couldn't afford to make. We did the best we could to make the payments as agreed, but one month we were only able to pay half of the bill, and the hospital was unforgiving. By the time the second MRI appointment rolled around, we were in collections for the first, so I postponed it.

The financial pressure from the hospital did not help my marriage. Things were already severely strained between us because the woman my husband had married had morphed into a deranged lunatic. He didn't understand what I was going through, or why I couldn't just "get over it." He'd say things like, "The past is the past! Why can't you just leave it behind?" And, "Why do you have to dwell on this bad stuff? Why can't you think about positive stuff?"

When I began drawing pictures in between therapy sessions to help me process trauma, his response to those was, "When are you going to draw some happy pictures? Like the person you want to be, instead of this sad person?"

I couldn't explain in good enough terms that the drawings helped me. He didn't understand that I was not *choosing* to dwell on my trauma, but that the thoughts and images invading my mind were intrusive, persistent, and painful. And as much as I fought to keep them at bay, they simply barged in anyway. But he, like anyone who doesn't grasp the symptoms of PTSD, or how they manifest and why, just couldn't make sense of my explanations. He remained frustrated and angry, and so did I.

Kali had given me hope during one of our final visits in December 2005, when she suggested I bring Mike with me to a therapy session. He agreed to go, and in that session, Kali gave him a revelation when she showed him PET scans comparing a healthy brain against one with PTSD. She explained the physical and physiological changes that take place with PTSD—all out of my control, and absolutely real. The session ended with Mike tearfully expressing his new understanding that this was happening "to" me, and was not something I could control or overcome with a stronger will. He understood now how much I needed his support, and saw how he'd treated me poorly from the beginning. We both cried, and that session took away some of the blame directed at me. For a while, anyway.

But it didn't change our external circumstances. As the months went by, the freshness of that hopeful session with Kali disappeared, and the prevalent truth was that Mike carried everything alone. It grieved me, and I pushed harder to heal. God knows the arduous pushing from the depths of my soul to heal. But healing is painfully slow, and in the beginning, visible only in the most subtle of ways. Most milestones go unnoticed by anyone who isn't intimately a part of it, and the slow pace of my healing aggravated everyone in my life. Mike and I had frequent arguments about the lack of change, and the lack of progress. He didn't see those subtle changes of healing and growth. He wanted the end result, and he wanted it much faster than it was coming.

In his peaks of aggravation he'd say, "Well, are you working every day towards healing? Are you doing something every day to get better?" Those questions grieved and hurt me, because he couldn't see that I was. He couldn't see the battle I fought inside, so very much like a battlefield during a raging war. I had a very real enemy, and it was the trauma I had endured as a child. I fought alone on that battlefield against hundreds of sword-wielding flashbacks, nightmares, terrifying images and thoughts that roared and came at me constantly. I fought alone in the dark with a heavy, ominous rain beating down on my soul and spirit, and it never let up. I was drowning in a suffocating oppression, and fighting so hard for my freedom. I wasn't going to stop, but some people in my life couldn't see why it took me so long to win. They couldn't see the baby steps that took me a little bit closer to my freedom. Mike couldn't see it, but I know he felt like he was drowning, too.

So I tried harder to *show* that I was getting better. Either my innate addiction to people pleasing, or the fact that I felt like a total piece of trash, fueled my guilt and shame over causing so much grief to the people in my life. It seems absurd, but PTSD was ruining my life, and I felt like I was ruining everyone else's. Guilt and shame inspired me to do stupid things, like my jewelry business and various website endeavors. Those clearly didn't work, but a new spark in my brain now urged me to do something different: school.

I believed it would show everyone my great strides to get well and help the family. I just didn't get it. You would have thought my clear-cut failures delivered pretty solid slap-in-the-face clues that my energy was best focused on getting better, not getting involved in monumental tangents that could potentially lead to my destruction, and the destruction of my family. But dang it—I wanted to help. I couldn't stand being unproductive, helpless, and the source of our gloom and despair. And no matter how you sugar-coated it, it was my fault. My family and friends argued that point to tears, "You didn't ask for PTSD. This isn't something you brought upon yourself."

Still, it was easy to look back and say, "If only I hadn't been abused. That's my fault, too." At the time, it wasn't self-pity. I believed it. Sandy did her best to change my mind. At first, I couldn't possibly believe her. I hated that little girl who refused to stand up to her abusers, and for letting it happen. I hated her for being weak, helpless, and silent. In one session, Sandy leaned forward, narrowed her eyes, and in a somber tone said, "I want you to picture your seven-year-old daughter, Lacey, right now. Now you ask yourself, if a man she knew and trusted suddenly pinned her down and molested her, would she be physically strong enough to push him off? Would she?"

Tears streamed down my face, "No."

"If she came to you and told you that Uncle Bill had touched her, would you be angry with her?"

"No way," I sobbed. The idea was unfathomable.

"And in her innocence, would you blame her for being molested?"

I pictured Lacey and her bright eyes, beautiful smile, and blonde bouncy curls. Her gentle nature, sweet spirit, and desire to help and please others. The thought alone of her being abused made me sick to my stomach, but should it happen, it would be impossible to blame her. A child is vulnerable, and naturally trusts the grown-ups around her; especially family, and those who show kindness to her. But still, I clung to the notion that I was somehow different. I wasn't Lacey. I just couldn't shake the blame that I held over myself for not being stronger—for not saying *no* to bad touch. I couldn't forgive myself. So what if no one had taught me about sexual abuse? I believed I should have known.

And now I had PTSD because of the abuse. I was one hundred percent victim, and angry about it. So I tried desperately to keep pushing PTSD away; avoid it, deny it, pretend I was getting better. I felt a confidence about going to school. I knew the things I was capable of before PTSD, and still believed I could somehow tap into that strength and overcome the disorder by being productive. But as the school term neared, reality set in. Sitting at my desk at home one afternoon, I thought about the homework, the study time, and the new schedule I would have to keep. I would have to drive to the campus, alone. I thought about being in a classroom full of thirty other students who would no doubt, eventually, want to talk to me. Get to know me. I would have to read textbooks, and at the time, my anxiety was so severe I couldn't read. Words on a page overwhelmed me. I couldn't absorb them, or the material as a whole. Trauma immersed my brain so completely, I couldn't take in new information and hold onto it. Kali had shown me scientific proof that this was a real symptom of PTSD. These panic-laden thoughts about school suddenly gripped my throat like a tightening noose, and a vise of terror inside my chest threatened to crush my lungs and heart. I couldn't breathe, and fear laughed as it cloaked me with its dark fabric. I knew that school was impossible.

I canceled the class, but I was unsure of the protocol, and too anxiety-ridden to find out. I couldn't even make a phone call, and was too humiliated and embarrassed to ask Mike for help. I knew he would be disappointed in me for quitting before I even started. I wrote a letter to the teacher and told him I was withdrawing from the class. I received a reply that he had received my withdrawal and had filled my seat with another student. I thought, *That's that.*

A few months later, in October, I helped Mike with an interior paint job for Traci's mother, Rita. The morning of our first day, I stepped out onto our patio, instantly refreshed with the autumn air I love so much. Fall is my favorite. The crispy, cool air that awakens your mind and senses as you take it in. The thin fog that drapes over trees, houses, and cars before settling on the ground. I grabbed the mail still in the mailbox from the previous day and tucked it into my shoulder bag along with the carrots, sandwiches and snacks I had packed for us. Mike locked the door behind us, and conversation began about the painting job—who would paint which room, what we would do first, etc. He had a spring in his step, and he touched me deeply when he opened the door to the truck, looked me in the eye, and *smiled*. I rarely saw that smile in those days. It was genuine, and it was for me. Driving to Rita's house, we laughed and carried on, reminding me of better days. Days before PTSD.

I leaned my head back on the headrest, gazing at my handsome husband as he spoke colorfully about his upcoming hunting trip. I knew how much these trips meant to him. He exuded a different energy when September and October came around. I understood it because I had felt it once, too. Hunting was something we shared before PTSD—before I lost the desire to do *anything*. But I didn't think about that. I thought about this remarkable moment. How we enjoyed each other's company. How he looked at me with a twinkle in his eye. I didn't want it to end.

Alone at Rita's house, he turned up the country music and we started prepping our respective areas—covering lights and taping around window borders. While I worked in the entry, Mike worked in the hallway adjacent to me. I remember a lot of laughing between us, which was a rarity during those difficult days. It seemed like a day of renewal with my husband, and I breathed easier.

On a break, I went into the living room and pulled the mail and the baby carrots out of my bag. As I flipped through the short pile of envelopes, I popped one of the juicy, orange veggies into my mouth, and then almost choked on it when I saw an envelope from the community college. Through the window of the envelope, I saw blue paper. In an instant, the rainbow of contentment around me shattered away in dark, jagged pieces. I felt heat swell in my stomach, and nausea rise in my throat. "Oh please, God. Please don't let this be bad."

I trembled opening the envelope, and nearly vomited when my worst fear appeared: it was indeed an invoice, for six hundred and eighty five dollars. "Noooo," I mouthed, doubling over with it clutched to my chest. This couldn't be! I wanted to scream it away. I wanted to rip it up and make it not exist, but it did exist, and I knew I needed to tell Mike. The sickness and devastation overtook me. It had been such a good morning. A *much needed* good morning. And I was about to ruin everything.

Suddenly, Mike walked into the room, saying something about Rita's one-eyed dog when he saw the look on my face and stopped.

"What's wrong!" he bellowed above the blaring music in the background.

I walked over to the radio and clicked it off. "I just opened the mail," I quivered, glancing down at the blue paper of misery. "We... Oh, God..."

"Oh, God, what?" he was nervous.

"We got a bill from PCC. Apparently, I didn't cancel the class correctly."

"How much is it?" His voice escalated.

"Six hundred and eighty five dollars," came my barely audible answer.

"Six hundred and eighty five dollars?" He stared at me with his mouth open, paint bucket in hand, while the amount registered painfully in his mind. "No! What happened? You canceled the class, right?"

"I really thought I did. I must not have done it right. I'm so sorry!" I was scared. I knew the pressure he was already under to make ends meet; and truthfully, we weren't making ends meet. My inability to work had put the weight of the world on his shoulders financially, emotionally, and physically. The ability to cope wavered as it was. I knew this would be the straw that broke the camel's back.

He left the room, and I held my stomach as it twisted and churned. I didn't know what was coming. I listened to the silence for only a moment, but the sounds that followed brought quick tears to my eyes. The sound of his own tears—an anguished, fed-up, exhausted, enraged sobbing—accompanied by the pounding of his fists against a wall. His sobs became screams of sharp profanity, and the words, "I work my ass off! And it's all for nothing! For nothing!"

My own tears were flowing now. I couldn't believe what I had done. My guilt and sadness clenched my guts like a fist around a wet rag, wringing out every last drop. I knew better than to go in that room, or try to comfort him. I knew he needed time and space. I knew I had blown it; really, really blown it. I looked around for a place to hide, which was dumb. I knew he loved me; he'd never laid a hand on me. But every person has his breaking point. I didn't know if Mike had just reached his. I thought about running out the front door and never looking back. I wanted to escape the moment, escape the day, and escape the pain. I wanted to rewind to that morning, walking out into our foggy street, seeing the smile on my husband's face again; seeing him smile at me.

I suddenly realized it was quiet. The ranting and sobbing had ceased, and I waited in silence on the floor. Moments later, he emerged, paint bucket in hand. I could almost feel my heart break into pieces when I saw the hurt on his face. His tears, still falling.

"Let's get to work," he said sharply. "We've got to get this shit done so I can get paid."

The words "I'm sorry" sat on the tip of my tongue, but I swallowed them. If I said them out loud, it might quiver the tightrope of grace between us, causing us both to fall. Mike disappeared down the hall, and I picked the blue piece of paper off the floor. I crumpled it furiously into a ball, far smaller than necessary, and fell doubled over onto the carpet. I sobbed long, silent tears until I didn't have any more, and then grabbed my paint bucket. Back in the entry, I got on my knees and began painting above the trim where I had left off. Neither of us spoke again of the blue bill that day, but I knew the moment I got home, I would start the process of fighting it. And I knew I would not speak of it again to Mike unless I had good news.

That news didn't come until February 2007. After two rounds of denied appeals, my dad graciously stepped in. He happened to be employed part-time at the community college, and fought for my case with the Board. As he created trails of emails with Accounting, directors, and others in between, I continued receiving invoices from the college with interest accruing. The last one I received threatened to send me to collections. I did not show any of these to Mike. I believed Dad was fighting hard, and I followed his advice to wait, and not pay anything. Though I prayed daily for victory, as February approached, defeat loomed on the horizon. That's when I learned that God is much bigger than appearances. After the Board reviewed letters and statements from my doctors, psychologists and therapists about my condition—even though I felt that breached some sort of Privacy Act—they decided to vote in my favor. The school rescinded my debt.

When I shared the news with Mike, he looked at me and said, "That's good." There was no hoopla. No dancing or rejoicing. But it was good.

"Please forgive me," I said. "I know I'm lucky that we got out of this. And I want you to know that I'm done. I'm done with tangents... with distractions. I've been trying to prove that I'm better, but I'm just sinking deeper. I'm sinking all of us, and I'm sorry. I'm so sorry."

"Just get better," he said. "Just go to therapy and get better."

I realized then that I had no business making any decisions at all. Mike didn't make me feel small in that moment, but I *was* small. Like a child, needing guidance from a parent; and the sooner I could accept that, the better off we would all be. Knowing that, however, did not make the mental shift any easier. I wanted to be the strong woman I knew I was somewhere inside. I wanted to overcome, but instead, PTSD had overcome me.

Like waterskiing, the more you try to control the rope and the skis, the more certain you are to plummet into the water. The key is to let the boat and the skis do the work, and you be the passenger, focused on simply maintaining your balance, and on the boat ahead of you. If you look up to avoid the water spraying in your face, you lose your balance. If you try to control the rope and pull it, rather than keep your arms straight and relaxed, you lose your balance. If you stand too soon, you'll fall. I was doing all of the wrong things in trying to move forward. I looked in every direction *except* the boat. I tried to do stunts and prove myself a pro, when I hadn't even learned the basics of simply letting myself be pulled. If a waterskier can't do that, she ultimately ends up frustrating everyone by her stubbornness and constant plummeting into the water. Only when you can humble yourself, admit you need help and surrender to it, will you succeed.

I needed to surrender. I needed to go to Sandy and say, "Fine. I'll do whatever I need to do. I'll talk about whatever I need to talk about. Let's do this."

It just wasn't that easy. It should have been, but when you're healing from childhood sexual abuse, a rebirth needs to take place. I'm talking about the developmental core beliefs built into a child's soul about themselves. You can't simply replace those beliefs with new ones. You must take a pick to the rotten soil of those lies and destroy it, and then gently prepare the ground for new soil. You plant new seeds of truth, and nurture it for a harvest of beauty and confidence. But that rotten soil is like concrete; and for me, the beliefs I had about myself were so solid, you may as well be trying to use a toothpick to break it. It wasn't gonna happen easily.

I remember a visit from my sister one day. She was frustrated with my healing progress—or the lack thereof. Deep in an argument, and flustered, she said, "I don't get it. Why can't you just replace the lies with what you know is the truth about yourself?" As devout Christians, we both knew the "truth" she referred to. But all my life, I knew that as truth for everyone else. In the deepest place in my heart, I believed Jesus died on the cross for everyone *but* me. That was my truth.

"It's not that easy," I responded. "I can't just say, 'Oh, okay, I'll just forget everything I believe about myself and change it to what *you* say is true about me.' That's *your* truth! I can't just believe it because you say I should!"

Still, I needed to be willing to give up my truth. And for me, that meant facing the demons that terrified me every night, and the ones that haunted me and pierced into my consciousness every day. I needed to start talking about the abuse and telling my stories. I needed to face the pain, and the horrors of those events; to lessen their power over me by telling them out loud. I don't know if anyone ever feels ready to take that plunge. I certainly didn't.

10

SHAKING HANDS
WITH PAIN

I tried. I honestly tried to talk about the past, but the fear that consistently rose up in my chest put me in such a state of panic, I'd freeze. I couldn't break through the wall if I wanted to. And no, I didn't want to, but I knew I *needed* to if I wanted to heal. It's astonishing to me, the power trauma can hold over you. For victims of sexual abuse, the power is exerted by the perpetrator, but that stifling power remains for years afterwards—sometimes a lifetime— if they keep it inside. But for *anyone* with PTSD, no matter what the source of the trauma, I truly believe that the only way to release its power over you is to confront it. To get it out. But I don't necessarily believe it has to be spoken. After three years of therapy, I still could not speak about my trauma out loud. I believe for some, it is just too frightening. Too traumatic to hear yourself say it. It was for me. A true ally will walk with you, alongside you, helping you seek out the right path that will bring you healing. It is not always conventional. There isn't one single method of healing that works for everyone. We are all so complex, with differing pieces to the puzzle that make up our individuality. We each hold our pain differently, our experiences, our memories. Though I have found commonality with others with PTSD in the symptoms, I know that *how* each of us arrived there is as unique an ordeal as it is terrifying.

I am so thankful for Sandy's understanding of this, and her willingness to let me write out my trauma. I frequented a forum online called After Silence, a private community for sexual abuse and assault survivors. I wrote in that forum many times, strictly to encourage and support others, but had never shared my own story. I knew it was time. I began sharing my story—one incident at a time—on After Silence, and then printed them out to bring to Sandy. She would read the story silently, always shaking her head, and then open a gentle discussion about it. But there were still things I could not share with Sandy, or with anyone.

We discovered that *feelings* continuously blocked my progress. It seemed I had a very limited vocabulary on the topic. I felt anger, sadness, or happiness, but I believed that anger was wrong, so I never connected with that emotion. But not just anger. I realized I couldn't express or connect with any type of difficult emotion at all. I couldn't put names to feelings. I couldn't identify them at all, and trying to brought on a panic attack.

Aside from my writings, I shared trauma with Sandy by way of drawings. In one session, I brought a picture for her that I'd drawn in colored pencil. A green, hilly field with a large, bushy elm tree to the left. Beneath the tree sat a little girl, seven or eight years old, with her arms wrapped tight around her knees. A pink, flowered sunhat and long hair hid her face. After Sandy studied it briefly, she turned it around to face me. Sadness crept across my heart, seeing that little girl so closed up.

"What do you see here, Nima," Sandy asked gently. "What is this little girl feeling?"

"She's sad," I whispered. I knew there was so much more that I just couldn't articulate.

"I think she looks lonely," Sandy continued, but the rest of her words were drowned out by the panic suddenly filling my chest. She used her index finger to focus my attention on the girl, drawing invisible circles around her as she spoke. But something about her finger going around and around her struck a defensive chord in me.

"Don't touch her!" I warned. "Don't do that—don't touch her!"

Sandy pulled her hand away, surprised, as I was. I began to weep.

"What happened just now, Nima?"

"I don't know," I cried. And I truly didn't. Whenever I spoke of the trauma, or the little girl in my pictures, I had no words to describe or define the reaction that came. Feelings rushed in at once like a rising flood pressing against a closed door, and then finally bursting through, filling the room in seconds. I drowned in it, and trying to isolate one feeling and describe it was impossible.

Sandy felt the time had come to try something drastic. Honed in on my grief and anger, Sandy knew those two things were obstacles to my healing. She had once participated in a grief workshop in California. People of all backgrounds and emotional burdens attended, and Sandy thought it was exactly what I needed to break through my emotional barriers. I resisted the idea at first, but was also frustrated by my lack of progress. I agreed to talk to Mike about it, and when I did, he did not hesitated to concede. Anything to help me move forward. So with a scholarship and more financial help from family and friends, I flew to California—alone—to attend the workshop. This in itself intimidated and frightened me. I suffered from intense agoraphobia at the time, so the idea of traveling alone, having to converse with others in a comprehensive manner, sifting through hundreds of loud people bustling and hustling around me, going through the security line with anxious people behind me, and officers scanning for any suspicious behavior, brought a rush of terror.

I practically hugged the California baggage claim when I reached it unscathed, but I needed to escape the crowd. Once I had my suitcase in hand, I stepped away and focused on stopping the trembling that vibrated through my limbs. I was to catch a bus to the workshop location an hour away. I sat on a cold, metal bench outside the airport, just beyond the car lanes, waiting for the bus to arrive. Dissociated, and still terrified of being alone in such an unfamiliar place, I prayed that I would just *get there* okay. The fear of the unknown muted me. After boarding the bus, we pulled out onto the freeway, where I gazed out the window and let my thoughts get lost in the traffic that reminded me of a crowd at a sold-out concert. I was so glad not to be behind the wheel.

I arrived at the workshop building around 9:00 P.M., and a woman greeted me with a packet of brochures and a workbook for the sessions. She said I'd be sharing a room with one other woman, Megan, who showed up a couple of hours later. Thankfully, she turned out to be a quiet one, too. I thought I was just lucky, until I read a statement in a brochure asking that all attendees kindly refrain from heavy conversation before the workshop began, as participants would all be in a "sensitive state of mind." *Thank God,* I thought. *They really thought this through.* Megan wandered off to shower, which left me alone in the room. I embraced the quiet, and ate one of the several protein bars I'd brought along.

The next morning, curled up in the corner of my bed against the wall, I felt numb. My stomach churned with nervousness about the workshop and what it would entail. Megan and I puttered silently around each other getting ready in the modest, narrow room, and took turns at the single pedestal sink and mirror to do hair and make-up. As I braved the hallways, clutching my notebook tightly to my chest, the fear coursing through my veins gave way to the silent smiles of others as I passed them by. The air was already charged with emotion. *Or maybe,* I thought, *it was a permanent fixture there.*

I wandered into the large meeting room that would be our main gathering place. About thirty chairs formed a "U," with the opening for the speaker in front of a large, beautifully crafted stone fireplace. Only three people occupied chairs, as there was still about twenty minutes before the session began. Nearly empty, just the way I liked it, so I could be the onlooker of people entering. Tracing discreetly along the left wall, I went to the refreshment table for a needed cup of coffee. I found it odd that there were no stir sticks for the drinks. Only for a moment did I look for someone to ask, but thought better of it and used a bobby pin from my hair. I slid into a chair at the "8:00" position of the circle—close enough to hear the speaker well, but far enough away to be unnoticed. As people filtered in, I wondered about their stories, why they were there, imagining I would find out soon enough.

Perusing the brochure, I saw that all the counselors were well-trained, and each one had been a part of this workshop for years. The brochure also emphasized that someone would always be available if you needed to step out to talk in private. I imagined that happened a lot, but I knew I wouldn't have the need. Slowly, people filtered in and filled the chairs, and the session began. One by one, staff members came to the front to introduce themselves, give tips for the sessions, as well as general rules of the workshop. A woman said that at one fifteen, the attendees would be introducing themselves, and then at five o'clock, we would get down to business with a session titled "Natural Emotions." *Here we go*, I thought.

I was so wrought with anxiety at the one fifteen session, I about blacked out just introducing myself, but I survived. At the five o'clock session, I learned that *all* emotions are natural—something I didn't know. I knew that happiness was good and expected, as was sadness, but never anger. I knew love and joy were natural emotions, but it shocked me to hear that anger, fear, jealousy, and grief were on that list as well. They said that those negative emotions were not only natural, but it was vital that I stay connected to my feelings no matter what they are. The speaker drew two columns on a whiteboard. On the left, he wrote the natural emotions. He listed Fear first, then on the right, made a list of ways we distort that emotion: panic, phobias, excessive worry, building walls, and anxiety. Next to Anger, he wrote "violence, rage, self-destructive behaviors, giving up, passive-aggressive behaviors and revenge." Next to Grief, he wrote "numb, depression, black hole, helplessness and hopelessness, remorse, guilt and blame."

I began to see that I was seriously distorted, and I was also in a room full of people very much like me. I guess that's why I was there, to help get the distortions sorted out and see things correctly. I knew I was full of self-blame and guilt, grief, and all the distortions of anger; but yet, I had trouble connecting with the fact that I was *angry.*

The next day they introduced us to The Mat. The Mat was thick and black—like a wrestling mat you'd see in a gym. They placed it at the front of the room, just inside the "U", for attendees to come up and get out their anger, grief, and whatever powerful feelings consumed them. *No way am I getting on that thing*, I thought. *No way in hell.* Before long, however, I realized I was the only one *not* getting on it. The staff never forced an attendee onto The Mat, but I noticed some people seemed anxious to get there— like The Mat was the reason they came. A staff member gave each person who went to The Mat a pair of gloves and a two-foot long piece of black, flexible rubber tubing. The counselor of that particular session handed them a large phone book, and then backed a few feet away. I noticed a stack of phone books off to the side near the fireplace. What came next seemed to come naturally for everyone.

The phone book symbolized whatever—or whoever—was the source of your grief and/or anger. I heard every kind of story: the death of a loved one, past abuse from a parent or trusted figure in their life, a divorce. I was moved by the display of messy, raw emotion I had only ever witnessed in the movies, and not a single one of them was the least bit concerned about who watched, or what we thought. They did not have to be told what to do, and there were no rules, except "keep the rage to the phone book," and nobody from the group could touch someone on The Mat or comfort them during their time there. I watched as person after person grabbed that black piping with intent, and then let loose, beating that phone book within an inch of its life. And at the same time screaming, yelling, vomiting words of familiarity that ripped into the phone book, and cut me to the core. Words that made me weep. Words that struck deep, but words I had never been able to voice myself.

I learned that many of the people there had attended the workshop more than once, and couldn't wait to get to The Mat. What was my problem? Embarrassment, yes. Fear, totally. Fear of looking stupid, fear of falling apart, fear of losing control. All definites. I simply didn't want to do it, and yet part of me did want to. My family, who loved me and wanted me healed, gave me the gift of attending this workshop. I came with the determination to give it my all. But I had not expected The Mat. I had not expected to be asked to put my feelings on public display. But I prayed, saying, "Lord, help me get to the mat. Help me trust You and the work You want me to do. Give me the strength now. Help me be me, whoever that is. Help me fight. I want to trust You. I want to be free of all this pain. Just help me get up there. Help me move."

I didn't believe I would be able to let loose like everyone else, but part of me wanted to try. Before I knew it, only two of us remained who hadn't been to The Mat. On the next break, one of the therapists approached me in the hallway. It was Valerie, a therapist I'd been drawn to since the beginning of the workshop. She was a heavy-set, attractive black woman with long, elegantly braided cornrows in her dark hair. Her smile spread out wide and inviting, and her arms emanated a mama's love that, for some reason, I wanted to crawl right into from the start.

"Do you think you'll be going to The Mat?" She asked, placing a gentle hand on my shoulder.

"Oh, I don't know," I heaved a heavy sigh. "I'm kinda scared." *Kinda scared* was an understatement.

"Oh, listen," she comforted. "All you need to do is go sit on it. Just see what it feels like. Don't talk if you don't want to. Just sit, and see what happens."

"Maybe…" I said.

After the break, Valerie eyeballed me. I smiled nervously as heat rushed to my face, and found my legs suddenly carrying me to The Mat. I knelt down, and took a deep breath, but nothing came out of my mouth. The therapist beside me, Nancy, asked if I could at least share a story from my past so that others in the room would know what I struggled with. The words, "I ran away from home when I was sixteen," poured from my lips. *Figures*, I thought. *Of all the stories…* As I shared, I did not beat the phone book. I did not scream. I didn't even raise my voice. I did not shed a single tear as I spoke of the week I lived on the streets in a foreign city, five hundred and eighty five miles from my cozy bed at home. But my voice quivered as I narrated the three rapes I endured there, giving an edge to the worst pain imaginable hidden in my soul. I remained disconnected, as I always did when sharing my story, because I could not connect to the feelings. It was a well-used wall that shielded me both from the emotions of the abuse I endured, and from others seeing the hurting me. Except, the fact that I felt unlovable somehow slipped from my lips.

What I had shared moved others in the group to surround me on The Mat. As I drew my story to a close, I could not look at them. I shook with embarrassment and shame... unworthy of their attention. I didn't know why they were there, or what they intended to do. Then Nancy surprised me by saying, "Now Juanima, I want you to look into the eyes of everyone around you. Go ahead. Look at them."

Did she know what I was feeling inside? Could she see the walls I had built around me right there on The Mat? She urged me again to look at them. It was one of the most difficult things I would do at that workshop. As I raised my gaze, and moved slowly across the many eyes looking at me, I melted with their returns of affection, love, understanding, appreciation, and even tears. *Were they crying for me?* I wondered. And then as if one woman read my mind, she nodded, tears streaming down her face.

Following the session, several women approached me individually, asking to hug me, telling me what an impact my story had had on them. I returned their embrace, but inside wondered what made me so special. I honestly didn't believe my words had any power, or that sharing my story would entice someone else to be brave enough to share theirs, as one woman whispered to me, trembling. She was the one person who had not yet been to The Mat. She promised me that at the next session, she would get up there. If I could do it, she could do it. As she walked away, I stood alone in amazement. *Sharing matters*, I thought. *Telling my story matters.*

I felt a soft touch on my shoulder, and turned to see Nancy. She asked to speak to me, and led me to a side room I hadn't been in before. Spread across the room were half a dozen other "Mat stations," set up complete with phone books, gloves, and black rubber piping. She shared a theory with me that perhaps my difficulty lied in displaying my anger in front of others.

"Definitely," I said. "I've never been able to do that. And especially here. I just feel like I'd be performing. Getting angry because I'm supposed to, but I just don't feel it."

"Well," she replied, "I understand that. That's why I thought perhaps we could try it here. In private. I believe you have anger inside that needs to come out, Juanima. Would you be willing to give it a try?"

I smiled. I knew I could never do what she was asking. It just wasn't in me. I never displayed anger to anyone. Ever. The shocking scene with my husband after slamming the cookbooks to the floor only reinforced to me that anger is better kept inside. I felt Nancy would not let me out of this easily, so I complied, and she led me to a station against the far wall. I was glad we were alone in the large room. I pulled on the gloves, and knelt down on the mat.

I chuckled nervously. The whole thing felt as wrong as trying to drink a soda on a roller coaster. It shouldn't be done. This didn't fit for me. I didn't *feel* any anger. I didn't feel there was anything to even connect to. As I sat there in silence, with Nancy beside me waiting patiently for my tirade, I wondered if there was something wrong with me. Everyone else in that group had tidal waves of anger they seemed to access from the deepest chasms of their being. And every single one I watched, I understood where it came from. It seemed right as rain. For them. So was there something wrong with me? Why didn't I have that anger? Surely, from all the men who abused me, I should feel rage for what they did to me. It's gotta be in there somewhere. Maybe I just hadn't accessed it with my mind yet. I closed my eyes. *Oh anger... wherefore art thou....*

"Maybe you could try just hitting the phone book with the piping," Nancy said softly. "Sometimes if we act first, the feelings come after."

With a heavy sigh, I again complied. I whacked the phone book with the piping.

"Again," she said. "Harder."

I whacked it harder. Nothing. I whacked it again, and again.

"Just let it go!" Nancy said louder, her voice rising with anticipation.

So I let loose and whacked the piping on the phone book like I was playing whack-a-mole, and I even managed to rip the pages up pretty good.

She smiled. "How does that feel?"

It felt ridiculous. "I don't know," I said, resigned. "It's just not there. I'm whacking the phone book, but... I'm just not angry."

"That's okay," she smiled. "Maybe it's just not time for that yet. You can't force those emotions. If it's not there, it's not there." I shrugged and nodded, just glad she wasn't going to make me keep torturing that poor phone book.

☙

At the next session, the woman kept her promise and went to The Mat, and I hugged her afterwards, proud of her honesty and bravery. I could tell she felt proud of herself, too. As the speaker, Don, began, he drew an upside-down triangle on the blank page of the flipchart. On the left corner, he wrote "Perpetrator," followed by statements such as "no one will ever hurt me again; I'll never tell you what's hurting me; tough, bully, taking it out on others; blame others, younger kids; angry and rebellious = The Judge." On the right corner, he wrote "Caretaker," and under that, statements like "Fix it; take care of people, siblings; be good; as adults, super responsible, super efficient; perfect = Minimizing." And at the bottom point, he wrote "vulnerable, helpless, powerless, I can't do it, I need help, losing your voice = Victim."

At the end, he said, "All these things we do, trying to manage our pain."

True, I admitted to myself. I had done all of those things, been all of those things. I thought of the persona I took on with Traci when she tried to access my deep feelings: stiffening up, acting tough and impenetrable. *I'll never tell you what's hurting me. You'll never reach that part of me. I'll never be vulnerable for you.* I thought of the position I tended to take in relationships with others, somehow always recruited as the counselor... the Band-Aid. In my close relationships, I would be the good girl, never making waves, never causing an argument, and diffusing one that started by manipulating the conversation into avoidance of it altogether. I hated conflict. It frightened me. Initially, I denied those weakling words at the bottom of the triangle. *That's not me at ALL,* I scoffed silently. *I am NOT a victim.* And yet I was, because I kept silent. Because in the dark, in the depths of my soul, came the voice of a little child crying out, "*I can't do it... I have no voice... I don't matter... I am helpless... I am useless... I am worthless.*" Victim. Don was forcing me to face my own despicable truths, and it hurt.

"Here's how you get out of it," he announced, pointing his black marker at everyone in the group. "Are you listening?"

Everybody's eyes were glued. I could see that his words rang true with all of them. On the board, in fat, black letters, he wrote FEELINGS. "Express. Your. Truth," he said with pointed emphasis on each word. "Take responsibility for your needs. Nobody can be for you—not Mom or Dad—what *you* can be for you. Days are past for getting the parents you wish you'd had. It's time to move on, and become the most that *you* can be. Take responsibility. And then do things differently. Speak up with your truth, and acknowledge your successes. Stop condemning yourself for not being perfect, or for having a bad day. You need to say, 'It's okay that I'm not okay today.' This is a process, people. Sometimes life long. You have nobody to perform for. Nobody to account for but you. Nobody to prove anything to. This is your journey. This is your time, and whatever you feel at any given moment is *ooookay.* It's okay. And the more you express your truth, whether just to yourself or to another person, the more you are growing and healing.

"Pain is universal," he continued, and drew a straight, horizontal line on the board with two large, half-circle dips like tires. "This line is life, and these dips are our wounds. We all have them." Then he drew dotted lines across the gaps, covering the dips. "We cover them up, conceal them, and hide them. But if we don't deal with that wound, it festers. It can cause infection. Putting a Band-Aid over a wound doesn't heal it—it merely covers it up. Eventually, you need to deal with the source of that wound. If your wounds are old and deep, it's going to take time. The feelings may be overwhelming, so you've got to handle them one layer at a time. You can't just dig it all out at once; you've got to treat it tenderly, with enormous love and care.

"It's a lifelong process of getting to the deep stuff. Our wounds will always impact us, but we can get to the point where it doesn't hurt our way of living, or make us hurt ourselves. Be patient with yourselves. Healing. Takes. Time."

I sighed. That "hurting ourselves" part put an ache in my stomach. At some point, I knew I would need to deal with that. I didn't want to cut. Obviously, the consequences of it far outlast the addiction itself. I put my hand over my sleeved forearm, feeling the twinge of guilt over the scars that lay underneath. Hundreds of thin, white stripes of torment, pain, and overwhelming agony. This is how I had chosen to speak my truth. To put a voice to my pain. If I were going to stop, I would need to learn to speak another way. I knew the time had come.

Don closed the session with more hopeful words. "There are many layers to your grief, and at the center of it lies its core. It will be painful getting there; but gradually, you will be able to appreciate other parts of your world. Five minutes of music, a tree. You will see and notice moments of beauty, and you will enjoy them. The greatest pain you suffer will not last forever. But it's so important that you continue the process. It's dangerous to become stuck. It's not a linear process—it's messy. It's all over the map. Please, please, remember to give yourself time. You have the right to grieve at your own pace."

I wished my family would realize that, and accept that. But it's difficult when your healing impacts so many others. I am not a lone island. I cannot travel this road without causing hurt to others. I couldn't help but feel guilty at all times for my pain. For the suffering I brought upon my family, my husband and children. Upon my siblings and parents, as they watched me go through the most horrific journey of my life while not understanding any of it. If there was any rage inside me, that's what it stood for. It stood for my hatred of PTSD. Hating that I couldn't control it. Hating that it controlled me. Hating that it had ruined my life, and stolen as much from me as the abuse itself. Stolen my joy, my peace, my happy life. My happy married life. I had no marriage now. Sure, he stayed. To my blessing, he stayed. But we had no joy, and no intimacy. We were barely surviving. We slept in separate rooms, and he did not hold me. There was the ritual kiss goodbye every morning as he went off to work, and the occasional hug to go along with it. But it was not the Oh-baby-I-love-you-passionately hug. No, there was none of that. It was a refuge. For me, a hug of hope. A silent pleading for him to stay. To not give up on me. And his return was just that. An assurance that he wasn't. And so if he would just return that hug, I knew we were okay another day.

⮧

On the last day of the workshop, the group filtered in for one last session. The staff had set up the room a little differently—in a celebratory fashion—with a path created through the center space of the "U" with large rocks bordering evergreen-colored paper. The speaker's spot had been replaced with a small, square table. I smiled immediately at the sight of the cozy fire they'd built in the fireplace, and sat a little closer to it than usual. Once everyone chose their seats, Nancy moved to the square table, and after an encouraging spiel about our bravery for attending, she said, "Remember, it's not about 'getting over' your loss. It's about moving with it, and doing things that symbolize and honor your grief. What are you going to do differently when you get home?"

Home... I immediately thought of my girls. Jordan, now four, and Lacey, now eight, were being impacted the most by my symptoms and anxiety. My anxiety was a constant thorn, because it always loomed around and through me. In my notebook, I wrote down safe things I could do with them when any of us felt anxious. Rather than letting the anxiety get control, I wrote down that I would, 1) draw colored pictures with them, symbolizing my/our feelings, 2) have a pillow fight, 3) throw rocks outside when we're mad, and 4) hit or scream into a pillow. I thought of a large square pillow Mike especially liked, and I would make that our "mad pillow." I didn't think he would mind. I also remembered a thick, rubber and plastic bat in the girls' closet that would be perfect for wailing on that big pillow.

Nancy announced the final exercise. We were each handed a small piece of paper. On that paper, we were to write down one thing we are taking home, and one thing we are leaving behind. We would share those things one at a time with the rest of the group, and then walk the path, indicating our journey home; but we were also letting others acknowledge us as individuals, and the progress we had each made at the workshop.

My nerves started their fire dance. I had no idea what to write, and the thought of speaking in front of everyone terrified me. But, it was the last exercise. It would be more embarrassing to be the one person who refused to complete it. Thankfully, she started at the opposite side of the "U," and since I was close to the fireplace, I would be one of the last few to go. But watching each person go to the table, write and announce what they were taking home, and what they were leaving behind, and then tossing the paper into the fire, my soul was moved. The written words were not taken lightly. They weren't "just words" for anyone. They were new life missions; statements of powerful growth that had taken place in each of them over the three days of the workshop. The words portrayed the voices of once-victims now taking charge of their lives and their destinies. Taking charge of their healing, and their futures. I looked down at my blank piece of paper, and the fear of speaking in public gave way to a sense of purpose. When it was my turn, my paper still glared white. With my heart racing, I walked to the front of the room and looked at the group. With cheeks flushed, prepared to say, "I don't know," the answers suddenly rushed in like wildfire. I knew *exactly* what to say.

"What I'm taking home," I said, "is my bravery for getting on The Mat. I'm also taking home the realization that I... *deserve* self-love and nurturing." The words came out like glue, but I realized instant power in saying them out loud to the group. Claiming them as my truth. I wrote that on the small paper.

"What I'm leaving behind..." I continued, "... is my silence." There was nothing else to say about that. Every single person knew exactly what that meant for me. It meant I would no longer be a victim to my past. It meant acknowledging that I was not helpless, and that I do indeed have a voice, and that my voice matters. It meant speaking my truth, whatever it was at any given moment, simply because it was my truth.

I wrote "SILENCE" on the paper, and tossed it into the fire. As I watched it burn, I felt empowered, albeit shaken. Making such a statement, and then watching it evaporate into eternity, sealed those words with promise. I would be held accountable for them. I would need to learn to receive my own feelings with the same respect I had always received the feelings of others. Not beating myself up, not tearing myself down, and never harming myself because of those feelings. Leaving behind my silence was a big promise, but I had found a new determination to grow and see it through. As I walked the path, meeting the smiles and proud eyes of those I passed along the "U," I stood a little taller, and for the first time in my life, I congratulated myself on my progress. I chose to see the small victories I had made in that emotionally disgorged weekend, instead of the long journey I knew lay ahead of me. In such a short time, I really had come a long way.

11

FEELINGS

Remembering brought indescribable pain. PTSD forced me to involuntarily remember horrific moments of my past on a daily basis, but healing required me to consciously remember the trauma that dismantled my manageable life as I knew it. And not just remember it, but hold it in my consciousness and let it become real; see it, feel it, connect to it, and accept it for what it was. I needed to acknowledge what it did to me, and how much it hurt. That is the agony and torment of healing, but it *is* the way to heal. You can't do it all at once. It takes a lot of time. There is also the issue of forgiveness, and forgiving myself, honestly, was at the top of the need-to list, as well as the most difficult.

The pain of my past oscillated near the surface, just beneath my skin, seeming to take on a life of its own. It wanted out, but I stifled it, so reluctant to give in to it. And not just pain. I so adamantly denied that anger and rage existed inside me, but I was wrong. It seemed the grief workshop cracked open another dark chamber where the rage had hidden, and now it seeped like lava into my mind and body, oppressing me and possessing me. It still boiled a week later when I went to see Sandy.

Traci accompanied me as always, taking notes of the things that I would not remember later. Sandy said she could almost see the rage exuding off my skin like steam from a boiler. Ever since the grief workshop, it had expanded and swelled inside me until it practically percolated out of my pores. I couldn't stand myself. I knew I had opened doors in California to the feelings deep inside, but I had no idea what I had started. I vibrated with rage right before Sandy, and I couldn't contain it. I couldn't pretend it didn't exist. It was bigger than me.

Without much discussion, she went to the tall, slender coat closet in her office and pulled out a phone book. She placed it in my lap as if she was handing me the key to the city, sat down in her chair opposite me and said, "Go. You know what to do with it. Rip it up. Go to town," she said, waiting patiently for my emotional release. It did not come. Instead, it only grew inside. Sandy had triggered a greater onset of the anger with the pressure to perform. I know she was trying to help me and set me free; but to me, she was pushing me to do something I didn't want to. And suddenly I'm back in Lynch's office with everyone around me chanting, "Just say it! Just say it!"

"No, Sandy. I'm not gonna rip the phone book." I muttered.

"But you have to, Nima. You have to get this out!" She was desperate for my relief, and I refused to let her have the satisfaction. "Nima, this is going to eat you alive if you don't get it out. I can see it on you! I can feel it from over here. You need to grab that page and just rip it. Then grab another one and rip it. Rip it, rip it, rip it!"

"I'm not gonna rip your stupid phone book! I won't do it!" I yelled, throwing the phone book on the floor. And then I cried, embarrassed by my outburst. I'd lost control. Again.

The room was still, other than the rapid breathing from my own mouth. My heart crashed like a battering ram against my chest, and I clutched it as a blackness began spreading through me like a tide, and across my vision. I was suffocating beneath my own rage, but still I couldn't release it. I would never release it while someone watched. I silently battled the oncoming panic attack, trying desperately to control my breathing. To slow it down.

"You are so stubborn, Nima!" she groaned, admittedly frustrated by my lack of cooperation. I felt badly for the way I'd treated her. I knew she was trying to help. I understood that there would be a great benefit to getting this demon out of me; but I just couldn't let it go. I stared helplessly at the floor, tormented by an onslaught of guilt and feelings of inadequacy, and more feelings of shame.

"I know I'm making your job very difficult," I whispered, struggling to get the words out. "I'm sorry. I don't mean to."

Sandy let out a deep sigh. "Okay, Nima. Let's step back." She sighed again, letting the tension subside. "If you can't do it here, then maybe you can do it with Traci."

I knew I wouldn't be able to do that either, but I didn't argue. "You guys need to do this," she continued. "Tonight. You need to try. Nima, you need to try. Kick everyone out of the house, Traci. You guys have a drink or two, or three, I don't care. Dim the lights. Get relaxed, and then work it out. *Get it out.* Do whatever you need to do. But you must do it, or Nima, this will kill you."

I couldn't disagree with her. The way I felt physically in that moment... I wondered why my heart hadn't burst. Why I hadn't passed out from lack of oxygen to my brain. I could feel this rage devouring me from the inside.

"We'll do it," Traci piped in. "We'll do it."

I had no energy or words to fight either of them.

&

That evening, as I waited for Traci to pick me up, Mike handed me a small gift bag. "Don't open this till you get there," he smiled. He knew this night would be daunting for me.

I hugged him. "Thank you, Baby," I said. "That's very sweet."

When Traci pulled up, Mike walked me out to say hello and dished out the regular teasing, underhanded insults at Traci that made us all laugh. I hugged Mike one more time, threw my overnight bag into Traci's white Honda Quest, and climbed in.

"Have fun!" Mike teased.

"Yeah, right," I laughed, mockingly. Then I smiled with gratitude, "I love you, Baby."

"I love you, too," he waved. "See you tomorrow."

Traci took my hand in hers as she turned the car around in our cul-de-sac, and made the short, silent drive to her house. Judging by the grin on her face, I knew she had the evening all planned out, but I didn't have the energy to ask about it. I figured I would know soon enough. I looked at the bag Mike had given me, and couldn't wait to look inside. I saw two giant York Peppermint Patties and a folded note on yellow lined paper. I opened it. "This gift is for two very special women to celebrate with. One to celebrate herself and the healing that she is getting closer and closer to. The other to celebrate herself as the compassionate and loving friend that she is. Enjoy, with love, Mike. P.S. If this is just an excuse to run around the house naked, you never need an excuse to love. P.S.S. Maybe you should close the blinds."

Traci and I burst out laughing. It was a running joke between our husbands that Traci and I had become lesbians in our intimate relationship. Granted, we hugged, held hands, and wrestled a lot through my healing. It was a unique friendship of two hearts touching in a way I'd never experienced before, but we were not lesbians. Still, we let them have their fun at our expense. The note deeply touched my heart. I knew my husband suffered right along with me, barely surviving, as I was. He could not hold me, comfort me, or listen while I spewed out horrid details of my past. Our intimacy as husband and wife took a back seat, but he was still my best friend. Never in my life have I known a man of such loyalty and sensitivity; of compassion and dedication to his family and to me. Though he didn't verbally throw encouragement my way on a daily basis, it was notes like this that I cherished and held onto. They showed his true heart. A heart that spoke in its own way, *I'm loving you through this the best I can.*

"Mmmm! Yorks!" Traci beamed.

"Mine!" I laughed, clamping them defensively to my chest. "Both mine!" I love Yorks.

The house looked dark when we pulled up, and she smiled compassionately when she saw the nervousness on my face. She squeezed my hand again before getting out of the car, and then waited for me to grab my bag. When I came around the front, she wrapped her arms around me and kept them there as we stumbled awkwardly into the house. I had to laugh.

Inside the house, I smiled. I could always count on Traci for an amazing presentation. The lights were dimmed, and I noticed several pieces of paper taped across the walls. As I read each one, my heart filled with appreciation for this amazing girl, who had walked me through three years of the darkest torture imaginable. She had stayed with me, held me, and got tough with me when I needed it. She hugged me, even when I tried to push her away. She let me know on a constant basis that no matter what, she would never abandon me. As I looked around the room at the candles, the pillows and tennis rackets (I chuckled, knowing what those were for), the encouraging posters covering the walls, I knew I was loved. In my darkest moments, I knew I was loved.

I read each paper on the walls:

'We cannot clearly reconnect with the Light unless we are willing to own and honor our experience of the Darkness.'

'It is our pain. It is our anger. If we don't own it, then we are not owning our self.'

'We cannot fully feel the Joy unless we are willing to feel the Sadness.'

'We cannot learn to Love without honoring our Rage!'

And another that said, 'God's anger is directed at sin, and thus is right.'

"Very philosophical, Ms. Traci," I smiled. Then looking at her thoughtfully, "Thank you."

"First things first," she smiled, and led me into the kitchen. There, she had a blender pulled out, tall, wide glasses, ice, tequila, and enough strawberries to make all the margaritas I wanted.

"You know me so well," I chuckled.

For the first hour, we spoke nothing about the real reason I was there. She turned up Norah Jones on the stereo and broke the ice with the ignition of funny memories and good laughs, something she was always capable of doing. Margarita consumption eventually made it easier for me to laugh. After three or four glasses of liquid courage, I felt ready for anything.

"You ready to conquer some demons?" She smiled.

"Let's do this thing," I slurred, cracking up at my obvious state of drunkenness.

Traci reduced Norah to background music, and we bumped hips, laughing, into the other room. In the living room, she had dragged the large ottoman of their sectional sofa to the side, and placed two large pillows on top of it. Two tennis rackets leaned against it.

"You gonna join me?" I teased.

"Well, I have some things to say, too," she said, folding her arms sternly across her chest.

"Okay then," I outstretched my hand. "You first."

In a flash, Traci's jovial demeanor turned solemn. She reached on top of a nearby console and grabbed an over-sized, white coffee cup, and set it down on the ottoman.

"What's this?" I asked, peering into the cup, "Paper coffee?" The cup was full of little strips of white paper, and each one had a word typed on it. The word on top said 'Mistreated.'

"I got these off the computer. I thought they would help you get in touch with your anger. You can pull out a strip of paper and then, I don't know, just start yelling, using that word." She pulled out the word 'Mistreated,' and stood to her feet. I could see her building up to something as she took the tennis racket in both hands, and raised it over her head.

She brought it down hard on the pillow and surprised me when she yelled, "You asshole! I hate you for mistreating my friend, Nima! I hate what you did to her! I hate how you hurt her!"

Her genuine anger moved me. She pulled out another word.

"Threatened," she read with grittiness, and set it down. Then she started pounding the pillow again, "You are an asshole for threatening my Nima!" *Whack! Whack!* I glanced at the pillow, flattened by her fierce thrashing. Traci was really getting into it, and my mouth hung open. She pulled another word. "Vulnerable!" *Whack!* "You abused her and hurt her when she was most vulnerable! She was just a child you assholes!" *Whack! Whack!* She pulled another word, and I was becoming lost in a confusion that suddenly swept through my soul.

"Scared!" She said, pulling another word. She screamed in anger. Like a mother defending her child, I witnessed Traci screaming in pain and anger for me. But the words... there was something about the words themselves. As she called them out, and made them real, and merged them with her own feelings about my abuse, a tornado of torment began rising from deep inside.

"You bastards scared my Nima! You terrified her! You made her afraid, and took her voice away!" *Whack! Whack!* "You took her childhood! ROAAARR! Come on, Nima!" *Whack!* "Grab your words! You have to do this! You have to get angry!" She was seething. Her face blood red, flowing with protective anger for me, her friend. But all the words... the tornado inside me only grew. I couldn't speak. Something was happening inside me that I couldn't articulate.

Numb, I pulled words one by one from the cup. *In Danger. Hopeless. Unseen. Sick. Not Heard. Misunderstood. Out of Control. Ignored. Disregarded. Disrespectfully Treated. Lied To. In Pain. Violated. Fearful. Stupid. Compromised. Anger. Battered.... Silenced....*

"No," I quivered. As I pulled out the last word, *Nightmare,* I was shaking.

"C'mon, Nima. You gotta do this! Stand up and grab your racket and just start hitting the pillow, even if you don't—"

"No!" I shouted, fed up with the whole anger thing. "It's something else!"

"What do you mean... something else?" Traci stopped pummeling the pillow.

"I... I don't know. Something is happening to me," I cried. The tears fell, but I didn't understand why yet. "It's these words. I don't know, Traci. I don't know what's happening."

She knelt down beside me. I took the words in my hands and sprinkled them on the floor like rose petals, turning the words up. My tears flowed like rain, and the pain came like knives into my chest. *Violated. Unseen. Battered. Ignored. Vulnerable. Silenced.*

And then it hit me. All at once, the meaning, the understanding, and the real purpose of the evening exploded into my awareness like a backdraft. It hit me so swiftly and with such intense force I doubled over onto the floor and wailed in torment as if I'd been punched square in the gut. Traci sat waiting, silent, concerned.

"Oh my God..." I stammered. I scooped the words up, crumpled them into my fists, and crushed them to my chest like I was trying to push them in. In broken sobs, I tried to explain what had just been revealed. "These words... are the feelings I never had for the abuse. They are the words I could never say... because I never knew them. I never connected to what they did. It happened to some other little girl. But now I know... oh my God, I know... that this is what they did to *me*. These are the words... This is what they did to me."

Thousands of tears broke through like a river through a shattered dam. The grief and realization of being so thoroughly broken ripped through. A broken dream, a broken heart, a broken body. The pieces of the puzzle came together so tightly, because for the first time in nearly thirty years, I had words for my pain. I was abused. I was raped. I was beaten and battered. I was vulnerable, and I was silenced. I was invisible, and I was ignored. I was damaged. I no longer saw my abuse dissociated, from the ceiling corner of the room. I was there. It was *me*. Beneath him. It happened to *me*. That little girl was me.

ॐ

The pain of making the emotional connection to my abuse took its toll on me. My soul was a bottomless reservoir of grievous tears for days, yet a shift was also slowly taking place. I suppose it would be difficult to heal from childhood sexual abuse if I could not first fully accept that it happened to me. And now I knew—not just with my head—but with my heart and soul. I had been disconnected emotionally from the abuse my entire life, but making that connection was critical for me to move forward in my healing. Once it was a part of me, and the knowledge locked painfully in place, I could go forward.

Yet now, for me, going forward meant going back. It meant revisiting the past, and telling my story, because secrets like that are poison. I think often about the fifty million people in the United States alone who suffer daily from the effects of childhood sexual abuse. I know the majority of them are just surviving, keeping their secrets locked desperately away, thinking their silence is saving them from a life of pain. But they are already living it every day. In hindsight, I can see how the abuse of my past slithered its way into my thoughts and self-image on a daily basis. Consciously, I was unaware that certain negative behaviors were linked in any way to the abuse I suffered as a child. As a young adult, I "walked away" from the abuse, determined to make a better life for myself. I did do that, and I was happy on surface levels. But beneath, there existed a dark chasm of worthlessness and shame that kept me from living a *full life*. A life of being me to the extent God created me to be. A life of expression and love, including loving myself the way God intended. Throughout my young adult life, I found it easy to be kind and loving to others, but one long look in the mirror made me revolt with disgust. I felt ugly. Deep inside, I was the ugliest person alive.

Be happy and live up to everyone's expectations, and your world will stay safe.

Keep the peace at all times; don't make any waves, and your world will stay safe.

Don't get angry, or if you do, hide it well and keep silent, and your world will stay safe.

I lived to stay safe, and meld with those in my life in such a way that I brought joy to their lives, and enjoyed a meaningful relationship, but they were free of risks. I wanted only to keep the peace in my relationships, which meant if I disagreed with someone, I kept it to myself. If a friend invited me to an event, I couldn't say no. If they needed my help, I showed up. I avoided conflict or hurt feelings at all costs. The consequence to that, of course, is that I never lived a fulfilled life. I lived to please others on a daily basis, and lived in fear of failing that mission. What seriously lacks in all of that, however, is being *me*; having an identity of my own.

Feelings of worthlessness, I believe, lay at the core of my self-destruction. If one believes they have no value, then there is little energy spent on enriching their lives; little energy spent on discovering who they are, simply because it doesn't matter. I spent my existence trying to gain approval from others. Even if I acted with a genuine, loving heart, I short-changed myself by never investing myself honestly in those relationships, or discovering my own identity.

The time had come to face my memories. To acknowledge each painful moment, and hopefully, in the process, reclaim the pieces of me that past evils had stolen away.

&

I sat wistful across from Sandy, watching carefully, protectively, as she scanned over my latest drawing. The picture, sketched in colored pencil, showed a thick forest of fir trees with a shore of lush green grass and sprouting weeds. Inside the woods, darkness wove through the trees like a river, beckoning the little girl who stood before it. She stood frozen in her favorite blue and white dress; her long, cinnamon hair pulled back from the crown and tied neatly with a blue ribbon in the back.

"What happened to her?" Sandy asked, with strong concern etched on her face.

"It's just a dream," I said. "But it's a recurring dream; one I've had as long as I can remember."

"Tell me," she said, almost in a whisper.

Taking a deep breath, I told the story of the little girl standing at the edge of the woods, and the man standing between two trees waving for her to go inside with him. The trees loomed and swayed above her head, but she knew these woods and was not afraid. She also knew the man, and did not fear him either. In real life, this was my home. Those trees were part of the ten acres that nestled our mobile home. Those woods contained endless memories of my

childhood: tree forts, BB gun wars, cops and robbers or cowboys and Indians with my neighbor, Greg, and endless hours alone, wandering in my own thoughts and comforting solitude.

"Who is the man?" Sandy interrupted.

"I don't know," I answered. "I can't see his face. It's blurred. But I see his clothes very clearly. Worn-out blue jeans and a blue plaid shirt."

"And what happens?" Sandy asked.

I continued the vivid details of the dream of me following him into the woods, and him telling me to stop when we reached a small clearing the size of a merry-go-round. There is an opening high in the trees there, allowing the sun to filter through with rays of warmth and light. The man tells me to lie down in the clearing, and it is here that I begin to tremble telling the story. I'm certain what I'm saying is a dream, and yet my body shakes, my voice quivers, and the words stick in my throat. When Sandy stops me to ask what I'm feeling, I say that I feel frightened, but I just want to get the story over with.

I do as the man tells me to, because I know I must. I lay on my back, and he is over me, and then I turn my head. I see a stick lying on the ground near my head, and I study it, noticing the sunlight that falls across it. It's a long stick, one that I could almost use as a walking stick if I went on a hike with my dad, if it weren't for the smaller branches that forked off the sides. My dad could break those off, though, and then it could be a walking stick. Maybe... or maybe I could just draw in the dirt with it. It is just me and this long stick, but I cannot reach it, and so I continue studying it from a few feet away. I smile at the sparse patches of moss that remind me of little fuzzy caterpillars taking a nap. I imagine the moss clumps are caterpillars. Those black- and copper-colored ones that curl up when you touch them. I wanted to be one of them. I wanted to curl up and go to sleep. I wanted to leave the woods and be alone again. I wanted to go home.

As I finished the dream, tears streamed down my face.

"I don't get it," I shivered, squeezing my arms tight around my shins in the chair. "I thought this was just a dream."

"Maybe it's not, Nima." Sandy assured. "Memories can manifest in many ways. Judging by your emotional and physical reaction right now, and by the vivid details you shared... I don't know. I think it's quite possible this happened to you."

"But I don't remember anything else," I argued. I wanted to believe it was a dream. "It's the same exact details every time, and I can't see this man at all. I can't see his face."

"Maybe your consciousness doesn't want you to remember who it is. Maybe it's someone significant in your life."

"I'm done talking about this," I said sharply. "I don't know what it is—a dream or reality—but I don't need or want to know anymore. I have enough memories that I know are real. I don't want to dissect this if it's not meant to be. I'd rather just leave it alone."

"Of course," Sandy soothed. "I think you're absolutely right. There are ways to retrieve memories, but I believe that when you're ready, the memories will come. There's no need to force it or push it."

I thanked God for Sandy's understanding and patience. She never tried to make me talk about things before I was ready. However, my inability to discuss other incidents made healing very slow and tedious. And so through my writing, I progressed and moved forward with Sandy. Through my writing, I remembered.

12

SHATTERED PIECES

I was seven years old when I took my first solo airplane ride for a summer visit to my grandma and grandpa's house in Nevada. My Uncle Rick was fourteen at the time, and lived with them. On the second day of my visit, the sun scorched and sizzled anything in sight. My grandma offered to turn on the sprinkler in their fenced, back yard for me, and I jumped at the opportunity. Grandpa worked that day, so I kept company with Uncle Rick and Grandma. The water had already soaked me from head to toe when Grandma poked her head through the sliding glass patio door, announcing she was going to the store for groceries and wouldn't be long. Her peach-colored toy poodle, Peaches, bolted through the door and joined me in the sprays, barking and prancing around my feet. Grandma laughed. I could go with her, she said, but I decided I couldn't possibly leave the cool water sprays. She waved as she closed the glass door, and I played alone with Peaches in the scorching heat to exhaustion. When I went inside the house, the shock of the air-conditioned living room caused me to jerk inward and I squealed dramatically. Streams of water dripped to the linoleum floor beneath my feet, and Uncle Rick rushed a towel over and wrapped it around me, laughing, clearly entertained by my childishness.

He wanted to show me his bedroom, so I followed him there. I liked Uncle Rick. He always made me laugh. I sat on his bed as he talked about the posters on his wall, and then he turned his attention toward me. That's when the tickling began. In a way, I enjoyed his tickling because of the attention, but I was so extremely ticklish, it didn't take long before I wanted it to end. As he dug his fingers playfully into my sides, I twisted and ached from laughing so hard and begged him to stop. He released his grip, and placed his hands beside me on the mattress while I caught my breath.

"No more," I chuckled breathlessly, but that made him start again. Within seconds, however, his tickling became slow and purposeful, and it felt different to me; not like tickling. He moved from hovering over me to being directly on top of me. He smiled at me, but that's when the confusion and icky feelings crept in. His hands moved again to the mattress, and he pressed, moving up and down, as a moaning crept from his mouth. Something felt very wrong to me, and a hotness flushed across my cheeks and through my stomach. The giddiness was long gone, and all I felt now was embarrassment and shame. This didn't feel right anymore.

The click and turn of Grandma's key echoed across the entryway, directly next to Uncle Rick's room. He jumped off me like he'd seen a rattlesnake, and Grandma entered, arms stuffed with bags of groceries. But as she walked right by the doorway of Rick's room, I couldn't move. Rick grabbed me and sat me up, and while Grandma talked to us from the kitchen, Uncle Rick came close to me and said, "This is just between you and me, okay? Our little secret?"

I stared at him blankly, and suddenly Grandma stood in his doorway with a smile on her face. "Hello? I could use some help with the groceries."

She thought nothing of the scene before her, or the blank look on my face. Uncle Rick followed her out to help, and so did I, after deciding to pretend the tickling had never happened.

❧

The following summer, I turned eight years old, and it was the first summer my parents allowed me to join my older brother and sister to pick strawberries at a local farm. We rode a school bus out to the strawberry fields, and most days people crammed inside it, looking to earn some extra money. I didn't especially like picking strawberries, but there was something astounding about those crisp, aromatic new, one dollar bills the farmer handed me at the end of the day when I turned in my flats of strawberries. I would take the dollar bills in both hands, handling them with the tenderness of baby kittens. I'd push them against my nostrils and breathe in their strong scent. Like they were fresh off the press; and so stiff, folding them in half and shoving them in my back pocket felt uncomfortable. But I didn't care. I thought about the gum I would buy, or maybe I'd save them up for something longer-lasting. I also enjoyed the chill of those early morning rides. Though I didn't particularly enjoy waking up early, the crisp morning air carried with it the freshness of a new day, and a fragrance of fir trees just washed by the early morning dew.

Whenever I stepped on the empty bus destined for the strawberry fields, I made a beeline for the back seat. There had been a day I thought sitting in the front of the bus was cool. It brought me close to the bus driver, which made me feel special in a "teacher's pet" sort of way, but I also felt more protected. I learned what an illusion that was, when bullying kids from far back in the bus began targeting me and my waist long hair with rubber bands and spit wads. I would feel the painful *thunk* of a rubber band at the back of my head, and reach back to find a tangled mess. Sometimes, with help, I could get the rubber bands out. Other times, I had no choice but to cut them out. Sitting in the front seat no longer felt cool or safe. But then, I learned I really wasn't safe anywhere.

One morning after boarding the bus to the strawberry fields, I dove into the back seat before anyone else had a chance. I smiled and stretched my legs out as far as I could. The seat was mine. I don't know where my brother and sister sat on the bus that day, but I knew they were there somewhere. As the bus bumped along the dirt and gravel roads to the fields, I stared out the back window watching the dust billow out from the tires in a continuous flurry. When I turned back to look again for my sister or brother, an African-American boy got up from his seat and walked towards me, smiling. I did not recognize him, but he looked at me with sun-shiny familiarity. He moved with a swagger, hitching his thumb in the wide brown belt holding up his jeans. His ribbed, white tank top already showed a layer of tawny dust. Within seconds he was at my seat, leaning over me. I glanced around nervously. Did anyone see this boy with me? Was anyone paying attention? I wanted to yell for my brother, but I was too shy. The boy grabbed my calves and slid me down on the seat. He glanced once to see if he'd drawn attention, but then his eyes covered me again and his hand rubbed up my thigh. I didn't say a word. He towered over me, but I didn't like his hand on me, and those icky feelings in my stomach were swarming again.

I don't remember the rest of the bus ride. I remember picking strawberries later and my older brother giving me a strawberry shampoo, but I didn't think it was funny at all.

≈

I was ten when my parents divorced, and I never saw it coming. My mother's pain revealed itself the day she walked out the front screen door with suitcases in hand, tears streaming down her cheeks. Across the wood porch she fled, and I went after her.

"Mom! Mom! Where are you going?" I cried out.

"Away!" she replied, with a voice strained and trembling from the tears.

"Wait! Don't go, Mom!" I cried, too, frozen and confused. Her feet carried her briskly away as if doom nipped at her heels, and freedom awaited her up ahead. She did not stop to say goodbye, but disappeared quickly into the woods, where a friend waited on the other side.

Several worrisome days passed before I saw my mother again. But on that day, we had no warning of the events it carried. An unfamiliar burgundy van pulled up to the trailer, and my mom stepped out. She hurriedly ordered us to pack our things because we were leaving, and quick. No questions. My siblings and I packed our suitcases, and within minutes we were driving down the long, gravel driveway, and I watched my home shrink in the distance.

"Where are we going?" I asked.

"We're going to a new home," my mom said quietly.

"But—what about my cats?" I asked, alarmed. There were twenty-two of them living on The Ranch, as we called it. Though most of them were wild, and only three actually allowed in the house, they were my pride and joy. I knew each of them by name. I raised them. I loved them. They were mine.

"You won't be seeing them again, Juanima, but they'll be fine."

"No! They'll die!" I cried. No one else would take care of them. I knew they would die. I felt my heart explode with grief and I sobbed into the back seat, watching my joy and hopes disappear with the woods and trailer I called home.

૏

To add to my confusion, I was introduced awhile later to a man whom my mom said was our new stepdad, Ron. I didn't even understand yet that she and my dad were no longer together. I didn't understand any of it. But we lived in a new house, and this man now slept in the same bed as my mom. My dad was alone, back at The Ranch, and I thought of him, and cried for him, knowing how lonely he must be. I felt the loss of him, and my own loneliness, stretch across my heart and clench my gut like a boa constrictor. Mom said things would be better soon, and I would be okay if I just gave it time, but I didn't see how it would be okay. I never got to say goodbye to my friends at school. I never got to say goodbye to my cats, or my best friend. I didn't get to prepare for not seeing my dad every day, or hearing him read the Bible to me at night by my bedside, and pray for me. My predictable, happy life was jerked out from underneath me like a rug. And I blamed this man... this new stepdad. He thrust my siblings and me into a strange, threatening world. I also discovered I suddenly had two new sisters. I didn't want two new sisters. I didn't want another dad. I wanted my own dad. I wanted my cats. I wanted things to be the way they were. I eventually realized, however, that I had no say in the matter. I was along for the ride, whether I liked it or not.

On Christmas Eve of that same year, my siblings, two stepsisters, Uncle Rick, and I slept out in the living room, spread out in sleeping bags around the Christmas tree like a pinwheel. Sometime in the middle of the night, a nudging on my shoulder pulled me from a dream. It was Uncle Rick, and he was climbing into my sleeping bag with me. Groggy and confused, I wondered if I was still dreaming; but glancing around, I saw the pinwheel of siblings illuminated by the lights of the Christmas tree. He moved in close to me, but there was not enough room, and it smothered me. He kissed my cheek, and then he was against me again, moving and pressing. I looked at the twinkling lights on the Christmas tree, and stared at them until they blurred into a single, shadowy light.

I missed my dad. My stepfather contrasted him like black and white. I found comfort around my dad because of his love for God. He emanated goodness, and though he made mistakes, like every parent does, he had a heart of love for his family. He was a rock in my life. My stepfather did not have this goodness. Ron spoke badly about God, and bad-mouthed my dad. Anytime I voiced how much I missed my dad, he angrily voiced how worthless my dad was, and that he didn't care about us. He said my dad gave us up. "That's a lie!" I'd scream in my dad's defense, but Ron never let up.

Ron drank a lot. Every day, he lazed in that brown recliner across from the TV and drank beer. To keep peace, I brought him beers when he asked, but cringed at the mixed smell of cigarettes and alcohol that permeated his clothes and his breath.

On alternate weekends I stayed with my dad, and I ached for those precious days. They always went too fast, however, and I dreaded the drop-off on Sunday afternoons at the Big Reds restaurant. I dreaded it, not just because I had to leave my dad, but because of the fighting that always occurred in the van as we pulled away. I'd plunge tearfully into the back seat of the burgundy van and sob, pressing my hands against the back window. Despite my tears, my dad routinely stood next to his car, waving his arms in the air, smiling as we pulled away. The further away I got, the more fervent his leaps and waves, until his jumps took him three feet in the air, as he wildly waved and yelled out, "I love you, Pooh! I love you, Pooh!"

"What a stupid idiot," Ron would mutter under his breath. My face would flush red with anger, but I always kept silent, waving until my dad disappeared from sight. "He doesn't really love you or want you, you know. He sees you because he has to. Your time with him is fake."

I knew he lied, because every single time we drove away and left my dad, my dad had that widespread grin on his face, and he jumped and waved his arms in the air until I was gone. *That's not fake love*, I thought. *He misses me, too.*

Once he disappeared from sight, I would shrink down into the seat and cry silent tears all the way home, listening to Ron's angry words about the pitiful man who raised me, but couldn't hold his family together. *But you're the one who ripped us apart*, I thought.

My freshman year in high school began with braces and solitude, except for my best friend from junior high, Amy Wright. I loved her companionship. During my sixth grade year, my mom and Ron had moved an unprecedented three times, forcing me into three different schools that year. I gave up on lasting friendships until Amy came along in eighth grade. She helped me with geometry, and we stuck like glue. In my PE class, I became attracted to a senior named Chad. He had what I called "puppy dog eyes," large brown saucers that twinkled when he laughed. But I saw something in

Chad—a rebelliousness, a carelessness—that struck a similar chord within myself. I watched him run lines in the gym one day, and stared a little too hard, not put off at all by his mediocre attempt at speed. He tried to impress no one. And then suddenly I realized he was looking back at me, and within seconds he stood in front of me, pulling his sweaty, sticky black AC-DC t-shirt away from his chest to breathe. I laughed, and he asked me out.

"Aren't you charming?" I grinned. Luckily, my mom thought so, too. And thus began my first real dating relationship. He respected me, and as the months went on, I felt I had found a pretty special guy.

❧

I saw nothing special in my stepdad, Ron. One afternoon, just before Thanksgiving of that year, my mom had taken a grocery-shopping trip, and I was home alone with Ron. I stood in the bathroom, curling my hair, when he suddenly appeared in the doorway. I glanced at him, and he stared back, leaning against the trim. "What!" I barked. He never looked at me at all.

He chuckled, folding his arms across his chest. He shook his head, and my stomach churned with discomfort from the way he looked at me. "You are so pretty. Just like your mom."

I turned my attention back towards the mirror. In the four years he and my mom had been married, I couldn't remember having one real conversation with Ron, let alone receiving a compliment from him. The one nice thing he ever did for me was teach me how to throw a Frisbee. He never took an interest in my life or in me as a stepdaughter. But now he held out his hand like I was supposed to take it.

"What!" I shouted even louder.

"Come on," he said, leering like a Cheshire cat. I stared at his hand, feeling a twisted confusion by it. The sudden niceness made me suspicious, and yet for four years I had hoped for this very thing from him: a kind word, a smile. His anger exhausted me, and created invisible walls through the house that I tiptoed around. So I put down my curling iron and looked up at him, curious, nervous, and afraid to say no. I took his hand.

I didn't like his hand. We crossed the living room, the dining room, and then he opened the sliding glass door and took me out onto the deck. In broad daylight, he sat down in a deck chair and put his arm around my waist, pulling me close to him. The churning pit in my stomach grew, and suddenly this felt very bad to me. His hand moved to my bottom. "Do you have a boyfriend?"

I shrugged. "Yeah," I said, "Kinda." He tilted his head and stared at me. Stared at all of me. "Does he touch you?"

I felt sick. Nobody had ever talked to me like this, or asked me questions like this. "I don't know," I whispered. He pulled me closer.

"Does he touch you like this?" He put his hand between my legs and rubbed. Then he stopped, and pulled me onto his leg so that I straddled it. He touched me again between my legs, and then took my hand and put it on his penis. "Right there. You go like this," he whispered. "Did you ever do this?"

"Don't," I quivered. But the sound was croaky, frozen by the panic creeping its way across my throat. He pulled me closer. "Did he ever kiss you?"

I felt bile rise in my throat. This felt so wrong, but I couldn't move my legs to run. Then he kissed me, and his tongue inside my mouth broke my terror like a hammer to a window. "Stop it!" I screamed and jumped off his leg, down the porch stairs, and bolted across the yard.

"Get back up here!" He yelled angrily. This paralyzed me. His anger frightened me.

"Stop what you're doing!" I cried, squeezing my body inward in efforts to extinguish the disgust and shame that now devoured my insides.

He laughed. "Okay, okay," he said, waving me to come back up to the porch. I refused, and that's when he came to retrieve me. He grabbed my wrist and pulled me up the stairs. "It's okay," he coaxed, "I'm not going to hurt you."

He pulled me close again and moved his hand under my shirt, pawing at my small breasts. He stared into my face, watching my

202 • JUANIMA HIATT

reaction—watching my tears. I swallowed the bile that threatened to come up, and then he stopped. I thought it was over, but when he opened the sliding glass door and stepped inside, holding out his hand again for me, I knew it wasn't. "Come on," he said. "It'll be okay."

My hesitation frustrated him, but then a loud grinding sound startled us both. I realized the sound was the garage door opening. My mom's car turned into the driveway, and my heart burst in my chest. Panic-filled emotions and thoughts flooded my head, and suddenly Ron grabbed my arm and hissed, "Not a word of this, do you understand? What we did was okay. I was teaching you things. But you can never tell your mother about this, do you understand? *You'll be sorry if you do.* If you tell anyone... you'll be very sorry." He let go of my arm and my mom appeared in the doorway.

"Hey! Can you help with the groceries?" she asked, and disappeared back inside. Ron followed her, looking back with a dark glare that embedded a fear in me so strong, I knew I could not defy his demand for silence. I believed he would harm me if I did.

Though the truth eventually came out, and though he never touched me again, the ignorance that invaded my home ruled. No one discussed what had happened. No one discussed how I felt about it, or how it affected me inside. The injustice sparked an anger in me that burned and grew, continuously fueled by the kindling of shame, worthlessness, and a sad realization that my value seemed to come in bringing sexual pleasure to men. And while my anger festered against those who ignored the event, I couldn't help but apply the obvious truth: no one really cared about me.

の

Chad seemed to care about me, however. He invited me to his senior prom the following spring, and of course I jumped at the chance. I didn't know any other freshman girls going to the prom, and that boosted my ego significantly. The night of the event, he picked me up in a gleaming, black sports car, and his jaw dropped when I came out in a full length, mint green dress with an iridescent overlay that sparkled and swooshed when I walked. By the time we arrived at the dance, my cheeks ached from smiling. His approving, stunned glances made me feel beautiful. During the prom, he held my hand and danced with me tenderly, then sporadically broke into goofy, jerky moves that made me laugh out loud. Nothing he did was conventional. At the end, he brought me home by curfew, and kissed me goodnight. I loved the lack of drama in our relationship, and he never pressured me to give more than I wanted to. That brought a level of safety for me, because my parents had raised me to wait until I was married to have intercourse. The idea of waiting for the right man, and having someone who respected me and adored me be the first one I made love to, seemed perfect. I wanted to wait.

꙳

Shortly after the prom, however, Chad's hands started walking. It became a nuisance to me, as he made progressive attempts to cross the physical boundaries I had established. Thankfully, when I said "No," he yielded, and never made me feel bad about it. I enjoyed being with him, and went to great lengths to spend unwarranted time with him. Still fourteen years old, but fueled by a taut rebelliousness, I taught myself to drive by stealing my sister's car in the middle of the night. The first time, I crawled into her bedroom after she'd fallen asleep, and silently removed her car keys from her purse. Using blankets, I formed a body under the covers on my bed, and placed an ankle weight on the pillow to mimic head weight. Then out the window I stealthily climbed, careful to leave it open a quarter of an inch so I could get back in later. Under the divulging lights of the street lamps, I slid quietly into the driver's seat of the small, brown, 1976 Toyota Corolla, shifted it into neutral, and pushed it to the end of our street before starting the engine. What stood against me, however, was that I had never driven a stick shift, and the street before me was at a forty-five-degree angle. Nothing like jumping into the fire with both feet. I puttered and sputtered up the road, only to kill the engine by faltering on the clutch. It was a frightening coast backwards down the street; but eventually, I made it to the top, and then I made it to Chad's house, where he waited in the shadows.

We went to our favorite park, which we chose because of its low lights and abundance of trees, allowing a slim chance of being seen by police. We lingered there one night, amidst a light fog and dew settling on my windshield. The air had a bite to it, but I cracked the window because it was starting to get foggy inside as well. Then Chad wanted to get frisky. He leaned over to kiss me, but the stick shift made it uncomfortable.

"Why don't we get in the back seat?" he smiled.

"Chad..." I shook my head.

"C'mon! I won't do anything you don't want me to." I looked at him, and believed him. Historically, we'd messed around, but always put on the brakes before it went too far. I conceded. We took turns climbing over the seat, and I shivered from the chill.

"Oh, you poor baby. Let me hold you," he laughed.

"It's cold!" I shrieked, as he squeezed me in a bear hug.

"Well, hmm... gee... close the window," he teased.

"You're the one fogging it up in here," I bantered. He grabbed me playfully, tickling and poking while I defended myself with punches to his arms. And then he kissed me, pressing against me with an aggressive force. "Easy, tiger," I warned.

This time, though, he grew impatient, and started unbuttoning my shirt.

"Hey! Stop it!" I said, smacking his hand away with a nervous laugh. His hands returned to the buttons. "I'm serious, Chad. Knock it off," and slapped his hand away again.

He started kissing me and said, "Fuck it," and shoved his hand up my shirt. Surprised by his roughness, I tried to push him off. "No, no, no, no," he calmly said, "Just go with it."

"I don't want to go with it! Get off me!"

He moved up and down on me, getting heavier, breathing in my face. He kissed my face... my neck. I grunted, trying to push him off.

"Chad! Stop it!" I yelled. My fear escalated, and he stopped listening to me.

"No, c'mon," he said, but he had already made up his mind. He ripped my shirt open, and I heard the *tink-tink* of buttons landing around me.

"Stop it, Chad!" I screamed. He touched me... kissed me... and held my hands over my head. I tried to wiggle out from under him but had no room to move. He got my pants down and a rush of terror flooded my body. "No! Chad! Stop it!"

I screamed again and begged for him to get off me, but he didn't listen, and he didn't stop. His weight grew heavier on me, crushing my chest, and I struggled to breathe. And then there was a sharp, stabbing pain that shot through my body as he pushed his way inside me. It wasn't easy for him, so he pushed harder and I kicked in what little space I had.

"Stop! Stop! You're hurting me! Stoooopppp..." I sobbed. The space closed in around me, and even when he removed his hold on my wrists, I couldn't use my hands to defend myself. I couldn't move at all. His hands grabbed at my sides and legs, manipulating them to make it easier for him to thrust. My lower body felt like it was breaking in two.

When he was done, he pushed himself up enough to see my face. "Hey, you okay?" he chuckled. When I didn't answer, he hunched over awkwardly to pull his pants up. "It is so damn small in here! It's like a closet."

I slid back away from him, trying to button my blouse, but my hands wouldn't work, and buttons were missing.

"I guess we'd better get home, huh?" he said, climbing back up to the passenger seat. "Holy shit—it's late."

Feebly, trembling, I got myself into the driver's seat. I have no memory of leaving the park, or the drive home, but when I coasted the car back into its spot in front of my sister's window, I remember stepping so slowly out of the car, not because I was trying to be quiet, but because I still felt the knives piercing into my body from the waist down. Every move, every step, caused a tear to fall. I leaned against the door until I heard the *click!* of it closing. Using the car to maintain my balance, I maneuvered along the side of it, glancing through the window into the back seat, when something stopped me cold. Blood... all over the seat. And then I looked down, and noticed the blood on me. I leaned to the ground and swallowed hard against the bile in my throat.

"Oh my God..." I strained with emotion, but I couldn't afford to make a sound. Panicked, I ignored the searing pain through my legs and midsection and climbed up through my window to get a wet washcloth, then snuck out again to clean the seat. I scrubbed with everything I had in me, but despite my best efforts, there remained three dark spots I could not erase.

I didn't sleep that night. I just knew Cris was going to ask me about the stains, even though she had no idea I was sneaking her car out at night. She didn't ask. She didn't see. But for months, I rode in the back seat of that car with those brown stains, constantly reminding me that I was a total loser who wasn't pure anymore. Every day I sat there, it reaffirmed to me that I was just a dirty, slutty, white-trash whore.

I stopped seeing Chad, but the self-perceived reality of the source of my worth grew roots into my soul. It was further reinforced when the weekly letters from my dad suddenly stopped coming, and our weekend visits dwindled because he'd be "busy" that weekend. In my young mind, I believed Ron's abusing me had caused my dad's withdrawal. Certainly, my mother had told him about it, and his inner response was that I was no good to him now. He was ashamed of me. The silence from my dad, coupled with Ron's repeated statements of, "He doesn't really love you or want you," began to sink in and take hold. I started to believe it. My dad really *was* rejecting me. And though he and I never discussed this issue, I was as certain about *it*, as I was certain about my own worth.

Worthless, but I sought power and control. My motivation for boyfriends was simply to reaffirm my worth, and yet I found power in my ability to seduce them. That's what it had come to. If I could finally lure a guy in who hadn't looked at me twice before, I felt powerful, but it also proved to me that what he really wanted was sex. Thus, proving my worth.

The late-night masquerades continued several nights per week, as I found my way to parties after dark behind the wheel of my sister's car. One night, at a house I can't remember, people I didn't know very well taught me the game of Quarters. It's a drinking game where you try to bounce a quarter into an empty glass, and if you make it in, you get to choose someone in the group to have a drink. Funny... the guys kept choosing me. That was the first time I got drunk. Still fourteen, I sat at the long rectangular table with six or seven other guys and girls, and I remember laughing so hard I fell backward in my chair onto the floor. The room erupted with laughter, and so did I, despite the lump on the back of my head from the brick fireplace I had fallen onto. But in that moment I realized the gift of forgetting. I realized alcohol could numb pain, and it also made me the life of the party.

Heading to a subsequent party at the same house, I pulled into a 7-Eleven to pick up some personal things, and edged by a police car that was just leaving. My stomach twisted in fear as we made eye contact, and he stared at me suspiciously. Spontaneously, I smiled and waved to him like a girl with a purpose, and he smiled and waved back. The Sweet and Confident Girl Act worked nicely. When I arrived at the party, someone approached me with pot. I looked at it, and took it without hesitation. At that point, I had little to lose. I didn't like it, though, because of the down it brought. I already battled depression, though no one would know it because of the confident smile I wore all the time. But at the next party, it was cocaine, and that's what hooked me. It took one inhalation for me to feel sharp-minded, alive, and powerful.

The weeks passed, and my extra-curricular activities remained undetected by my mom. But late-night parties weren't enough. My life became a high-risk cesspool of shoplifting and compulsive lying; but I was never caught because of the smile, and I knew how to pull a score. I found a great clearance on lingerie at Fred Meyer one afternoon, and spent fifteen minutes around one rack, pulling tags off of beautiful negligees and stuffing them into a blue shoulder bag that I had also stolen. I deflected any suspicion by smiling and making small-talk with people who approached the rack, or store clerks who walked by and caught my eye. Then I took fifteen more minutes just to walk around the store, stopped at the checkout to buy a single scarf, and walked out with the scarf in a grocery bag, and the blue shoulder bag stuffed with the stolen lingerie. Lingerie I would never even wear.

It became a thrill for me, and an almost daily excursion after school on my way home. Even if it was just a candy bar, I stole it; but for more expensive lifts, I had to cover myself by making an additional purchase. My one near miss was the day I stole a rhinestone anklet. It sparkled with shimmering black stones like I'd never seen, and I ripped the tag off and dropped it into my coat pocket. I lingered awhile, and then stopped at the counter to purchase some black eyeliner before walking out of the store. I'd walked about ten feet from the building when a woman came out and said, "Hey! I know what you did! You! You wait right there! Don't you move!"

She disappeared back into the store, and I knew she was off to get security. No way in hell was I sticking around. I bolted down the alley beside the store and hid behind a dumpster. I heard the hysterical voice of the woman, followed by a man's voice asking exactly what she had seen. After several minutes, it grew silent again. When I was sure the coast was clear, I ran to the back of the large building and hopped the fence, which placed me right at my street. My house stood directly across from me. I unlocked the door and ran inside, laughing, and patting myself on the back for my undefeated record.

The two "me's" became more defined into the day child, and the night child. At school, I had normal friends and excelled in drama and volleyball. I sang in the choir, and learned I could actually sing. I started a cake business out of my home with my best friend, Amy. But at night, alone in my bedroom with torturous thoughts and depression, the darkness in my spirit consumed me. I didn't realize, however, that my hurt and anger was seeping out at home. A touchy attitude, refusal to do what I was told, and an irritable tongue were grinding on my mother's nerves. My deep, stifled anger drew more attention to myself than I'd wanted.

I was meeting up with some friends one night, Tobin and his friend, Matt. I sat in the darkness of my room, waiting for the slumbering silence to settle a little deeper, and for "12:55" to show on my clock. The silence hung in the air so thick, I heard ringing in my ear from nowhere in particular. I was focusing on that when the phone rang. Jumping from my bed, I grabbed it before the first ring ended.

"Hello?" I whispered.

"Hey. It's Tobin. Just telling you that we're still on and we'll meet you in the Fred Meyer parking lot."

"Are you crazy?" I scolded in a hushed tone. "It's one o'clock in the morning! You probably woke my mom! I gotta go. I'll see you there." I hung up the phone and dove into my bed, faking sleep, while my pulse pounded like a steel drum in my head. When five minutes passed and my mom hadn't emerged from her room, I assumed I was in the clear. I slipped out after making the blanket-body in my bed, and hopped the fence over to the back of the Fred Meyer building. I jogged to the front of the store, where Tobin and Matt waited under a street lamp. I reiterated what a dork Tobin was for calling my house, and then let it go. We walked together under the bright lights, and then over to an adjacent, graveled trailer lot where little light shone and shadows loomed. Tobin didn't live in my city, so we rarely saw each other. I appreciated Tobin because he wasn't complicated, and he made me laugh. I loved him like a best friend.

In the midst of updating him on my new school, a sheriff's car suddenly skidded onto the gravel, its lights whirling and siren bleeping, and then another followed suit. Matt ran. As one officer took off after him, the others arrested Tobin and me, and placed us in the back seat of the police car. I shook, terrified.

"You kids trying to break into some trailers?" the officer asked, shining his flashlight across our faces.

"No," Tobin quivered. "We were just talking."

"Uh-huh," he replied with disbelief.

I didn't think my life could get any worse until a pair of headlights swept across my face, and when I turned to look, I recognized my mother's car. I watched with absolute horror as she pulled into the Fred Meyer parking lot. It dawned on me then that she knew I'd be there. I moaned like a criminal sentenced to the electric chair. The officer had been watching me closely.

"You know that car?" he asked.

"It's my mom," I sobbed.

I don't know what happened to Tobin, but after the officer spoke with my mom, he pulled me from the police car and sent me over to my mom's car. I wanted to run the opposite direction. Neither of us spoke a word during the short trip home, but I felt her fury vibrate across the car like invisible electrical currents. I knew she'd had enough with me. When we got inside the house and into my bedroom, the yelling began. There was no waiting until morning. She went to her room and returned with one of Ron's belts, and released her fury on my backside. She'd never done that before. Ever. But clearly, she didn't know another way to let me know how much pain I'd caused. How much trouble I'd been. I screamed and cried as the belt lashed repeatedly across my backside. And then she stopped.

"I've had enough of this!" she yelled. "Of all of this! I can't do this anymore! I can't control you anymore! You're going to live with your dad!"

Her words were a slap in the face. "No, I'm not!" I screamed back. The rage billowed in my throat. He didn't want me, and I hated him. "I won't go! I'd rather live in a foster home!"

"Fine!" she yelled. "That can be arranged." Then I heard the slamming of her bedroom door.

I slid down to the floor and sobbed, holding the back of my legs as pain radiating across them. The thought of moving to my dad's devastated me. I had finally made some good friends, and now I would have to leave them. Again. I grieved the fact that nobody understood me. Nobody really knew me. I knew I hurt my mother, but the pain inside me needed somewhere to go. I couldn't handle it on my own, but I had no choice. I understood that in my world, everyone else needed to live their own lives, and that the disagreeable things got swept under a rug. Maybe my pain was just too big for everyone to handle. Or maybe, I wasn't the only one dealing with pain. I know now that my mom suffered in ways I didn't understand at the time. But back then, I had never felt so alone, and so completely abandoned.

As I slid under the covers of my bed, and faced a sleepless night, the hope in my heart dwindled. I saw nothing good ahead of me. My world had officially shattered.

13

FALLING

 ♦1987-1988♦

The next morning, my mom retracted the foster home option, and informed me I'd be moving to live with my dad after the school year was over—the summer after my sixteenth birthday. I hated my life.

The day I walked into his small house on a busy, main street in Hillsboro, I seethed with bitterness and rage, and I didn't understand at all why he was so overjoyed. It *had* to be an act of some sort, trying to pretend everything was great, when in reality, everything was falling apart. He reached out to embrace me with the ear-to-ear grin I had loved so much as a child, but I reeled back, ran down the hall, and locked myself in my bedroom. I left a moment too late, though. The crushed expression on his face had seared into my retina. *Fake love*, I kept telling myself. *It's all fake.* To his inmost dismay, I kept my distance the entire summer.

On the first day of school, my stomach burned with an insatiable fire of fear and anxiety. All I could think about were the friends I had left behind at my other high school. I didn't *want* to start over! What would the kids be like at the new place? Would anyone like me? I hated being the new kid. I drove to the high school in my sister's old Toyota Corolla, which she had sold me for two hundred dollars. The same car with the ever-present dark stains in the back seat. But by the time I touched the front double doors, I had shifted to the day child, and she walked in with purpose and confidence, and survived those first days. I met Darcy, and we quickly bonded—not because we shared similar interests, but because we shared a similar pain. I joined the party scenes again, but this time it was better. This time I had a friend.

At home, I hid two-liter bottles of alcoholic coolers in my closet that I drank every day after school. My dad tried to give me space, but he gave me too much. He never entered my room. Never knew what I did behind that door. I wavered between the conflicting emotions of rejection—believing he just didn't care enough to come in—and gratefulness that he left me alone. But he never knew what I did behind that door. Never knew how I hurt myself.

Though Darcy often kept me company within the confines of my small bedroom, in my soul I longed to have that discussion with my dad, asking him why he rejected me, and why he wasn't there for me. I refrained from asking him because I was too afraid of the answer, and hearing the words out loud. Not that it mattered. I did a fine job of reconfirming my worthlessness on a daily basis. The self-loathing and disgust became a constant companion, and I grew to despise the thing that seemed to attract aggressive, evil, violent hands: *my body.* I hated being pretty, and often fantasized about scarring my face so guys wouldn't find me attractive.

Though I had not yet discovered cutting, I found other ways to indulge in self-punishment. I quit caring about my body, and turned my anger on myself. Food became an enemy, and if I wasn't avoiding it completely, I threw it up when I did eat. However, because of my lifelong aversion to vomiting, I established a fairly consistent ritual of starving.

One night, Darcy and I went to a party. I noticed maybe ten people mingling against walls and on the sofa when we walked in. I also noticed drugs or alcohol in almost every hand, and that guys outnumbered the girls three-to-one. That made me uncomfortable. I lingered around the fireplace most of the night, as it gave me full view of the room, and nobody could sneak up on me or approach me by surprise. I admired its construction, with beautiful stones in variegated neutral tones, and a beautiful oak mantel, decorated with evergreen plants and candles for the winter holidays. But I loved the warming fire, and stared at its tall flames, mesmerized by their flickering and dancing.

A guy interrupted my trance, coming too close for comfort, and stuck a joint in my face.

"You sure are pretty," he smirked. "Welcome to the party. They call me Mouse."

"Mouse?" I chuckled, and took the joint from his hand. "Okay." I didn't need to ask why people called him Mouse. His ears were testament enough.

He lit the joint for me and backed away, the smirk still plastered on his face, as if anticipating my reaction to the thing in my hand. I put the joint to my lips and inhaled deeply, and suddenly found myself in a time warp, sitting on the floor with Darcy, munching down a bag of peanut M&M's and laughing so hard that I peed my pants a little. Later, I bumped into Mouse again.

"You have a great smile," he said with a gallon of charm. "I've been watching you."

Great, I thought. *Another one I need to watch out for.* But the longer the night wore on, the more comfortable I became with Mouse. His charm, his smile, and sense of humor. He had a way of making me feel at ease.

"How old are you?" I asked him in the hallway to the kitchen, giggling and drunk.

"Not too old," he said softly, leaning against the wall. He stuffed his hands in his pockets and stared, his gaze burning through my clothes. I felt it, and shivered.

"I need to go find Darcy," I said, and wobbled back down the hall to the living room. I needed to tell her it was time to go.

I found her putting on her coat, about to walk out the door with some guys.

"Hey!" she laughed. "I'll be right back. We're going to get some more alcohol."

"What?" For the first time, I noticed the other guests had left.

Mouse came up behind me and looked at Darcy wavering in the doorway. "Go ahead," he said, flashing an alluring smile. "I'll take good care of her."

I no longer trusted Mouse, and something about his smile made me nervous. I heard the guys outside call to Darcy, "You comin' or what?"

"You'll be fine," she said, taking my hand. "We won't be gone long. Mouse will take care of you!" She giggled and slammed the door. I stood there, frozen, listening to her laughing outside, listening to the car doors slam, listening to them drive away. I strained to hear the engine until it was gone, and the only sound left was *him* breathing. He was still standing there, and that's when the fear took over.

I don't know what he said to me next. I don't remember. But I know my feet were glued by the front door, and I remember every detail of the entryway. I remember the coats hanging there, the boots on the floor. It was fall. Caked mud coated the boots and the floor around them. Whatever grown-ups lived there didn't make the kids shake off the mud before coming in the house. I was focusing on that mud when I suddenly found myself on the floor. He took me down so fast, I hit my head on the linoleum. Mouse touched my head sympathetically until I tried to get up. Then he pressed his hand down on my chest.

"Let me up!" I said.

He smiled again. "It's okay. We're just gonna have some fun."

"Get off me!" I said, louder. When he put his weight on me, panic flashed through my body, and I screamed until I felt the burning of his hand across my cheek. That silenced me.

"What'd you do that for?" he said, still grinning. "What the hell are you screaming for? I said I'd take care of you."

When I kicked at him, he stopped being nice. I screamed again but his hand crushed down over my mouth, bruising my jaw.

I saw the mud again. I saw the coats. I reached for those coats with my eyes as he used his free hand to push my pants down. "Just relax," he said.

He laughed at his own clumsiness in removing my pants, but he finally had them out of the way. The ice cold tile beneath me jolted the nerves in my back and backside as it came into contact. My mouth burned from the vice-like grip of his hand. As he paid less attention to his hand on my face, it moved up over my nostrils, and the shock and terror of suffocation surged through me. I bucked against his body with all my might, but it only enticed him. He groaned with excitement about his opportunity to do what he wanted with me. He put his full weight on me and drove himself in me with brutal force. This made me scream, and I whipped my head side to side until I was free from his hand; but no one heard my scream, and the pain radiating through my lips and cheeks from his return grip made me stop.

I see the boots, and I want to put those boots on to run away in. I don't care about the mud. I see myself, trying to run in the boots across a luxurious wheat field where the millions of tips look like golden feathers bowing and whispering in the wind. A beautiful rain sprinkles lightly down on my head, and I look up to the sky at the slice of sun peeking above a cluster of gray and white clouds.

That is the last memory I have of that night. I don't remember him getting off me, but I remember lying there on those frozen tiles, and my body is numb. I don't remember how my clothes got back on. I don't remember Darcy coming back, but I know she did. I don't remember going home, or my conversations. But I remember his ears... the flashy smile... the pain shooting through my body. My spirit breaking again. I remember that.

৵

As hope faded from my spirit like a twig carried out to sea, I grew tired of living. Darcy and I brainstormed and made a plan to end our pitiful, dismal lives; but one day, sitting far back in the school theater, watching my classmates practice a scene for an upcoming play, I realized I didn't want my life to be over. I just couldn't take the pain anymore. I found Darcy and proposed we leave; run away, and start new lives, and leave the pain behind. The trip would be permanent. I believed that would work for us. A new hope ignited within me when she agreed.

For months we planned the trip. We perused the white pages and created false names for ourselves, and solidified a story: We were sisters, and our names were Sylvia and Celeste. Our parents had died long ago in a car accident, and we had decided that when we turned eighteen, we would pack up and move somewhere new, taking only our suitcases and the clothes on our backs.

We decided to leave mid-December, before our high school's Christmas break. The night before we left, Darcy spent the night. Earlier that afternoon, I had talked my dad into letting me make his bank deposit for him. He appreciated my helpfulness, elated by my effort to actively participate in our relationship. At the bank, I deposited his check, and then promptly withdrew it from the ATM. I returned his card, and the receipt for the deposit. He thanked me profusely. The guilt gnawed at my stomach, but I dismissed it, convincing myself that it was something I had to do.

After packing my suitcase, Darcy and I locked ourselves in the bathroom to color our hair. We both chose fiery red to support the image that we were sisters. My older brother was visiting from the Airforce at the time, and he shared my little brother's room directly on the other side of the bathroom wall. At one point we got carried away laughing, and his fist pounded angrily against the wall. "What the hell are you guys doing? It's one o'clock in the morning! Get the fuck to bed!"

We hurried, and quit talking. We certainly didn't want to risk my dad getting up, even though he knew we were leaving. It was part of the plan. I had explained to my dad that through our drama class, we had formed a thespian group, and a new girl was joining. So at 2:00 A.M., Darcy and I would join the others in our group to go to her house and drag her to Shari's Restaurant in her pajamas for breakfast. He believed the story, and he loved seeing me finally laugh as I told him about the prank. If only it were real.

In addition to our full suitcases, Darcy and I packed some things we'd try to sell if we ran out of money. At 2:00 A.M., I walked to my dad's bed to say goodbye. It dawned on me as I watched him sleep that I would never see him again, or my brothers. Yes, they were family, but family had taken on a new meaning for me. Before, I believed family was sacred, and you stuck together through hard times. Now I knew that hard times were meant to survive alone. Family ignored underlying currents of pain, and just like me, put a smile on their faces and went on with their lives. But my life felt like a never-ending battlefield, so I needed to leave my family.

I created chaos around me. I caused friction. I knew I burdened my family. But my heart was broken. As I watched my dad sleep, I saw him through the eyes of that little girl who admired him so much, and looked up to him. The little girl who cherished bedtime, when he would read the Bible and pray with her. Who helped her learn to cook, and watched and cheered when she did crazy stunts on her bicycle across the school playground, while inside he trembled in fear for her safety. I grieved. I ached for that simple, joyous love. I still loved him, deep inside. But it was not enough to heal us.

My eyes burned with the threat of tears, and I stiffened. I needed to make this quick.

"Dad..." I whispered, gently nudging his shoulder.

He stirred groggily, and looked up at me. "Hey, Pooh," he smiled. "Everything okay?"

"Yeah," I replied. "We're leaving now."

"Okay. See you when you get back." He said with a tired, croaky voice.

I won't be coming back, Dad. Tears welled up and I kissed his cheek, "Bye, Dad. I love you."

"Love you, Pooh."

I returned to my bedroom, closing the door behind me as the tears flowed. My stomach ached.

"Are we really doing this?" Darcy asked.

"We have to," I said as I lifted the window. We slid out with our suitcases, closed the window, and loaded our stuff into the Corolla. I didn't look back as we drove away. I was leaving behind fake love, a hopeless future, and—I believed—the pain of a million tears. I had a rock-solid determination to start over, and find something real. Something good.

中

We left Portland, Oregon, on a Greyhound bus to Reno, Nevada. On the long ride southeast, we sat at the back of the bus, where a small group of guys played card games across the seats. Other than them, the bus was empty. Darcy and I sat quiet. In the silence, I tried to come to terms with my choice to leave my family forever. With no one to act for on the bus, my smile faded, and I felt the darkness. I felt the sadness in my core over the truth of who I was. As a child, my parents made me believe I was special. I had dreams of who I would be when I grew up; of course then, I had powers like the Bionic Woman or Wonder Woman. I was powerful and resilient. My dreams had no limits.

But now I knew it was all a lie. I wasn't born for great things. I was trash. My dad always told me, "God doesn't make junk," but God sure made a mistake with me. My uncle, the black kid on the bus, my boyfriend, my stepdad, Mouse. They saw my true purpose. And if their goal was to use me up, they succeeded. If they wanted to steal my love for themselves, they did that, too. They took it all, emptying me of all good things. Now I knew I was born to be used.

"Hey, gorgeous," I heard from the guys behind us.

Darcy and I looked over our shoulders.

"Yeah, both of you. Why don't you join us for a friendly card game?"

Darcy and I looked at each other and shrugged. It was going to be a long trip. Why not? I put a smile across my face, and Darcy and I joined them in the back. After a couple of hours, we chided like pals. They asked our story—where we were headed—and we told them the story we'd rehearsed so many times. Our answers came as fast as truth. Impressive, to say the least.

Then I got the look from one of them. The one I knew by heart. The look that said, *You're beautiful, and I will have you.*

He went to the seat furthest back in the bus and waved at me to join him. As I looked at him, smiling mischievously, I knew what he wanted, and I knew that I would not resist him. I was sixteen years old, and I had gained a new perspective of my true purpose, which was to fulfill the lustful needs of men. Though I did not want it, and though my soul screamed with its injustice, I knew I could not fight it because I would never win. This college boy didn't look mean or violent, but images of Mouse flashed in my head. *Neither did he.* This college boy smiled, with no inhibitions whatsoever. He did not care that he had just met me. He didn't care about my heart, my life, or what made me happy. He wanted one thing from me, and it was the thing I knew now I was supposed to give. Another piece of my soul.

I rose from my seat, and with each step towards the man, remnants of my humanness fell away. The leftovers of self-love, self-respect, dignity, and purpose. Pieces of the girl who cherished life, who believed in love and happiness. I stood next to him, cloaked with a darkness that numbed my spirit, and hardened my heart. He pulled me onto his lap, and while he took what he wanted, I went to another place where I felt no pain. Where I felt no sense of time or existence. Where I felt nothing at all. And that made it easier to forget.

☙

When we arrived in Reno, the cold, biting air shocked my senses. Walking into the station, trailing our suitcases behind, I noticed a large clock showed a little after 9:00 P.M. For a moment we stood dumbfounded, wondering what to do next. We knew the best way to lie was to do it assertively, so we scoured the lobby, searching for our best chance for a good start. And then we saw him. A security guard who looked to be in his mid-twenties. I told Darcy he reminded me of John on the TV show CHiPS with his flaxen hair and boyish face, except he was heavier. We approached him, and introduced ourselves. I laughed when I saw him name tag: John. What a coincidence.

"We're both eighteen," I said, maybe too eagerly. "We came here to start a new life, but... we have no clue where to go to get settled. Can you help?"

He smiled. "You came here... to start a new life... at nine o'clock at night in the dead of winter? And you have nowhere to go?"

"Uhh—" I said, and looked at Darcy. "Yeah, we're not too bright, I guess."

He laughed. "I guess not, but everyone makes mistakes, right?" John's demeanor matched his baby face: kind and sincere. After just the right amount of flirting on our part, he offered to meet us after he got off work at 11:00 P.M., and said he'd show us where we could stay that night.

"Just wait for me at the McDonalds down the street," he said. "I'll get there as soon as I can."

It was nine thirty when we walked into the thick, deep-fried aroma of the fast-food restaurant. My stomach gurgled and growled like a baby tiger, and couldn't wait to sink my teeth into one of their chicken sandwiches. Darcy and I grabbed our meals and devoured them while sitting on tall, red barstools at a narrow table directly against the restaurant windows. Our backs faced the entrance doors. At about ten fifteen, the doors opened and four men entered. Darcy and I stopped eating to stare at the reflection of the group in the window. They looked like a mutinous, punk rock band, all dressed head-to-toe in black leather and chains. As they stood in line to order food, I looked over my shoulder at them, and that's when I saw it was not four men, but three men and a child, who couldn't have been more than eleven or twelve.

Watching their reflection, they took their food to a table nearby. Before long, their attention was on us. Darcy and I grinned at each other, not sensing any danger from these men, but rather, an exhilarating buzz of adventure and mystery. The flirtatious energy became a pit in my stomach, however, when they rose from their table and came our way.

I enjoyed them more from a distance. They seemed larger-than-life, and when they stopped to talk to us, I thought about asking for their autograph. Instead, they made our acquaintance.

Shade was the leader of the group and stood over six feet tall. Close to his side was Tommy, the kid. He nodded at Darcy and me but quickly looked away. I saw a sullen hardness on his face that I recognized. I just hid mine behind a smile.

He looked like Shade's little sidekick, dressed similarly in black jeans and a black leather jacket with rivets across the chest and waist hem. Damon stood in the background, and one glance at him sent a shiver up my spine. Sinister eyes shadowed beneath long, black greasy hair that hung loosely over his face, emphasizing a blanket of acne pits across his face. He smirked when he caught me staring, and I looked away. A fourth man, Jason, stood at the back, quiet and distant. The one, I figured, who didn't want to be remembered.

While Darcy gave the rehearsed speech about us, I studied the kid. I wondered what his story was, and felt sad for him.

"Wanna hang with us?" Shade asked. "We can show you a good time."

"No, thanks," I said. "We're waiting for someone."

"I thought you said you just got here."

"We did," I said. "It's a security guard we met at the station. He's showing us a place to stay tonight." Did we share our story a little too freely? Maybe there was wisdom in staying silent, and not talking to anyone, but it was a little late for that.

"Pssh. You don't need that guy. We can take you right now! We got a great place to stay, right guys? And," he sneered, "We can show you more excitement than a lame security guard."

Darcy and I made a decision that would alter my life forever. Maybe it was the magnetic pull Shade seemed to have on us, or maybe our exhaustion had depleted our smart brain cells. Either way, we left that restaurant in the company of peril.

Darcy and I followed them on foot down the steep city road, and we drew closer together when they led us to a filthy, rundown motel located in an alley near an industrial area. A foul-smelling, acrid odor shocked my nostrils. Dark and eerie alleys branched off in every direction. All instinct warned me to grab Darcy and run back to where we came from, but the guys corralled us into the room, and closed the door behind us. Tommy dove onto the only bed in the small studio and crawled up on the pillow. Jason left the room, and all that remained was Shade, Damon, and little Tommy, who moved to the chair next to the bed at the wave of Shade's hand. Tommy didn't talk much, but hid his face beneath long, curly brown locks. Shade brought out some beer, and as everyone went about their business, my apprehension dwindled. The guys seemed casual enough. Even Damon, who gave me the creeps, kept his distance and bantered with Shade.

Later, the door opened, and Jason jumped inside with a duffle bag over his shoulder and two large copper-colored bags of cocaine cradled in his arms. He kicked the door closed with his foot and peered uneasily out the window. When he seemed satisfied, he dumped everything on the bed. I shifted uneasily, and so did Darcy. He took a huge vanity mirror off the wall and laid it on the bed next to the bags of cocaine, then moving quickly and quietly, he set a bag on top of the mirror and sliced it open. Snowy white powder spilled out onto the glass. Jason leaned over and removed scales and other apparatus from the duffle bag, and began weighing and packaging the powder in smaller amounts. Only for a moment did my inner addiction for the drug scream, but the uneasiness in my gut quenched the desire completely. Something told me I didn't want to be a part of this. I backed away from the bed and eased into a corner of the room.

When Jason finished, he left with the duffel bag, and took Tommy with him. I stayed in the corner, disconnected, while Darcy sat on the bed with Shade, drinking a beer. Damon had disappeared into the bathroom. When too much time had passed, Shade hollered at him. "What the hell are you doing in there? Get out here!"

"I'm busy!" came an angry, muffled reply. Shade laughed.

"What's he doing in there?" I asked.

"Gettin' high, most likely," he answered. "Heroine. Maybe other stuff. Who knows?"

The pit in my stomach grew painful. I moved over to the window, and touched the dirty, beige curtains hanging over it. I wanted out of there. I felt a dangerous energy in the air that made my hairs stand on end.

"Let's go back to McDonalds," I said to Darcy.

"Not yet," she said. "I'm having a good time. I wanna stay."

I pulled the curtain back a bit and peeked out, and Shade yelled at me to close it. I jolted back, startled by his outburst. "Get away from the window," he said.

Damon emerged suddenly from the bathroom, and the anxiety in my gut turned to terror. He looked crazed with his arms stiff at his sides, vibrating like a tuning fork. His eyes were wild and bulging, his jaw and fists clenched, pumping invisible stress balls.

Shade laughed at him, "Dude, you really fucked up." It was clear he'd taken in too much, but Damon told him where to shove it.

I turned back towards the window, even though Shade wouldn't let me look out. I thought of John, the nice security guard, and wished we'd waited for him. I looked at the doorknob on the door and saw myself turning it and bolting from the room. Darcy would catch up to me eventually. The panic rose in me when I felt Damon behind me. His face at my neck, hot breath spreading down, he slid my hair back over my shoulder like he might kiss me there. I tilted my head to block him.

"C'mon," he said.

I wanted to leave, and suddenly the words were coming out of my mouth, "I want to leave!"

I went for the door and Damon slammed his fist into it. "You can't leave!" he yelled.

"Why not!"

"Because there are punks with guns out there, bitch. And if you open that door you're dead." I shook my head. "You don't believe me? Look here, you stupid bitch!" He whipped back the curtain and pointed to multiple places in the alleys. Sure enough, I saw them: Men with rifles and hand guns darting back into the shadows. Their enemy. "They'll kill you, too, if you walk out that door."

I started to cry and Damon laughed at me, "Oh, you gonna cwy like a wittle cwybaby? Wah! Wah! Wah! You gonna cwy wittle cwybaby?"

I turned away, trying to stop the tears, but the terror consumed me. I felt his eyes burning into me, and then his demeanor shifted and he tried to comfort me with a seducing hand. His charm made my stomach churn.

"I think I'm gonna throw up," I quivered.

"Go ahead," he whispered, trying to coerce me away from the window.

"Leave me alone," I pleaded, disgusted by the touch of his clammy hand on my neck. I pushed it away, wanting desperately to leave, but knowing I couldn't. He touched me again, dragging his finger along the back of my neck. I shrugged and shivered his hand away. Like a pesky bug, his hand returned. I whirled around and screamed with cornered fury, "Fuck off!"

In an instant his hand hit my face and knocked me to the floor. I was dazed, and my whole head throbbed. I tried to get up as he screamed names at me, "Fucking bitch! You fucking cunt!"

I got on all fours to crawl away, and he grabbed a fistful of my hair and flipped me onto my back.

"Aaaaah!" I cried. He grabbled my hair in both hands and started pulling—dragging me. I screamed for him to stop.

"Damon, leave her alone," Shade said flippantly, as if this was my big brother teasing me.

Damon ignored him and kept dragging me. I screamed for help, and the silence fell like icicles into my heart. Some hair pulled free from my scalp, so he grabbed more. I kicked my legs to try and ease the force of his pull, and caught a glimpse of Darcy through my tears. She sat on the bed, cradling a beer in her hands, and that was the moment my world shifted. She was all I had left in the world, and she didn't move to save me. No one did.

Damon dragged me into the scanty bathroom, growling and grunting with a violent rage. He pushed me on the floor and kicked me against the bathtub like a ball to the curb. He grabbed my legs and slid them where he wanted them. I kicked at him dizzily, pain flowing over my body like water. I sat up and swung a fist at him. He dodged and landed a punch to my face. The blow forced my head to the floor and against the tub. I tasted blood in my mouth, and felt a warm liquid oozing down my face. Much more than my tears.

I weakened against his drug-induced craze, and my kicks as he pulled my pants down landed in the air. Still, this angered him, and I caught punches to my legs and side. I heard another zipper. When I tried to move he hit me again. His hands grabbed and grasped and ripped at me like a wild animal, pulling my clothes off, pinching me and punching me at my resist. His adrenaline surged like electric jolts through his limbs, like he could have sprinted for miles without stopping. But there weren't miles... just the suffocating walls of the bathroom, and they were closing in on me.

When he rammed himself inside me, I screamed again. The violence of it... I knew I was going to die. The miles... were the hours he pinned me beneath his sweaty, surging body. Nobody came to the door. Nobody came to help.

Damon didn't tire, and I became his rag doll. Numb... limp... empty. Time stretched into a kaleidoscope of pain and torture, and for a while, I disappeared. But then he suddenly grew even angrier. I wasn't doing something right. He pulled out a knife.

"See this, cunt?" he hissed. "If you don't cum, I'm gonna slice you up. You get me, bitch?"

I must have passed out, because a sharp sting on my face sucked me back into his world. "Hey! You hearin' my words, bitch?"

I heard him...And I knew I could never do what he was asking. The only way I knew to survive was to disappear—to let my mind fall into a dark abyss of emptiness. What he asked of me was impossible, but it was do or die. I believed his threat. I had felt the cold, steel blade of the knife against my thigh. He continued raping me as forcefully as when he began, and I lay aware, broken, and lifeless. I can't explain how I did what I did next. It's the single most difficult thing for me to admit, and shame still fills me now as I write the words. My body responded to his vile act, while tears soaked into my hair. But then a merciful darkness swept in, and there was a calm, and a quiet inside.

æ

I woke up to Darcy tugging on my arm. "Come on," she whispered. "Come on, get up." I had no strength. And in the light I saw the floor and suddenly felt sick. Blood. As Darcy helped me stand, I caught a glimpse of the mirror, but could not look in it. I couldn't bear to see The Nothing. Darcy led me out to the bed, and I saw the room was empty. The sun shone brightly through the window that, hours before, was the barrier between us and a violent death by artillery. I would have welcomed the guns. I would have given myself to the guns, had I known the alternative.

She sat with me on the bed and held me, and nobody came to bother us. As I shivered, trying to get a grasp on what was real, I was glad to be sitting there alone with Darcy. I was glad she hadn't left. But there were no words to say now.

After awhile, Darcy helped me to the shower. I felt sick from the pain, and struggled to stand on my own. I grasped the wall for stability, screaming silently, hurting so much. Hurting everywhere.

"We have to get out of here," she said. "They're coming back. We have to leave."

When I was cleaned up we left the hotel room, pulling our wheeled suitcases behind us, unsure of where we would go next. We thought of John, and decided we would try to find him. Maybe he would help us, if he could forgive us for standing him up. I needed to put the rape behind me and pull up my mask. The one I used every day. The one that says, "Nothing bad happens to me. I'm fine. I'm a happy, confident girl."

Darcy and I returned to the bus station that afternoon and found John. He was disappointed that we didn't meet him like we'd promised, but we put on the smiles and flirted until he forgave us. We asked if he would still help us find somewhere safe to stay.

"There's a hotel," he said, "A nicer one that I have connections at. I can get you guys a really good deal for the night—maybe sixty bucks?"

We cringed, knowing that would leave us with enough for one more meal. John offered to foot the bill for us. This time, we waited for him to get off work, and met him at a hotel in the heart of the city. I was caught off guard when John showed up with a friend, but a few minutes of conversation put me at ease. His combed, strawberry-blonde hair, khaki slacks and light blue button-up dress-shirt dazzled like a comfortable summer day, refreshing and easy company compared to the terrifying darkness of Shade and his evil gang.

John led us upstairs to our room, carrying with him grocery bags of beer and cooler bottles. The room was modest but beautiful: a studio with a kitchen, barstools beneath the counter, a queen bed out in the open, and furniture in light oak. The sun shone in with a new hope, and the more we visited, the more I started to believe everything was going to be okay. John's friend, Brian, was indeed kind. He smiled and chuckled a lot, and when he pulled pictures of his wife and two beautiful children out of his wallet, I relaxed even more. John and his friend both had a great sense of humor. The room filled with laughter, and for the first time, I enjoyed myself. I was forgetting the bad stuff.

After a few hours, our drink supply ran low, and John offered to go get more.

"C'mon, Brian," he said, walking to the door.

"Nah, you go. I'll stay here with the ladies if that's alright."

John paused, and there were glances between all of us. I don't know if Darcy told John what had happened to me—or whether he could see something had happened—but I sensed his sudden protective stance.

"Come here," he waved his friend over. Brian joined him near the door and they spoke in hushed tones.

"Dude! What's the big deal?" Brian laughed. "I'm not gonna do anything! I'll just keep 'em company while you're gone. Come on."

John looked at me, asking with his eyes if I was okay with this. I shrugged with mine. Uncertain. I didn't believe Brian would do anything, and I knew John wouldn't be gone long. But the obvious deception behind my experiences nagged at my consciousness. I couldn't trust my own instincts anymore.

His friend blurted, "Just go already! Hurry back. I'll take good care of them."

Take care of them, I thought. I'd heard those words before. So John threw his hands up and said, "Okay! I'm going." He looked at Darcy and me, "I'll be back soon," he assured. I smiled.

When John left, our jovial conversation continued with Brian. I finished my cooler, and then Brian said to Darcy, "Hey... Celeste? There's a paper in the hallway. Would you be a doll and go get that for me?"

She slid off the barstool and walked over to the door with Brian right behind her. He chuckled about something as he opened the door for her, and as soon as she stepped into the hallway, he closed it. Then he locked it. I had been sitting on the bed and jumped to the floor.

"What are you doing?" I asked nervously.

He was still chuckling, "Just relax, Sylvia, we're just gonna have a little fun."

"No, we're not. Please let her back in." Darcy pounded on the door, demanding that Brian let her back in.

When the pounding didn't cease, it was amazing... how quickly he turned. He moved like wildfire to the door and through gritted teeth said, "Listen to me, you little bitch. Stop that knocking or you're gonna get it, do you hear me? Now you just put your little ass right down there on the floor and wait—until I *decide* to let you back in. You get me?"

Darcy didn't respond, but she stopped knocking. The silence choked me with a death grip. I prayed that Darcy would go get someone. *Get help. Please bring back help.* But then I heard fabric against wall as she slid down to the floor. Brian walked toward me, smiling, shrugging like a ruffian. I stood there frozen, arms limp at my side and scared to death. Inside my head I was screaming, *'No no no!'* But nothing came out of my mouth. No screams. No fury. Just frozen fear.

"Now c'mon," he said, holding his hands out reassuringly. "It's okay, girl! We're just gonna have a little fun, you and me."

"I want Celeste," I whispered.

"Well, she ain't coming in right now. So now that it's you and me, why don't you just lay yourself right down there on the bed and we'll have our own little party, huh? Whadya say?"

He came to the side of the bed and got so close I could feel his hot breath on my neck. I frantically shook my head no, and that triggered his anger like a bull released from the holding pen. His hand struck my face with such force, I fell backwards onto the bed. My head exploded with pain, but I was not going to let this happen to me again.

Filled with a sudden vengeance, I got to my knees and yelled, "Don't you do that again, you son of a bitch!" The shocked expression on his face mirrored what I felt inside, but instead of deterring him, it energized him.

"Well," he sneered, "the little bitch has a mouth!" He slapped me again and as I fell backwards, I heard the zipper of his pants. With my eyes clenched shut, I gripped my head with trembling hands, and I knew by the swiftness by which he came onto the bed that I was in trouble again. I suddenly felt his hand over my forehead, and then a shooting pain across my scalp as he grabbed a fistful of hair and pulled me up to my knees. I cried out.

"Let's just see what that mouth can *do*, you little bitch."

"No!" I screamed, tears streaming down my burning cheeks.

"Do it!" he said again, and jerked my head towards his erect penis. When I refused, he gripped my hair tighter. "I'll hurt your friend. You'll never see her again, is that what you want?"

"No," I cried. He jerked me forward, shoving my mouth on himself. I choked and gagged as his grip tightened and moved my head back and forth, ignoring the violent pummeling of my fists against his legs. He finally shoved me backwards.

"You're a worthless cunt, you know that?" I crawled away from him, curling into the fetal position against the headboard, trying to bury myself into the pillows, hoping he was done with me. But I heard the laugh again. He was laughing at *me*. "But I'll bet you're good in other ways," he muttered, and reached for my pants. He pulled them off me effortlessly, and I couldn't fight anymore. My face seared with pain. I tried to curl up in a ball but in an instant he jerked my legs down and apart, jumped on top of me and thrust himself inside me. I screamed, and his hand came down over my mouth.

"Just enjoy this, bitch," he said; and he raped me, holding my arms down until he was done.

When he pulled away from me, I curled up. He threw my pants onto my head, and I heard him pull on his clothes. I stayed covered under my pants, not wanting to see anymore. I wanted to hide for the rest of my life.

He laughed at my withdrawal. "Tell your buddy John I had to go, right? Can you do that for me? Oh, and another thing," he said, zipping up his pants. "Better not say anything about this. I'll find you. And you and your little friend will get hurt. Yeah?"

I heard the door open and he was gone, and Darcy came running in. She jumped across the bed and held me, crying, "Oh, Nima! Oh my God. I'm so sorry." Her body shook with broken sobs. I had no more tears.

I pulled my pants from my head and sat up. I couldn't see my underwear anywhere.

"Nima—" Darcy whispered.

There were no words as I slid my toes painfully through one pant leg at a time, and with Darcy's help, got to my feet. The bathroom was an excruciating journey away, as each step exacerbated the stabbing pains and burning through my legs and midsection. When I got there, this time, I did look in the mirror. The girl staring back at me was an image of disgust. A weak girl, proven powerless time and time again. A pathetic girl who men chose as a punching bag for sport. *My purpose.* The little six-year-old girl who dreamed of being an artist and a singer, who had a love for everything on God's green Earth, was stupid and foolish. As I stared at the jagged black stains of mascara across my eyes and face, and the prominent red handprint on my face, I felt a deep repulsion.

They were the marks of a useless degenerate. Something I used to believe didn't exist because of the love and compassion I felt for all humankind. But I felt no love now. Certainly not for the thing whose reflection I now glowered at. I picked up the water glass on the sink, and with a boiling, hateful fury I smashed it into the mirror, screaming with the rage that surged through my veins. The glass shattered in my hand, chunks of it falling into the sink. I picked up a piece and sliced it across my hand, and then John walked in.

He froze in the doorway when he saw me. His eyes swept over the bleeding hand, the tear-streaked make-up, and the red stain left behind from his friend's hand. He dropped the drinks to the floor, and his shocked face turned to a crimson rage. His eyes welled with tears, and the words spit from his lips, "You don't leave, Sylvia. You don't leave! I'm gonna go get that son of a bitch!"

"No, John—" I yelled after him. But yelling was useless. He was gone.

I don't remember seeing him again after that. I don't remember the days that followed. I was raped a third time by the week's end, but the fragments of my dissociated consciousness have spliced the memory into images without story. Without sense. I cannot write it here.

≈

On our last night in Reno, Nevada, we had nothing left. Our pockets were empty. We connected with Shade again, and he knew of a man who could help us. In exchange for providing Darcy and me with false birth certificates, drivers' licenses, and other forms of identification, he would become our Sugar Daddy, until we could get on our feet. At least that was the promise. That someday we'd get on our feet. *Prostitution?* I thought. *Why the hell not. I'm not going home, ever. What choice do we have?* I had no worth or value, and I'd given up hope for anything good ever happening to me again.

Darcy and I dragged our wheeled suitcases behind us up the steep sidewalk in downtown Reno at 10:30 P.M. I looked longingly into the windows of the McDonalds as we went past. My stomach churned painfully with hunger. I held onto Shade's promise that the man would take care of us when we arrived. He said everything would be okay. I'm not sure why we trusted him, but we didn't have any other options.

In the days there of lost memory, Darcy and I had made friends, and they walked beside us now. There was Peter. I remember meeting Peter. I remember him sitting on a high concrete roof with his head in his hands, sobbing about his sad life and talking about suicide. We told him life was worth living, and that he shouldn't kill himself no matter how bad things got because somehow, life would get better. I believed this for him. I knew my life was already dust; it had no significance at all. Peter didn't kill himself that day, and now he and a few of his friends kept us company on our road to our supposed freedom.

Our amiable bantering came to a halt when a police van suddenly pulled to a stop in front of us—right up on the sidewalk. The entire lot of us froze in our tracks. As two officers stepped from the van and approached us, Darcy and I held hands. They asked the kids one-by-one if they had some place to be, and those that did were sent away. Peter had no choice but to leave us, and looked at us with regret as he walked away. Darcy and I felt like the broken links of a chain. We couldn't even pretend we had a place to be.

With charm and giggles, however, we made a grand attempt to lie our way out of arrest, and told our rehearsed story. But when the issue of guardianship came up, and who was *alive* in our lives that could come to claim us, we failed miserably. The officers decided to take us downtown to discuss it some more. We had the officers laughing, and even talked them into buying us a McDonald's meal before piling into the back of the police van for our ride to the station. But sitting in the back of the van, alone, Darcy and I trembled from head to toe. *How were we going to get out of this?*

At the station, we sat face-to-face with a crotchety woman with no patience for our theatrics or charm. The two officers who had brought us to the station stood next to her desk. As the questioning began, Darcy and I maintained our rehearsed story of being eighteen, and were just looking for a new life in Reno. The woman typed all of this shaking her head. When she was done, she handed us a form with written Miranda Rights, as well as some other statements we were to sign our initials next to. The form ended with a single question: Do you wish to speak with us now?

"What does this mean?" I asked the lady, who sat peering at us, annoyed, over her wing-tipped glasses.

"It means," the officer beside her said, "that if you're lying, you'd better tell the truth now or you'll be in a lot of trouble."

Darcy and I exchanged worried glances. *How far were we willing to take this?*

"I need to talk with Celeste," I said.

"Go ahead," the woman said, waving us into the corner of the room.

"I think we're screwed," I whispered. "I think we need to tell the truth." My stomach gnawed at the prospect of going back home, and by the frightened look on Darcy's face, I could see she felt the same.

"I don't want to," she quivered.

"I don't either," I said, holding her hand. "I just don't think we have a choice anymore."

Darcy agonizingly agreed, and we returned to the desk.

"You'd better get a new piece of paper," I told the woman.

"And why is that?" she sneered.

"Because... we lied. And now we're going to tell you the truth."

∽

That night they put Darcy and me into separate, adjacent cells, with a thick, stone wall between us. I shivered in the frigid air of the cell, feeling the cold in my bones. Aside from the twin metal bed that creaked like a rusty hinge, the room provided a single toilet and aluminum mirror above an old pedestal sink. Inside the cell, away from Darcy, I sobbed. Losing her companionship was like losing a rib—a piece of me. I pounded on the door and yelled to anyone who could hear me, "Please let me be with Darcy! I need to be with Darcy!"

They yelled back at me to shut up, that she was just in the cell next to me for crying out loud. Darcy and I screamed for each other for hours, the fear of the unknown and grip of isolation terrifying us both. When they refused to allow us to be together, I threw myself on the bed and punched the stone wall.

"Darcy!" I wailed, hitting the rough, gray stone repeatedly with my fist.

I heard the muffled cry of my friend on the other side. Neither of us slept that night. I wasn't ready for this to end. I wasn't ready to stop running.

~

My mother, and Darcy's father, flew down from Oregon to pick us up. On the plane ride home with my mother, there were no questions, and no discussions. I don't believe either one of us knew what to say. When I arrived home to my dad's, the reunion was bittersweet. I *was* glad to see him, but I also realized things would only be more difficult now.

To my surprise, he never brought up the money I had stolen. He did not yell at me for running away, or for betraying his trust. He hugged me and cried. I still believed this affection was fake, and I continued to keep my distance. I continued to hurt... and hurt him.

In an effort to cheer me up—and welcome me home—my dad offered to take me to a friend's ranch for a long weekend. His friend, Larry, had horses he said, a beautiful wife I would really like, and a couple of young children. I didn't want to go. The last thing I wanted to do was meet new people and have to work overtime to keep my mask up. However, the idea of being around horses appealed to me. We'd had a couple of horses on The Ranch named Rodney and Paris, and my siblings and I adored and cared for them. Sadly, we'd had to sell them because of financial difficulties. I was ecstatic about the idea of riding again, so I agreed to the trip.

Larry's family was very kind, just as my dad said they'd be. His wife, Linda, led me out to their stable right away, and before I knew it, I was up on the back of one of their strong mares, trotting through their fenced, grassy field. It was a freedom I had not felt in a long time, running against the cool wind, squeezing my knees to her side and releasing the reins to fly like a bird. As I breathed in the crisp, winter air, the hardness of my heart began to chip away. The moments of being on that horse—of flying—caused me to forget Reno, and the torment of that ordeal. For a flame was stirring inside me, and for a moment, I let it be real. I let it flicker and dance in my spirit, and it put a smile on my face that wasn't forged. For a moment, I let myself feel hope.

14

THE VAULT

❧1988-1989❧

My dad woke me early the next morning and said he needed to leave for a while to do a job: an appraisal of a property not too far away. He needed to photograph the property and write up the preliminary report, and asked if I wanted to go. It was something I'd done many times with my dad. I enjoyed taking pictures and learning about his business; but that morning, I decided to hang back and help Larry's wife around the house. She'd also promised another horse ride before the afternoon. My dad hugged me goodbye, and I returned the embrace. I thanked him for bringing me. The house was silent, still asleep, so I decided to surprise Larry and Linda by cleaning the kitchen. I was so focused on washing the dishes quietly, I didn't hear Larry come in behind me.

"Good morning," he said, in an early-morning grogginess.

"Hey!" I said, whirling around. I giggled. "You scared me."

"Sorry," he laughed. "What are you doing? You don't have to do the dishes."

"I know," I smiled, turning back to my work. "I want to. You guys have been so nice."

He came closer, looking over my shoulder at the work I'd done.

"Actually, you're the nice one," he said softly. His voice took a strange turn that bred an uneasiness in my stomach.

I was still in my loungewear, a red and white football jersey that my friend Amy had given me before I'd moved, and blue shorts. Larry stepped closer, until I felt him against my back, and his thick, brown beard bristled against the skin of my shoulder. I'd already been fooled in Reno to think that a kind face meant a kind man. Larry fooled me again. A kind face means nothing.

I whirled around to face him, alarmed at his intrusion. His hand moved up the front of my jersey, inside, and stopped at my breasts. I stood frozen, shocked and betrayed. He pawed at a breast and leaned in to kiss me, but the shuffling of his wife's slippers across the hardwood floors made him reel back in a flash. She suddenly appeared around the corner.

"Hey, honey," Larry turned and greeted his wife, taking her hands and kissing her on the cheek.

"Good morning," she smiled, apologizing for her messy appearance. "What are you two up to?"

Larry turned to me and smiled, "Uh, nothing much. I was just thanking Juanima for doing the dishes for us this morning. She sure is a treat."

"Wow," Linda said. "Thank you, dear one!" She came and gave me a hug, then pulled back and looked at me strangely, cupping my face in her hands. "You okay, honey? You look a little pale."

"I'm fine," I whispered, and smiled. "I'm fine."

"Hmm... maybe you should go sit down," she said softly. "I'll whip us up some breakfast."

"Okay," I said, and walked widely around Larry.

He avoided me throughout the rest of the day, but that night, I couldn't keep it inside anymore. When my dad came to my bedside to kiss me goodnight, my body shook, and I burst into tears.

"Pooh, what is it?" He took my hand, and I sobbed into his chest. I wanted to tell him about Larry. The words burned at the back of my throat. But I feared the confrontation. I feared Larry's denial. I feared being called a liar and splitting up their family, and I adored Linda and their kids. I pulled away and buried my face in my hands.

"Ron molested me," came the muffled words. I was sure he already knew, but it'd never been spoken about between us.

"He what?" His voice trembled. The silence that followed was deafening.

"When I was fourteen." I looked up at him for the first time. "You didn't know?"

"No, I didn't know." He sat back on his heels. "I'm so sorry, Pooh. I didn't know."

My heart softened a little for my dad in that moment. I was glad he didn't ask for details. He didn't know what to say, but he listened, and he wrapped his arms around me and hugged me. He got angry about it, and that helped me feel better, too. We left Larry's house the next morning, and I said goodbye to everyone but him. I embraced Linda and the kids, thinking I'd miss them and the horses, but I wouldn't miss Larry at all.

The following Saturday morning, there was a knock at the door. I peeked out from my room and asked Dad who was here, and he told me Larry was stopping in for lunch. The thought of Larry erupted the fountain of fear and anger I had suppressed the day he touched me.

"No!" I yelled. "He can't be here! He can't be here, Dad!"

My dad stalled at the front door, his hand suspended above the doorknob. Surprised by my outburst, he looked through the door window at Larry and stepped back. "Why can't he be here, Pooh?"

The tears were already flowing. "Because he touched me, too, Dad. When we were at his house, and you were gone. He touched me." I retreated to my room and slammed the door.

Larry did not come in the house that day, nor did I ever see him again. I don't know what my dad said to him, but they never spoke again either. I guess parents don't always know how to respond when a child tells them they were abused. I don't remember talking about it with my dad after that. I don't remember ever speaking of Larry again.

A few days later, however, my dad found me sobbing in a heap of worthlessness on my bedroom floor. The walls I had held up were crumbling, and I was weakening against the intense feelings of being unlovely, unlovable, and unworthy of love. I felt my dad's hand on my shoulder. Here I was, living in a house with a man who I didn't believe loved me, yet he sure put on a believable act of kindness and affection from day one. *Just how long can a guy keep up this act?* I wondered, but he continuously reached in, and sometimes tried to step in whether I wanted him to or not. He said it was because he loved me. I just couldn't believe it.

He lifted me up and helped me to the living room, which also accommodated his queen-sized bed. He sat me down and placed a manila folder on my lap.

"Go ahead, Pooh. Open it up," he said.

I did, and through my thick tears, saw at least a dozen hand-written pages on yellow, lined paper.

"What is this..." I asked in a strained, raspy voice.

He sat down next to me. "Those are journal entries I wrote after you ran away. I didn't know if I'd ever see you again." His voice cracked. "I was scared to death, Pooh. I was so scared I'd lost you. Just please... please read them."

He rose from the bed and walked into the kitchen, leaving me alone with his writing. I barely made it through the first paragraph before I burst into tears again. There on the page were written words from the dad I cherished as a child. Words from a kind-hearted, devoted father whose love had no ends and no boundaries. Words I knew to be true because when he wrote them, he believed they'd never be seen by my eyes. He didn't write them to win me back or because he thought it was what I wanted to hear. As far as he knew, I was dead. He wrote them because they had to be written; because they spoke the despair and devastation that pierced his heart every moment of every day, knowing I could be gone forever. He wrote love in its purest form.

I suddenly felt his arm take residence around my shoulder and pull me in. I melted into his chest, sobbing out the years of pain and rejection I had held inside.

"I didn't think you loved me, Dad," I struggled to speak through the tears. "I thought Mom told you about Ron, and when you heard about it, you were ashamed of me. And that's why you quit writing me letters. That's why you didn't want to see me anymore."

"Oh, Pooh. No. The first time I heard about it was when you told me at Larry's. I didn't know. I'm so sorry. I never stopped loving you, Pooh. The letters..." He sighed with regret. "It wasn't because of anything you did. It was me. I was hurtin', Pooh. When your Mom left, I just kinda... fell into this darkness. I never meant to hurt you, Pooh. I hope you can forgive me."

By now, he was crying, too, and we just held each other as the power of reconciliation and forgiveness swept through us both and joined our hearts together again.

"I'm sorry, Dad," I said. "I'm so sorry for everything. I'm sorry I stole your money."

"I forgive you, Pooh. Clean slate, okay? I'm just so glad you're here. I'm so glad you're home."

❧

Later that spring, the school board notified me that I wasn't going to graduate from high school because I was failing many of my classes, and my escape to Reno had cost me precious time and dozens of missed assignments. My only option, if I wanted to graduate, was to attend summer school that year, and I would have to achieve a C-grade or higher in all of the classes. Alone, I felt hopeless in ever making it happen, despite my new determination to shape up. However, my dad made a promise to me that if I would give one hundred percent commitment to the classes, he would be there to help whenever I needed it.

I committed to the classes, and sure enough, he was there when I felt exasperated, exhausted, and wanted to give up. He cheered me on, and I completed the summer classes with a B-C average. The Board told me that if I kept my grades up through my senior year, I would walk that line to receive my diploma.

❧

That summer, on a weekend visit to my mom's, I took my younger brother, Josh, gallivanting around the local mall. As we walked through the food court, a man grabbed my attention. Attractive, slender, with hair dark and wavy like a midnight ocean. He sat at a table with some friends in the center of the food court, so I took Joshua to a table nearby; far enough away to not seem obvious, but close enough that, just maybe, he'd notice me. I sat facing his direction. If he would just... look... up. He did look up, and I looked away. Then our eyes met again, and I smiled. He nodded, and smiled a crooked grin.

Enamored, I watched Joshua inhale his root beer, and as he slurped the last drops, he glanced up at me. "Why are you smiling?"

I shrugged and drew imaginary circles with my index finger on the tabletop, and then a shadow grazed across my hand.

"Hi," a voice said.

I looked up into startling, dark-wash denim eyes. "Hi."

"I'm Marcus."

"Nima," I smiled coyly. "This is my younger brother, Josh."

"What's up?" Marcus said.

"Nothin' much," Josh replied, propping his head up on the table with his hand.

"Hey Josh, how'd you like to go play some video games at the arcade over there?"

"Sure!" Josh jumped to his feet. Marcus handed him a dollar bill and he ran with it. "Cool! Thanks!"

"I'll be right here!" I called after him. "That was nice of you, Marcus."

"Eh," he grinned. "I had ulterior motives."

There was something electrifying about Marcus. He pulled me in with his charm, animated humor, and the charisma of Prince Charming. I knew I would see him again. What I didn't see coming, however, was the plunge I would take with him into our own dark abyss. We became a couple, but cocaine made us a threesome. I was happy to have my white powdery friend back, and even better, I wasn't alone anymore. Marcus brought laughter into my life again. He made me feel alive. Cocaine made me feel powerful and in control, but it became an addiction—a companion I couldn't do without.

I got a job at Godfather's Pizza a few blocks from home, but the salary didn't provide much for my extracurricular activities. I had a car to maintain if I wanted to uphold my life of freedom. The stains in the back seat had faded, but not the dirt it left inside me. My dad had co-signed a credit card for me as a reward for my increased responsibility and maturity. When cash was low, I took out cash advances on the card to buy cocaine, and the debt grew. The truth is, I wanted to believe I was responsible. I wanted to believe I could control the torment inside me by nurturing the habits that kept me numb, while simultaneously being a trustworthy and mature young lady who made my father proud. I could take cocaine to school to get me through the day, drive out the thirty miles to Clackamas on weekends to spend time with Marcus and his reckless friends, and still keep a good head on my shoulders and do the work I had promised my dad I would do.

I believed that I could cover the pain with drugs and alcohol so thoroughly that it didn't exist. I believed that if I lost myself in a relationship with a twenty-one-year-old man, and filled every free moment with volleyball, drama, friends and hobbies, I would forget about the darkness inside me, and the self-hatred and anger that sliced my spirit into a million little pieces if I ever gave it attention. So I had to ignore it, and keep busy enough to where I would never notice its existence.

But it grew.

༄

One night at the pizza restaurant, the guys and I worked together to clean the kitchen for closing. They'd become friends of mine over the months that I worked there, and we had a laid-back rapport. But this night, things were different. Maybe there was a full moon, stirring the animal instinct inside them. *Or maybe it was just me, existing on the edge of insanity.* It started with teasing, as one of my pals, Duane, chased me around the stainless-steel covered island in the kitchen. I screamed playfully, throwing a towel at his face to deter him, and then a handful of cheese when that didn't work.

Another pal joined in. "I'll get her!"

They got me, and tickled me against the island. I laughed until the other three joined in. The lack of air space became stifling and threatening in an instant, and when one of them groped at my waist, something snapped. I screamed like my life depended on it, and as a group they jolted upright, staring at me in stunned silence. I grabbed a butcher knife and jumped up on the island, slicing wildly through the air as a warning to anyone who dared take one step closer.

"Get away from me!" I screamed again. "Get away!" I was sobbing now, as the guys looked blank and confused at one another.

"Nima, what's wrong," one said.

"Dude, she's lost it," said another. "Just get back. She's lost it."

There was a room to the side of the kitchen—about the size of a bathroom stall—that housed a chair, a small worktop, and a phone. I leapt off the island and locked myself in that room, stumbling around frantically like a crippled fly in a glass jar. I picked up the phone to call the manager, and it shook violently in my hands.

"What the hell just happened?" I heard one of them say.

"Did you do something to her?" Another asked.

"I didn't touch her!"

Terror consumed me, and I struggled to dial. When I finally made the call, my manager, Rob, answered right away.

"Rob? I can't work here anymore," I cried in broken words.

"What? Who is this?"

"This is Nima. I can't work here anymore."

"Are you at the restaurant, Nima? What's going on? What happened?"

I couldn't answer in words. I sobbed into the phone.

"Listen—don't leave, okay? I'll be right there. Just stay right where you are and I'll be right there." He hung up the phone, and in five minutes I heard his voice in the kitchen.

The guys were still there, baffled by what had happened, and seemingly concerned. I hid from them all, hunkered down on the floor in the booth, holding myself together with my arms. My head swarmed with doubt as I listened to the defensive rise of their voices, trying to give an explanation to Rob about what had taken place. For a moment I wondered if I'd really gone off the deep end, but the terror pulsing through my body was definitely real. I was scared out of my mind, and I still clung to the knife.

I heard a tap at the window, and Rob let himself in. "Nima? Hey, it's me. Why don't I take that knife from you, okay? Nothing's going to happen to you now."

He closed the door, and knelt down beside me. I handed him the knife.

"Do you wanna tell me what happened?"

I shook my head. "I quit," I said. "I just need to quit."

"Listen," he said, trying his best to calm me. "I think we should talk about what happened. The guys said they weren't trying to hurt you or do anything to you, but I want to hear your side of the story. I'm hoping this was a misunderstanding, and we can work it out. I don't want you to quit."

"But I need to quit," I said. "You can't fix this. No one can."

"Okay," he said, "Okay. Why don't you sit up in the chair? At least you can get off this dirty floor. You want a cigarette?"

I didn't care for cigarettes, but I nodded emphatically for it now, and pulled on it like a parched traveler with a drink. As I stood to my feet, I peeked into the kitchen. The boys were gone.

When I finished the cigarette, I took my first deep breath. "Thanks for this," I said, holding up the orange remnant.

"I wish you'd tell me what happened."

"I can't. I just got scared."

"Listen, why don't you take a few days off before you decide to quit, okay? You're a valuable part of this team, Nima. I'd hate to lose you."

The thought of coming back to the restaurant and seeing the guys again filled me with shame. Though I felt certain at the time that they were going to attack me, there was a thread of doubt now. I suddenly felt ashamed and stupid.

I told Rob I would think about it, but a week later I handed him my resignation. I couldn't bear to show my face there again.

❧

The paranoia poked and prodded at my mind on a constant basis. All it took was a certain look from a guy: the tilt of his head and a smirk, as he scanned over my body like a copy machine. The raising of his eyebrows that said, "Hey baby, I approve." Poisonous words on a flickering tongue. Somehow, their eyes looked right through me to the quivering, vulnerable child. They looked at me like they knew the truth about the dark secrets I kept. I attracted abusers like a moth to light. They somehow saw the fear I tried to hide behind the smile, and with the flick of their brow, they let me know. I became their prey.

I saw "the look" one day in school from a guy that, on a good day, made my skin crawl. He carried an ominous silence. A darkness you could feel. I couldn't help but look up at him once, and saw he had his eyes on me, too. His boorish thoughts registered on his face as I passed by, and after that, I couldn't shake the disgust that traced across my skin like an army of hungry insects. The familiar feelings lingered at the surface: worthlessness, shame, self-hatred for what I was. Not *who*, but the *thing* I was.

I made my way to drama class, but something in me threatened to erupt. Once the class was in full gear, I quietly exited the theater while the teacher gave shouting instructions to an actor on stage. I rushed to the girl's bathroom and locked myself in a stall—I couldn't shake the bad feelings. I had a vial of cocaine in my pocket with a tiny spoon attached to the lid, and I inhaled some of the white freedom into each nostril. But instead of making me feel powerful, it seemed to stimulate the anger that swarmed inside. I was jaded by the vile mistreatment I continued to endure. I was a slave to injustice; I couldn't escape it. My hands trembled as I replaced the lid on the vial and wept. Then I heard the loud clang of the main bathroom door as it hit hard against the doorstop.

"Oops. Nima? Are you in here?"

I knew the voice. It was a fellow student from drama.

"Yeah," I replied, steadying the quiver in my voice as much as I could.

"Mrs. Gardner is wondering where you are and if you're okay."

"I'll be back in a minute. I'm just not feeling well."

The door banged shut with an echo through the small room. I exited the stall, but the anger was boiling now, and I couldn't seem to push it back down. With a groan, I slammed my fist into the cream-colored brick wall over and over, until a pain shot up my arm, warning me to stop. I couldn't open my hand at first, and feared I'd broken it.

"Oh my God, Nima. You're so stupid!" I said aloud as I stared at the purple and red bloody mess on my knuckles. *How are you gonna hide this one?* I had acted completely out of impulse, something I had rarely done until now. And somehow, I had to find my way back to class without letting anyone know what I had done. The last thing I needed was attention to my pain.

I looked in the mirror and with my left hand, wiped away the black mascara streaks and practiced smiling. I jumped up and down to gain momentum, and attempted to match the smile with perky body language. But my hand was a bloody mess.

Pain blazed through my disfigured hand as I held it in the cold water flow. I dabbed it carefully with paper towels, and wrapped a long strip of toilet paper around it. Then I took a deep breath and looked in the mirror again. The red splotches across my cheeks were fading. *Good to go.*

I returned to the theater through the double doors that opened directly down by the stage, where Mrs. Gardner stood in the same spot she had before. The entire class paused mid-scene when I walked in, and Mrs. Gardner turned around. I swung my right arm behind my back and smiled weakly as she quickly appraised me head to toe.

"Are you all right?" she asked.

"Yeah, I'm okay. Thanks."

She tilted her head down, peering at me over her red-framed glasses perched on the bridge of her nose. She held her gaze for an uncomfortable minute. "Okay then," she said quietly. "Return to your seat, please."

She turned back to the students on stage and shouted more instructions as I edged along a row midway up the theater and hunkered down as low as I could in one of the black seats. My hands still trembled, but I had once again managed to fool my way through a grown-up confrontation by someone who really cared about me, and maybe could have helped me. But I believed it was too late for me. I believed I was on my own, because I'd learned the hard way that screaming—or even talking—got me hurt, and nobody cared enough, or listened long enough to the pain, to direct me down a different path. My path now was *bearing it* because nobody could take it away from me.

Now, I wish I never would have quit screaming. Never would have quit talking. But I'd given up, and taken a vow of silence to my torment. I would continue to uphold the system that seemed to be working well for my survival. But looking at my throbbing hand, it seemed my system was cracking.

჻

I skimmed through the rest of my senior year and graduated by the skin of my teeth. On the morning of the ceremony, I jolted awake in Marcus' bed in his Clackamas apartment. I'd forgotten to set the alarm, and was running precariously late. As I grabbed the wrinkled skirt and blouse out of my bag and pulled them on, drums pounded in my head from my careless drinking the night before. I groaned. There was no time to even iron my clothes. I left Marcus asleep in the bed, and ran to the bathroom mirror.

I gaped in horror at my shallow, tired face and long, permed hair that jutted out in every direction like a clown's Afro wig. I was a mess, and had no time to straighten up. I opened up my make-up bag with trembling hands and the contents spilled out across the floor.

"Oh my God!" I screamed in exasperation, humiliated and ashamed of myself.

Marcus ran in, eyes bulging in a panic-awakened state. "What! What happened?"

"My graduation, Marcus! My fucking graduation starts in an hour and look at me! I look like hell and I have to get out of here now!"

"I'll drive you," he said. "You can get ready in the car."

"Get ready in the car—" I mumbled, picking up my scattered make-up. I fingered water through my hair and draped some lotion over it to calm the frizz. The truth about my irresponsibility hit me like a punch in the gut. I breezed past Marcus, standing helpless in the doorway, "Please drive fast," I begged.

෨

In the parking lot of the Convention Center downtown Portland, I fled in my high heels to the front doors, pulling on my gown and hat as I ran. Marcus was on his own to catch up. Inside, I raced down the hallway towards the girl's dressing room, but braked midway when I saw the long line of students already entering the double doors into the arena. I nearly tripped on my own feet as I stumbled to a stop.

"Juanima? Merrion?" A gentleman asked, spotting me. He stood at the double doors guiding the students through to the auditorium, where hundreds of parents and family members proudly anticipated their children receiving the award for such a poignant milestone in their lives.

I nodded.

"Get in right here! You're supposed to go through next!" He pointed sharply to the empty space that was meant for me and I slid in, walking through the doors two seconds later to take my seat in the crowd of other seniors. I walked in shame. I couldn't believe I had cut it so close. I didn't even have a chance to look in the mirror. I had no idea what I looked like. If I was even presentable. The embarrassment gnawed at my stomach. Even when a few friends waved excitedly when they saw me, I could barely look them in the eye. I realized how far down I had really sunk. I almost missed the graduation I had scarcely achieved.

My parents, none the wiser, congratulated me outside when the ceremony was over, and I smiled and cheered along with them, returning the many hugs I received with the utmost enthusiasm, as if everything had gone just the way I'd dreamed. But I was far from living a dream.

ಶ

My identity was divided.

I had ambition for a good career, and felt success would compensate for the damage I was doing to my body, mind and soul. During my senior year in high school, one of my classes had focused on career building. When asked to choose a career path, I wavered between being a lawyer or a psychologist. I interviewed several professionals in both fields, and after meeting with one Hillsboro attorney, she offered me a part-time job in her small firm. I started as an office aid, running errands, making copies, and filing. After graduating, I didn't waste any time getting my own place to live. I rented an apartment in Southeast Portland, quit the modest law firm, and joined a legal temporary agency. They immediately placed me as a receptionist in a criminal law firm downtown Portland, with the possibility of permanency after six months. The first week, I proved my ability to adapt to high-pressure situations, given there were thirteen busy incoming lines to the firm, and I received only two hours of training before the former receptionist left me for good. She couldn't wait to hightail it out of there. That should have been my first clue.

I handled the job, but after six months, my unhappiness peaked. Three of the thirteen phone lines were dedicated lines from prisons. Inmates called constantly, and while half of them genuinely wanted to speak with their attorney in the firm, the other half of the calls were sexually explicit and derogatory, directed at me. I couldn't take it. In addition to the disturbing—and sometimes frightening—calls, I hadn't developed many relationships within the firm as the atmosphere as a whole was overly serious and unfriendly. I assumed dealing with criminals on a daily basis made the attorneys that way. Either that, or they were already that way, and dealing with criminals felt like home. The one exception was Alan Smith. He was the only attorney who smiled, made jokes, and spent time talking with me.

When my six-month term neared its end, I gave my notice to quit. On my last day with the firm, I looked for Alan to say goodbye. Someone said he was away at lunch, so I left him a note and made my way down the stairs towards the exit door. Halfway down, he walked in.

"Hey, Juanima. Where are you off to?"

"Actually, today was my last day. I'm leaving. I'm glad to see you, though, so I could say goodbye."

He came up the stairs, meeting me in the middle.

"Dang," he smiled. "I'll sure miss you around here. You were the only light in this dark place."

I chuckled sheepishly, and gave him a hug. It seemed natural, as I had enjoyed our friendship while I was there. But in the midst of the hug, he pressed me against the wall of the stairwell and kissed me. Hard. Nausea kicked on like a flipped switch, and I pushed him away.

"Alan! Oh my God—what are you doing?" I demanded.

"I thought you wanted that!" he smiled.

"I'm eighteen, Alan! You're—"

"Thirty-nine?"

"Thirty-nine! Oh my God! What in the world made you think I wanted that?" I didn't wait for an answer, and ran out the door. My bus was five blocks away, and I ran the entire distance in tears. I was so sick of my niceness being misinterpreted. It was always... misinterpreted.

৵

Shortly before Marcus's twenty-second birthday, he asked for my hand in marriage. Still eighteen, and completely against the wishes of my parents, I gave him an enthusiastic yes. When his birthday came around, his roommate and friends threw him a surprise party in his apartment. Marcus and his roommate, Jason, kept the simple, two-bedroom flat in immaculate condition. Its contemporary furnishings and off-white walls, spotless. Jason flashed his style and his money like a new sports car, and he blew a lot of his cash on marijuana plants and cocaine.

His birthday present to Marcus was an eight-ball of cocaine, carved into the numbers "22" on top of the large glass coffee table.

"Happy birthday, dude," Jason said. "It's all yours."

It's sad that it was the only present I remember, but Marcus was extremely grateful. So was I, as I thought about the credit card in my purse, maxed out on cocaine, that I would now have to contend with. Guns N' Roses blared through the apartment as I kept my eye on the white powder on the table, making sure Marcus's friends didn't get greedy. But he didn't seem to mind when a few gathered around and helped themselves. I'd like to think I was protecting it for Marcus, but honestly, I wanted to scoop it into a baggy of my own and hide it away for later.

Marcus handed me a rolled up dollar bill and grinned, raising his eyebrows teasingly. I smiled, cut away a small line with the razor blade resting there, and inhaled it. Then I threw my arms around him and said, "Happy birthday, Marcus. Thanks so much for having a birthday."

He laughed. When someone else approached the cocaine-etched numbers on the glass, he saw my glare. "Don't worry about the coke," he said. "Let's just enjoy ourselves."

He took my hand and led me to a group standing around the kitchen.

"Now we're talking," I muttered. "I'm starving!" As I nibbled on chips and dip, someone handed me a mixed drink, which I promptly downed. Another one followed, and another. A friend standing near the stereo waved me over. Giggling, feeling the buzz of the drinks I had just slammed, I bumped into a girl in the group and she handed me a joint I could not refuse.

It turned into a drinking-drug frenzy, and all I could do was say yes to it all. A shot of tequila, a beer, a wine cooler, a line of cocaine, a sniff of crack cocaine, and a puff of a joint laced with who-knows-what. And creeping into my awareness was the misery and self-hatred I hid so deep. Over the next several hours, I lost track of what I was ingesting, drinking, or inhaling, trying to push the misery back down; but instead, it was as if everything I did opened a door letting more of it out. Before long, it was staring me in the face. I was in the middle of a beer when a monster wave of dizziness rushed through me. My knees buckled, and Marcus caught me.

"Whoa, Nima. You okay?"

"No," I whispered, seized by a pain in my gut. "I need to lie down."

"Come on," he said, guiding me down the hall into his bedroom. Through a haze, I saw his red and blue comforter and collapsed onto it with my head at the foot of the bed. I tried to move my arms, but it was like lifting a car. Marcus slid my legs up on the pillows.

"Marcus—" I croaked weakly. "I don't feel right."

"You need to sleep, I think," he said, stroking the hair off my forehead.

I couldn't argue. I couldn't speak at all. The room went dark as Marcus and the other two who had gathered left me alone, closing the door behind them.

What happened next was terrifying. It seemed like endless time. There was a burning in my throat. A heaving of vomit from my immobile body. A flash of light. Then darkness again. Voices, panicking. Hands on my shoulder, shaking. Hands on my neck, pushing in. A shout.

"Marcus! Marcus! Get in here! She's got no pulse, man. There's no pulse!"

A girl crying.

Another voice, "We gotta call nine-one-one!"

"We can't!" Another argued. "Are you crazy? The drugs, man!"

"Fuck the drugs! She's got no pulse!"

The voices faded. Darkness. Silence. Endless time.

A light, coming through the window. Fuzzy air. Breathing in. The daylight shocked my eyes as I tried to peer into it. Marcus sat perched beside me.

"Oh babe… you gave us a scare! We thought you were dead. You had no pulse."

"What time is it..." the words burned in my throat.

"It's two in the afternoon," he answered. "How do you feel?"

"Like shit," I joked. "Oh my God... I hurt."

"What did you do last night? Don't ever do that again!"

"Don't worry," I whispered. The sharp pain pulsing through my brain alone was enough to dissuade me. I smiled, and fell asleep again.

ༀ

A few hours later, I woke up to voices in the other room. Marcus peeked into the room and let me know he was going to drive a few people home, and would I be okay while he was gone. I nodded, and decided it was a good time to shower and wash the nauseating remnants of the night before off my body. The hot water felt like healing rain as it covered and soaked every inch of my weary body, awakening the senses and reminding me I was human. I *was* human, and I had nearly died the night before. I could not forget the voices. The panicked yelling out that I had no pulse. To call nine-one-one, but nobody doing that. I remembered the fading voices of friends as they closed the door, silently hoping I wouldn't really die. I leaned into the streams of water and thanked God for keeping me alive; for giving me another chance.

But someone did die that day. Scott, a dear friend of mine and Marcus's, made a choice to drive home drunk, and lost his life in a motorcycle collision. It devastated both of us, and my relationship with Marcus began to deteriorate after that. Marcus drank more, and exploded in anger if I did or said something that upset him. I began to distance myself from him, and stayed in my own apartment more and more. Staying there, however, became more uncomfortable when my roommate began selling pot out of her bedroom. And because she was prone to carelessness, I constantly feared the cops would show in the middle of the night, tipped off by some fed-up neighbor.

So when I heard a loud banging on the front door at one o'clock one morning, I knew my life was over. But then I peered through the peephole and saw Marcus. He used the door to support his drunken weight with both hands up high and his head hanging down, swinging side to side between his shoulders.

"Open the door," he mumbled, not knowing I was there. Then he yelled, "Open the goddamn door!"

"Go home, Marcus. You're drunk." I muttered through the wood.

"I'm not drunk, you bitch. Open the door." He pounded louder on the door. "You better open it!"

He'd never spoken that way to me before. I moved against a wall in the hallway, and slid down to the floor with my head in my hands, shielding my ears from the pounding that was growing louder. His drunken anger scared me, but I knew if I didn't let him in, the banging on the door would eventually trigger a chafed neighbor to complain and eventually call the police. I didn't want police there, so I let him in.

He pushed the door into me, knocking me to the floor. As the boisterous yelling ensued about what a bitch I was for not letting him in, I stood up and moved back against the wall, away from the spit flying with his harsh words. Marcus had never hit me, but his fury as he paced before me with clenched fists, strained neck and reddened face made me want to duck and cover. Trying to talk him down only angered him more, and at the peak of rage, he grabbed the pajamas at my chest and raised his fist back behind his head. For a split second, he hesitated, and then drove his fist an inch from my face, straight into the wall.

I screamed, and pushed him away from me. "Get out, Marcus! Get out of here or I'll call the police!"

He stood dazed by the giant hole he'd left in the wall, and then abruptly staggered out the door. I rushed to lock the door behind him, and fell to the floor and sobbed. The relationship was over. I was not going to be a battered wife.

෨

The breeze crossing over the grassy hill carried a chill with it, and I wished I had brought a jacket; but I appreciated the sun bearing through the clouds, and it gave enough warmth for me to ignore the goose bumps on my arms. I was nineteen years old, and as I sat alone on the quiet hill below the city park waiting for Marcus to show up, I reflected on my life. There was much regret, and so much pain. It seemed I had set myself on a path of destruction, and in my heart, I knew that I was the only one who could take myself off of it. But I felt lost. What do you do when pain consumes you? How do you get rid of it? I didn't want to talk to another shrink, but I didn't want to hurt—or be hurt—anymore. I didn't want to hurt myself anymore. And what about God? My dad had always told me that God doesn't make junk, and yet I felt like an exception to that. Maybe my dad had it wrong, because I couldn't break free from the fact that I felt damaged, broken, and unlovable. I thought Marcus loved me, but real love isn't violent. I looked at the bright ruby on my wedding ring finger. It was a little unorthodox, the ruby. But it was beautiful, and I knew I couldn't wear it.

I thought of the years I'd filled my body with drugs and alcohol, trying to drown out the screams I heard inside. It'd become a program—a custom of my daily life. And though it brought relief in the moment, the crash was inevitable. The aftermath, when I was left staring at an empty mirror with nothing but a reflection of pain, torment, emptiness and ugliness. When I looked in that empty mirror, I believed my dad was wrong. I *was* junk. God didn't really care about me, for there was something deeply wrong with me. Something broken. Something unfixable. I didn't know if I'd ever be good enough for real love, but I knew I couldn't go down this road anymore. I didn't want to be so drowned in darkness that the next option was death. I needed to retreat. I needed to back away from it all. I needed to start over.

The baggage of my past was also suffocating me. Memories of being raped, molested, abused, beaten, and rejected, haunted me daily. It was time to stuff it all away. It was time to disconnect myself from it, and I believed I was strong enough to do that. I made a decision then to just... shut it off. To never think about it again. To run forward so fast, there was no choice but for the memories to be left behind. I was going to start fresh, a new Nima. A new life. New goals, new relationships. No more drugs. No more drinking. No more partying. A new Nima.

"Hey," came a startling voice behind me. I'd almost forgotten he was coming.

"Hi," I smiled lightly, with a tinge of sadness for what was coming. I feared his reaction.

"I'm sorry about the other night," he said, settling down in the grass next to me.

"Yeah... I know, Marcus."

We sat together in silence, and he put his arm around me. A gentle, apologetic gesture that I did not push away.

"I can't do this anymore, Marcus. I'm afraid of where this is going, if we don't just stop it now. I don't want a life like this. I don't want to be afraid all the time of making you mad. I don't want to do coke anymore." He took his arm away and pulled his knees up. "I know there's something good out there for my life, and for yours, too. I just don't think it's meant to happen to us... together."

"Maybe not," he answered solemnly. I was surprised by his lack of resistance. "I guess—I probably need to get my shit together, too."

We looked at each other for a long moment, aching for what was lost, regretting the hurts that still remained, grieved by the future that wasn't to be. I pulled the ruby ring from my finger and placed it in his palm.

"Yeah," he chuckled remorsefully, "I guess you won't need that anymore."

"I do love you, Marcus," I said and hugged him, and then pulled away when his embrace grew too tight. "I gotta go. Maybe we can talk later."

I jumped to my feet and rushed down the hill before he could see my tears. I didn't look back. I didn't wave goodbye. I needed to close the door quickly on the past, before the onslaught of doubts came in and made me change my mind.

༃

I still had my work cut out for me. Only by the grace of God was I able to quit cocaine cold-turkey, though it did help to eliminate the sources in my life. But I still couldn't shake the gnawing... the deep knowing that there was something wrong with me. I shut off the memories of my past, but I couldn't seem to escape the abuse. I worked another temporary job with an electrical company, and the foreman, a man in his forties named Richard, shared the same humor and friendliness that Alan Smith had at the criminal law firm. Richard and I joked around often, and then one day when I went to his desk to give him blueprints he'd requested, he slid his giant hand up the back of my skirt and rubbed my bottom. I cried out and spun around to face him, never to forget the pleased—almost innocent—look on his face. "What?" He'd said, mocking my upset.

I fled from his office, and ran straight to the owner and told him I was quitting the job. No notice. I grabbed my purse and ran to my car, shaking almost too severely to drive. But no way in hell was I sticking around.

When I later worked at a high-tech firm as a buyer, vendors customarily took us to lunch in attempts to woo and charm their way into getting preference—or at least maintain the favorable business relationship they'd acquired. I had gone to lunch a couple times with Mark, a vendor I had chosen for several hardware parts for our company projectors, and I was comfortable with him. He picked me up from the office one day in a shiny black SUV, and the first thing I noticed as I climbed up into the passenger seat was the "new car" smell. Lunch with Mark was pleasant and casual, and driving me back to the office, he talked about his family, wife and children, holding up his wallet to show me the cascading accordion frames of all of them. Then he put it down and pulled off of the road onto a gravel turnout.

"What are you doing?" I asked.

He chuckled, tilting his head to the side with a questioning look.

"What?" I laughed.

He said nothing as he grabbed my shoulder and pulled me into a kiss. I pushed him away and slapped him. I was as stunned as he was by the stinging red print on his cheek.

"I'm sorry," he replied. "I shouldn't have done that."

"No. You shouldn't have," I snapped. "Take me back, please."

"Please don't say anything," he said. "I really do love my wife. I don't know why I did that."

"Just take me back, Mark." I hid my trembling hands under my purse and slid as close as I could to the passenger door.

&

Each incident became a drop of worthlessness I placed into the invisible bottle I kept in my soul, which also contained drops of emptiness, inadequateness, and nothingness. But I would put it away, because I couldn't let anyone else see it. I couldn't admit to anyone that I ever felt those things. I couldn't let anyone see I was weak. I was determined to dominate my past and the effects it had on my life. I was determined to shut off all emotions relating to the rapes, the abuse, the rejection and demeaning acts I seemed to continuously fall prey to. The past became a door: tall, and thick like a bank vault, with five kinds of locking mechanisms that no one could ever access. Not even me. I leaned into it with all my weight. With gritted teeth I braced my arms against it and pushed, pushed, heaved and pushed until it clanged shut with a powerful, irrevocable seal.

After a year and a half at the high-tech firm, I quit my job and enrolled full time at Multnomah Bible College, setting my sights on youth ministry and music. To become someone new, I had to change the scenery. Attending that school was the best thing I could've done at the time. I immersed myself in biblical studies and had some amazing experiences there. I learned who I was in Christ. I learned I didn't need a man in my life to be happy; and, as a matter of fact, I made a promise to God that I would avoid relationships until I was secure with myself, and healthy enough to choose a *good* man—the right man—for me. Obviously, my track record stunk, and I knew it was because of my own faulty perceptions and shattered self-esteem that I continued to draw into destructive relationships. Though I left Multnomah after a year, I continued to cling to God, kept busy with church activities, and surrounded myself with positive people. Four years later I met my husband, Michael, a gentle, loving man who cherishes me, has a heart of kindness which he constantly extends to others, and embraces our family with love daily. When I met him, I had truly changed from the heart. I had a joy inside, and a new confidence. God had honored my promise, and He had not forgotten me.

But I had forgotten the vault. I believed, because no one had ever told me differently, that if you lock something away, it stays there. I thought that shutting that door and walking away from all those dark years was good enough. It's a statement I've heard a hundred times: "I've put it behind me." But when you put it behind you, when you lock it away, it doesn't die. It grows like a cancerous tumor. And over time you realize there were bits and pieces of it you'd missed—such as the core beliefs I still carried that I was unworthy, unlovable, and unimportant. But I coped with those beliefs. I felt I could deal with that. I couldn't deal with the trauma, but I thought I was safe from that. I was wrong.

You can't lock away trauma. Like the naïve belief when I was sixteen that running away would actually solve everything; that I could leave the pain behind and just start over. No. It follows you. It might stay out of your way and give you space for awhile, but eventually, and generally when you least expect it, it springs upon you like a wild animal. If you run, it will overpower you and take you down.

I made it almost fifteen years before the vault door came crumbling down, and then I nearly drowned from the contents. But I'm still here—still fighting—and I'll never stop until I'm free.

15

LOOKING BACK
AND HEALING NOW

❧2011❧

*And I go blindly forward, uncertain of tomorrow; but
I move forward anyway. That's what faith is all about.*

Though healing from childhood sexual abuse has brought
immeasurable pain, I have also been given the opportunity to start
afresh. I can start now, figuring out who I am; who God created me
to be. It's never too late. I have shared my past with you, and
revealed the secrets that lay for years like a sunken ship in the
depths of my soul. And through sharing, I discovered that not only
is it freeing, but it has a purpose in my life. You are reading these
words—my story—and I only hope it has helped you in some way to
understand PTSD and the recovery process, and if you are suffering,
to know you are not alone.

There is no magic remedy to heal PTSD, but if you're willing
to work hard, commit to it, and have patience, you will get there.
Today, writing this, I'm not completely healed. Anxiety still runs
through my veins and is difficult to calm. But I am full of hope,
because I have seen so much change. It started out so small, like my
first breath without tightness in my chest, or the day I made it
through a grocery shopping trip without bursting into tears in the

parking lot, or leaving my basket of unpaid groceries in the aisle while I fled from my perceived chaos in the store. I rejoiced the first time I slept through the night, and the first time I pushed through a full-blown panic attack on my own. My first day without dissociating. These may seem like meaningless milestones, but it proves you are moving towards healing. It's important to think and accept positive thoughts; to congratulate yourself over your small steps forward.

PTSD is a disorder just now in its baby stages of understanding, but I have hope in a future of healing for those who are suffering, if they can only learn to hang on and keep fighting. It's not easy. Healing is a long journey, and in the early stages especially, hopelessness can envelop you with suffocating constraint. The symptoms are at their peak, life is the most horrifying and bleak, and you are overcome with confusion and fear at the onset of a disorder that has abruptly stolen all control of your mind. But PTSD is a war that can be won.

You must decide to heal, and commit to stay the course. I remember standing at a crossroads and having to make a decision to either remain a prisoner of the storm, or turn to face it head-on. This decision was agonizing because it's easier to stay in denial, but it won't bring freedom. I also knew if I didn't fight, my relationships would crumble—starting with my marriage. So I gave myself an ultimatum. There could be no going back, no giving up, no matter how severe the pain. But I love the Bible verse, Jeremiah 6:16: "Stand at the crossroads and look... Ask what the good way is, and walk in it, and you will find rest for your souls." Notice it says "ask." I believe it's important to ask for help, to find the way to healing that will work for you. I longed for rest for my soul, and it was like reaching into a dark abyss. My soul was a constant upheaval of chaos—a storm that never calmed—but it's not that way anymore. Recovery starts with asking for help, and not giving up after the first four or five therapists don't work out.

My journey to healing has been a plethora of decisions over time to just move forward—away from whatever dark place I was in—but that's how you heal. PTSD became less overbearing when I perceived my healing as daily journeys. If I looked too far ahead—sometimes even an hour—I easily got overwhelmed. I had to live moment to moment, focusing only on getting through that moment; and though it caused great inconvenience at times to my family because I couldn't commit to anything beyond the moment in front of me, it was what I needed to do to survive.

My friends and family learned they couldn't just show up at the door and say, "Hey, you wanna go grab a cup of coffee?" Before PTSD, I enjoyed spontaneous activities, but this disorder rips apart every solid thing about a person. It changed my personality to the extreme opposite of what everyone knew about me, and I could not adjust back to that person. I believe the core of Nima was still there—the traits that make me who I am—but PTSD tampered them and pressed them down beneath layers of fear, anxiety, and panic, and "happy" just cannot exist in those conditions. Family and friends now needed to adjust to a new, frightened girl, who was suddenly just trying to survive in a private, terrifying world where darkness prevailed and monsters sprung out at every corner. I felt there was no safe place for me.

The change alarmed my family and friends, and everyone responded in their own way. I've learned through PTSD that people love based on their own personality and experiences, and are limited by the same. Love can be confusing—even messy at times—but if we can learn to see love through different lenses, there is greater opportunity for peace, acceptance, and forgiveness.

My two brothers were mostly silent when I developed PTSD. They simply didn't know what to say, or how to help. And though initially I was hurt by their lack of involvement, I eventually accepted that that was how they had to deal with my disorder. I love them dearly, and I know they love me. Love comes in different colors, and is sometimes subtle and invisible, but an open heart knows it is there. There were times when our phone calls were mostly empty and awkward, but just hearing, "Love ya', Nima," became good enough for me.

My sister was not silent, and ironically, caused the most friction for me in my healing. To love, however, means seeking to understand the motivations of others. I understand now that Cris saw my life being threatened. She was convinced that in the dark throes of PTSD, I was going to die, and she wasn't going to let that happen. I did not see her forceful intrusions as love at the time. When she took me to Starbucks and presented me with a book called *Healing is a Choice*, I felt judged and misunderstood. When I gave her a private, detailed journal entry that I had written about my uncle abusing me, and she showed it to him because she wanted him to see how he had ruined me, I felt betrayed, humiliated, devastated, and enraged. It set me back in my healing for weeks. I had recurring nightmares of him showing up at my house, breaking through the door, and attacking me on the couch where I slept.

When Cris came to my home and told me that what I needed to do was sit down with my whole family and just open up to all of them and let them into my living hell, I felt controlled. Love can sometimes seem one-sided and full of flaws. I know my condition scared her, and she saw no one else intervening to save me. She took that on as her job.

You can't do that to someone with PTSD. You can't control their healing. You can't make them take steps in a certain direction. You can't make them open up to their loved ones and just spill out the trauma that has pulverized their once-stable lives. One of the greatest challenges for both the person suffering from PTSD, and the hopeful supporters, is finding an effective way to communicate with each other. PTSD is extremely complex. There is no quick fix, and when PTSD shatters a person's world, they have no words to describe or explain the turmoil that's raging inside. What helps is for a supporter to be patient with the sufferer; to be loving and supportive, rather than trying to impose their own solutions.

There is no one way of healing that works for everyone. Because we are each beautifully, uniquely, and intrinsically designed, and made up of the fabric of our experiences, our journeys to healing will be just as individualized. It's important to go slow, and for the supporter to be patient while the sufferer finds what will work for them. Sometimes, the most effective help is hopeful encouragement and quiet reassurance that the sufferer is loved and valued no matter what.

I understand it is difficult to be patient when it feels your world as you knew it is falling apart. For the sufferer, finding someone who specializes in trauma and PTSD will ease your burden and help you understand what you're dealing with. For the supporter, I believe it is equally important to find your own circle of support. The weight of this disorder and its affect on everyone it touches is too heavy to carry alone. Also, for both the sufferer and supporter, open, *gentle* communication about your struggles is important. Do your best not to hide or avoid, and do your best to love and understand.

My family needed an understanding of this disorder. What *I* needed was love and encouragement; to hear the honest words, "I don't know how to respond to this, and it scares me; but I love you, and I'm going to see you through this." I also needed to understand that my PTSD was not just affecting me, but every person in my life who loved me. I felt like I was drowning in the middle of shark-infested waters, but imagine what a family would feel to see their daughter, their sister, or brother, drowning. I understand that one might take drastic measures to save them from death. To save them from themselves.

I love my sister, and I have forgiven her for everything she ever did that hurt me. We are working slowly but surely at rebuilding something new. Something stronger. Something balanced and real, and I could not do it without placing God in the center. It has helped me to understand the motives behind her actions over the years. She just wanted to reach me, but without understanding my inner turmoil of PTSD, she came across as forceful and intrusive.

During the intense years of therapy over my past, grievous feelings of rejection resurfaced about my mother and her choice to let Ron come back after he'd abused me. I realized for years I had waited for her to take it back. I had waited for words of remorse, but they didn't come. Then, on Easter weekend in 2006, she called me.

She told me she'd had a revelation about her decision to take Ron back, and how devastated I must have been. In the utmost sincerity, she apologized and asked for my forgiveness. "If I could take it back, I would in a second," she said. "I'm just so sorry I did that to you."

I sobbed into the phone, and told her I had waited for years for those words. I forgave her, and released an incredible burden of rejection that had weighed on my heart for two decades. Our relationship changed after that. Though I had learned to be friends with her through my young adulthood, I missed the intimacy as mother and daughter. When she acknowledged her mistake of years ago, I found a new respect for her, and she found a new tenderness for me. She became a great advocate in my healing from that day on, even attending a few therapy sessions with me, and some with my sister. My mom surprised us both in one session by sharing some of the abuse that had happened to her in her past, and as we drove home, I felt more connected to her than ever. She tried diligently to support me as I rode the tumultuous waves of PTSD, and her love was perfect. Never intrusive, never pushy, she opened the door of her heart for me to come in whenever I needed it. I only needed to ask, and she'd be there.

I remember the day when she came to my home and sat with me on our evergreen-colored sectional couch. The pain of PTSD was private and agonizing for me. I could rarely even put words to it. What I longed for in that moment with her was to be her little girl; to be held, because the anguish inside me was so overwhelming. Without speaking, I laid my head on her lap, and curled up in the fetal position. She rested her hand on my head, and weaved her long fingernails as a comb through my hair. We remained there, silent, for several minutes. It was precious time to me. It was healing time.

My dad and stepmom, Gail, like the rest of my family, helplessly watched my mental and physical plunge into depression and isolation; but I loved their cautious, yet ready hand to walk with me through my painful journey. They patiently sought ways to help me and love me without being intrusive. They were protective when others wanted to forcefully intervene and hospitalize me out of fear for my safety. Wisdom told them that hospitalization was not what I needed at that time. Thankfully, no one pursued that.

When I took my therapist's suggestion to move into Traci's house for a couple of weeks, some of those within my circle of supporters responded with resistance and doubt. There were feelings that my relationship with Traci was co-dependent and unhealthy. Feelings that I wasn't supposed to be there. But what I appreciated about Dad and Gail was that instead of judging, and deciding on their own whether or not it was the best thing for me, they came in person to see for themselves. On that sunny afternoon, we sat outside at Traci's patio table and talked. While I don't remember our conversation that day, I remember their love, gentle questions, and how they *listened*. I remember their warm, accepting embrace at the end of the visit when they said, "You're doing the right thing, Nima."

I remember the tears I shed because being there, away from my husband and two daughters, was one of the hardest things I'd had to do for myself, and to have the reassurance and encouragement from Dad and Gail was so uplifting, and so needed, I wept in their arms.

And my dear Traci. We were conjoined through the roughest waters of my healing. She was a God-given gift whose friendship was critical in my journey, and without her, I would not have survived it. I know that for certain. She also became the temporary "third leg" of my marriage, taking on the emotional partnership, which allowed Mike to focus on his role as husband and supporting partner, working, and taking care of the girls. I don't believe my marriage would have survived without the support she provided.

≈

I can look back over the years of picking up the pieces of my shattered soul, and see the many stages of growth. But growth only came after that gut-level decision to never give up. The future of my daughters, the need for me to break the generational chain of abuse, and the realization of what their lives would be like without me, was the basis of my decision. Anyone who wants to heal from PTSD must find their own reason to fight, and then not let go. There can be no Plan B. Aside from my children, it was a hope—a promise—that I clung to, of a better life ahead.

If you're reading this right now and saying, "I have no hope. I have no dreams. Not anymore," I encourage you to hold on. The beginning was like living underwater, trying to hold my breath. There was the constant threat of drowning as I held on to that last thread of an already-frayed rope. Darkness progressively got darker, and in the depths of it, I remember thinking *This is it. It will never be different from this.'* A future seemed impossible for me. I saw no hope; I had no dreams. I didn't think I ever would again. I wanted to die so much of the time, but I held on. If I felt I had nothing left, I'd see a glimmer of hope in the eyes of my daughters and hold onto that. At times my faith was but the size of a mustard seed, but that is all God requires to move in your life.

I forced myself to continue therapy, even though I knew it would rip me apart each and every time. I forced myself to continue doctor visits, even though I'd crumble into an embarrassing ball of tears every time I did. I went because I knew somewhere in the world, there were answers to my pain, and answers to my physical symptoms occurring with PTSD. I went because even though I wanted to give up, I didn't *want* to give up. I wanted to believe there was some kind of good life ahead for me.

Your thoughts are pivotal in your healing. What are you telling yourself about you and your future? One thing that kept me going every day was getting some sort of positive reinforcement about who I am, and where I'm headed. Find a resource that encourages you. Get involved in groups that include other sufferers of PTSD. Just don't allow yourself to fall into the easy trap of isolation. Find support. There were times I was a crumbled, fragmented, exhausted heap of rage and spent emotions. It's healing to have a friend on your side in those times.

๛

Healing happens in stages and progresses very slowly. I learned I couldn't put a timeline on my healing—no one can—and it was important for me to be patient with myself, and patient with the process. I may not have total healing yet, but I am stronger. I received an amazing compliment a few weeks ago from the mom of my daughter's friend. She said, "I don't see you as different [from others] at all. You're a strong and confident woman, and very brave. And I'm glad you're not scared to talk about [PTSD]. That just shows how strong you are, and that you're not ashamed of it."

I cried when she said those words to me. I had taken the risk of telling her I had PTSD, which I rarely confess to anyone out of fear of revealing my true self, and my daily struggle to survive. I have carried so much shame from this disorder, and from my past abuse. I have not felt strong, and certainly never confident. I have carried fear of being seen as different, and being shunned because of it. It is shocking to have those fears inside, but then hear the words, "You are so brave," directed at me. Me? Brave? Confident? Strong? Yes! It has taken a long time to capture the essence of my journey and how far I have truly come already in my healing. If you are fighting for your life with PTSD, you are brave. You are courageous, because not only did you survive the trauma, you are surviving it again day after day after day. You keep taking a single, if albeit tiny, step forward. You are strong and courageous!

A friend of mine recently told me his wife suffered childhood sexual abuse. He was so saddened by my experiences, and I told him, "Please don't be, because they made me who I am today, and I have healed so much, and I'm actually looking forward to my future now."

He added, "But it still haunts you."

I realized something so beautiful in that moment. No, it doesn't haunt me! Not anymore. Through relentless healing and perseverance, I can honestly say I am no longer agonized by the things in my past. Writing this book, there were many times I shed tears of sadness, as the memories are still so fresh, and the emotions still raw. But my past does not haunt me because I am brimming with hope, and hope transcends sorrow and darkness. Hope is like a friend who takes the hand of grief, and walks always towards life. I know if I keep walking in that direction, my life can only get better.

I no longer wish I had a different past. I have actually learned to embrace the trauma that ripped my life to pieces. You might think, "How is that even possible? Embrace?" Yes, because pain and suffering changed me; and though being in the midst of it felt like the worst possible injustice, and so unfair, surviving it—and healing—produced a strength and awareness I didn't have before. I don't think I would have such a strong desire to help others if I did not know suffering like I do. There is so much pain in the world, and my suffering pales in comparison to so many other's; but some of my greatest moments of comfort came from the understanding of another individual who had also suffered. The knowledge of world suffering is so apparent, and yet when we're in the midst of our own suffering, we feel no one else understands. It can be the most paramount state of loneliness. But I can give someone else the gift of understanding now. I can reach out beyond myself and give purpose to the pain I have suffered. You never know when reaching out just might save a life.

Even in the early years of PTSD, hiding within the walls of my home, living in fear and darkness, I tried to reach out to others. If anything, it got my pain off my mind for a while, and opened my eyes to the need around me. I made dinners for the neighbors when they were struggling through a crisis. I listened and consoled a neighbor when she had her first panic attack, and suffered from horrible anxiety. I gave encouragement and love whenever I could, even if I didn't get any in return. It felt good to help, and every time I did, it scratched away at my feelings of worthlessness.

I do a fine job of pretending I'm a normal mom. I also do a fine job of containing my anxiety, and keeping a smile on my face for the kids. I cherish the solitude when they're at school, and try to never waste a minute; but when they come home, I greet them at the door with a smile and a hug, and ask about their day. Pretending and containing has gotten easier over time, but I know my love and smiles are worth it when Lacey says, "Mom, you're so cool. You're not like other moms. You're not crazy and all bossy. And even though you have anxiety, you still love on us. And I know you're gonna be healed one day and you won't have PTSD anymore." Sometimes my daughter brings tears to my eyes with her words. I spent many years feeling crazy from PTSD. Sometimes God knows just what I need to hear.

Or when Jordan, who is eight, cups my face in her little hands and says, "Mom, of all the moms I could have picked, I picked you because you're the best there is."

I often don't feel like the best mom. I often feel like the worst mom. I cannot always hide my anxiety. I cannot always walk confidently. I still crumble. I am still wary of public places and still tearfully approach grocery stores at times. I still dread going outside of my house and having to get into my car to run errands. My stomach churns when Jordan asks me if we can take a walk to the park. I love spending time with her. I do not love going to the park. I still find it difficult to *play.*

But it's important to do what I can, so I push myself out of my comfort zone every day. I try to give my children the normal life they deserve, and keep the family flowing the best I can. I do this by always looking forward towards the hope of complete healing and freedom. My strength comes in having a spirit of tenacity; accepting that hard days are a part of my life right now, but believing there will come a day when I will see the glory of freedom.

Every day is still hard. The anxiety doesn't subside, and I have chosen to stop drowning it in alcohol, which means I have to *feel.* I have to find ways to deal with it. Sometimes it is still overwhelming, and I have to get away by myself to breathe. But my family understands. Communication is key; I cannot hide behind PTSD. Maybe to the outside world, I can pretend, but I can't always pretend within the walls of my own home. One of the first and most important lessons I gave my girls was that Mama's anxiety was *not their fault.* In the early years—the worst years—the girls were so small. I could not control my outbursts; and though I never, ever struck them, I could not always contain the rage. I still grieve when I remember the shocked jolt of their little bodies whenever a yell or a scream escaped my throat. I can still see their frightened tears, and me crumbling to the floor in my own tears, ashamed of myself.

But it's what I did in those moments that determined the future of my children. I couldn't pretend it didn't happen. I couldn't walk away, lying to myself that they'd get over it. I'd want to run from the room—embarrassed and overcome by the panic in my chest—but I would embrace the girls instead, in spite of my own tears, and apologize with a heavy heart. I would squeeze them and say, "Mama loves you two so much. I'm so sorry I yelled. I have anxiety, and it's just so bad right now."

One time they asked with quivering chins, "What's anxiety?"

I said, "It's when you feel so upset your chest is tight, and you feel like this," and I clenched my fists up by my chest and tightened my whole body, and gritted my teeth and made a groaning-growling noise similar to what they had done when upset or frustrated. "My anxiety is really, really bad, and sometimes I yell. But I should never yell, and it's never ever your fault when I do. I'm so sorry. Will you please forgive me?"

They both nodded, and we hugged again. It was agonizing and humiliating to admit—even to myself—that I had, and was responsible for, horrible behavior and losing control; but the girls understanding my anxiety and PTSD released them from taking on a burden of guilt and false responsibility for my disorder. I truly believe that the honesty I shared with them during those hardest times instilled the openness we have in our relationships today. I am not a perfect mom, but I love them with an unbreakable love, and I cherish every moment I have with them. Today, they understand my anxiety is not their fault, but a part of PTSD that I struggle with daily.

అ

I am still running the race. I'm not where I need to be, but thank God I'm not where I used to be. I haven't self-harmed since 2007. My scars, however, are prominent, and Lacey has asked what they are from. One day, I will share the story; but my answer was, "They're from a long, long time ago, when I went through a very hard time. It's in the past, though, and I'm okay now." Once in awhile, she'll take notice of them and say, "Poor Mama..." as she runs her finger sadly over the raised, white stripes across my forearm. And I put my hand on hers and say, "It's okay. They don't hurt me anymore."

I gave up trying to hide them all the time, and have tried to make amends with them. I am not at peace with them yet, but the scars are something I cannot change nor do anything about. I'm certain that people have noticed them, but I have accepted that they are a part of me. A part of my story, symbolizing a time in my life when the pain was too much to bear, and I did what I had to do to survive it. I did not learn as a child how to cope with the inner torment of child abuse. Most of us are not taught as children how to cope with trauma; but as adults, we find something that works and we stick with it, even if it's unhealthy. Some drink to erase or numb the pain. Many use drugs. Many exercise or work to extremes, and still others sleep their day away. I self-harmed, and then like most abuse survivors and PTSD sufferers, I continued my existence with a smile, and pretended I was normal.

I so badly want to be perceived as normal.

With self-harm, my triumph came first in recognizing the unhealthy behavior, and then giving it everything I had to stop. Self-harm is an addiction, and can be as difficult to quit as smoking or narcotic drug use, but it is not impossible. It took the same determination that it took to get through therapy. The same determination I still carry that one day I will experience peace and freedom from the debilitating anxiety. It took one day at a time to stop cutting, and many failed attempts. The point is to keep trying, and find someone to encourage you and support you in your efforts. Never let your failures become your settling place. That is giving up, and will never get you success, freedom, or healing.

Success builds from a plethora of failures. It's learning from your mistakes and getting right back up again, and again, and again. It's wanting to get well bad enough that you refuse to settle into a fixed state of avoidance. PTSD will not heal on its own; in fact, without action, it generally worsens over time. Healing is painful, but it gets better over time, little by little. Moment by moment, the burden becomes a little bit lighter.

Fortunately, as awareness and exposure to PTSD have increased through the medical field and the general public, more information and resources are available than ever to help a sufferer get better. Though medications never worked for me, I know they have helped diminish the symptoms for many, and aided in overcoming those sleepless nights. I also know that covering up symptoms is not a permanent fix. Medication does not erase what's happening inside. I remember my favorite doctor telling me one day during the early trials of medications, "This may help ease your symptoms, but you need to face what's tormenting you."

There are many ways to hide the symptoms and bury the pain, but those measures will only prolong the inevitable uprising of the trauma that landed you with the disorder in the first place. Flashbacks, nightmares, and intrusive thoughts of the brutal rapes and molestations I'd endured hit me on a constant basis—and only intensified—until I started facing those events head on. It was the hardest thing I've ever done, and more painful than enduring them the first time. But facing the trauma, by whatever means works for you, will break its power over you, enabling you to start gaining control over your mind—and your life—once again.

You must *decide* to stop living in fear of your past. Fear is like a door to a room full of your worst nightmares, but you have what it takes to open that door and push your way through to the other side. You must realize that there *is* another side. It won't be easy, but you'll get stronger as you fight, and if you don't give up, you'll find peace and rest. Focus on reaching the other side, and you'll break free from your prison.

༄

I believe one of the crucial steps in healing is forgiveness. Sometimes, it's easier said than done; I often forgive with my heart before my feelings catch up. I eventually realized that people were going to offend me and hurt me because they just didn't "get" PTSD, and I learned that it only hurts me to hold a grudge. So I continuously chose to forgive. Some of the most hurtful words ever said to me since I've had PTSD were by a family member. Granted, she was intoxicated at the time, but they struck me at the core and tore deep at my heart. She accused me of acting disabled.

Acting disabled. My only act with PTSD was feigning normalcy, so no one would know how bad off I truly was. How suicidal I was. How difficult it was just being around them because my mind screamed for isolation and solitude. No one understood the anxiety that ripped up my insides like a paper shredder every time I had to go to a family function—especially on a holiday like Christmas or Thanksgiving. No one knew that I guzzled a sixteen-ounce bottle of vodka and soda just before the party so I could walk in with a smile, and not the panic I felt inside. No one understood how I trembled when I saw a family member approach me at those parties, because I knew they would ask how I was, and what I've been up to, and I would have to make something up. I knew they wouldn't understand my truth—the terror I lived with every day—and I didn't want to make anyone uncomfortable. So I'd smile, and I'd laugh, and I'd pretend everything was okay.

Perceptions get skewed, and sometimes judgment can be so laced with anger, no amount of explanation will diffuse it. The most difficult part for me was having to walk away from it, judgment still hot in the air, while the pain of being accused of faking a disorder seared into my heart like a hot iron. It devastated me, but I forgave her. I forgave her many times before the feelings caught up, but you must do what it takes to be free of it.

I forgave my abusers. All of them. And certainly not for their sake, but for mine. Unforgiveness creates the perfect soil for growing resentment, bitterness, and hatred. Those things are like poisonous weeds in your soul, and they fester and grow until they become part of your character. I couldn't stand to harbor those feelings inside me because my whole fight has been for freedom... not bondage. When I forgave my abusers, it released me from that bondage, and I gave the burden of revenge to God. It says in His Word that He is our avenger. I believe that all the men who harmed me have been dealt with—or will be. I also feel sorry for them, because I know that one can't carry on sins like that and not feel miserable and tormented inside when you're alone with yourself. They are confronted with that, while I am free from it.

હ

Things started looking up for us in 2008. I survived another MRI and learned my brain tumor was benign. Also, I had fought for Social Security disability benefits for three years, and finally won my case. The award was retroactive to the onset of PTSD, and in 2009, Mike and I purchased our first home across town. We are now blessed to have the most thoughtful, loving, genuine neighbors I could have ever hoped for. They have been a great encouragement to me, and are constantly reaching out to me and my family. We consider them family, too, and our kids have become the best of friends. It's been such a positive change in all of our lives.

My husband and I have made great strides in our marriage, and work daily to keep things positive in our home, and between us. We work together to repair what's been broken. One of the things we have back now, that I missed so much, is laughter. Yes, I am finally laughing again! In the "old days," Mike and I played so much together... We are finally having fun again.

I have so much respect for him—even more than when I married him—because he honored me with a firm commitment to our marriage when things were at their worst. We *both* suffered immensely during those years. Everyone in my family and my closest friends suffered, and sacrificed parts of themselves and their lives to keep me afloat. But my darling husband was a champion and a rock, even though inside he was crumbling, too. The heartache that my PTSD brought into our lives seemed unbearable and irreparable at times, but he kept believing in me. He decided to hang on, too, and fight for us.

He hid his grief—as I did—for the sake of the girls. Oftentimes, I would greet him at the door after a hard day of work and see the fatigue and distress in his eyes. For a moment, there would be honesty and deep hurt; but when the girls came running around the corner screaming, "Daddy!" his whole demeanor shifted. He'd drop whatever was in his hands and kneel down so they could leap into his arms. His smile, however forced, was always genuine to his girls, and everything was okay when Daddy came home. I believe his greatest support came in providing normalcy and consistent caring for the girls. Mike sustained us, took care of us, loved us, and gave everything of himself, when he was getting so very little in return. I don't know how I got so blessed to have received such a gift as my husband, but I treasure him more everyday, and will never stop working to be the very best wife I can be. He deserves it. He's my best friend.

&

Your symptoms—and essentially, your life—will improve if you keep pressing forward and do the work of healing. Never lose hope, and give yourself the gift of grace, patience, and forgiveness as you go. Be patient with others who are trying to walk with you; give them time to understand what you're going through. *Help* them understand.

Have courage. It's inside of you; you just need to access it and then use it as a sword against your fear. Fear is the primal enemy of those with PTSD. It kept me in a box—never living. It ruled me, until I stood up to it. Fear has stolen so many years of my life, but when I finally began fighting against it, I realized I am a conqueror. *We are all conquerors.*

I combat fear by living outside my comfort zone. That means getting out of bed every day, exercising, eating right, and taking care of myself. It means going to the store (even though I still feel like crying sometimes about it), but now I go early in the morning when there are fewer people to contend with. I do hard things every day rather than live in avoidance, and I have seen that over time, it's become easier to do. I also notice that today, things don't frighten me like they used to. When you push yourself to do the things that you're afraid of, you grow stronger mentally, your courage grows, and you realize you are capable of so much more than you realized!

I love how my relationships with my daughters have grown over time. The bond I was so concerned I'd never have with Jordan is like concrete now. I have a powerful connection with both of my girls, because I loved them despite my pain, and I show them every day that they are the most important part of my life. I build them up, and make them feel loved and cherished. It brings me to tears at times to see their confidence and self-assurance—attributes I lacked throughout my life because of the abuse. I so desperately want my daughters to grow up liking themselves, and it brings so much joy to my heart to see it as their reality. I could only nurture this in them because of my own healing, and changes in my own perceptions about worth and self-love. Going through healing doesn't just change your *life* in a positive way—it changes your relationships. It changes how you interact with people, and how you affect people. Everything changes when you're not stuck looking at your prison walls.

It took time for me to understand I was worth fighting for, and you are worth it, too. Since we can't see the future, I can't tell you how it will be worth it for you, or in what ways your life will show the fruit of your toiling and heart-fueled labor. But I can tell you that when you make that unwavering decision to heal, something happens inside you. A shift takes place, and hope comes in. Your strength increases, and after a while, those rough patches don't take you down quite so low. You'll see more bright spots in your days, and a light at the end of the tunnel.

I was afraid of my feelings for so long, but now I am able to name them, face them, and talk about them openly. I am amazed now at the ways I have changed and grown, and developed confidence and a positive spirit I thought I would never have again. And I've come this far because of one gut-level decision to fight this battle, even if it took the rest of my life to win. I am better now because of it, and I will only continue to get better.

I learned that PTSD is not my identity. I am Juanima Hiatt, and I am fighting against a ravaging disorder called PTSD, and I will win. PTSD is not my future—it does not define me. In 2003, my life took a tragic, unexpected turn that had the potential to destroy me and all of my relationships; but I fought, and today, I'm smiling again. The trauma that brought on PTSD was not my fault. The symptoms I experienced that shattered my sanity and spirit were not my fault, nor did they mean I was weak, incapable, or crazy. There are physiological reasons for the symptoms that come with PTSD, and there is help available. Believe there is a way through for you.

I am awake now, and I know I've got what it takes to fight this battle another day. I am stronger now. My past no longer weighs heavy on my shoulders. The events that traumatized me are now a means to give others hope and courage to fight their own battles. Nothing is impossible. Healing is *very* possible. Just reach out. Take a deep breath, and step forward. You are strong and courageous. Don't be afraid of the pain, because on the other side of it is a freedom you have never known. You can make it if you hold on tight, have faith, and never give up.

"For I know the plans I have for you," says the Lord.
"Plans to prosper you and not to harm you.
Plans to give you hope and a future."
~ Jeremiah 29:11

RESOURCES

WEBSITES

www.aftersilence.org ~ A non-profit organization, message board and chat room for rape, sexual assault, and sexual abuse survivors and victims.

www.ncbi.nlm.nih.gov ~ Covers all facets of Post-Traumatic Stress Disorder including causes, symptoms, tests, treatment, prognosis, complications, and prevention.

www.ptsdinfo.org ~ A gateway to four specialized websites offering a wealth of information on and support for PTSD, including the National Center for PTSD, Gift From Within, The Dart Center for Journalism and Trauma, The National Center for Victims of Crime.

www.pandys.org ~ Support and resources for survivors of rape and sexual abuse.

www.emdr.com ~ EMDR (Eye-Movement Desensitization and Re-processing) is one of the most helpful, non-intrusive forms of therapy available to people who suffer from PTSD.

BOOKS

The Courage to Heal: A Guide for Women Survivors of Child Sexual Abuse by Ellen Bass and Laura Davis (2008)

The Courage to Heal Workbook by Laura Davis (1990)

Allies in Healing: When the Person You Love Was Sexually Abused as a Child by Laura Davis (1991)

The Post-Traumatic Stress Disorder Sourcebook: A Guide to Healing, Recovery, and Growth by Glenn R. Schiraldi (2009)

Resurrection After Rape: A Guide to Transforming From Victim to Survivor by Matt Atkinson (2008)

Battlefield of the Mind: Winning the Battle in Your Mind by Joyce Meyer (1995)

Waking the Tiger: Healing Trauma: The Innate Capacity to Transform Overwhelming Experiences by Peter A. Levine (1997)

The Body Remembers: The Psychophysiology of Trauma and Trauma Treatment by Babette Rothschild (2000)

Trauma and Recovery: The Aftermath of Violence – From Domestic Abuse to Political Terror by Judith Herman (1997)

For more information visit:

www.juanimahiatt.com
www.facebook.com/juanimahiattauthor
www.theinvisiblestorm.com
www.facebook.com/theinvisiblestorm

Email: juanimahiatt@gmail.com

Made in the USA
Charleston, SC
24 June 2012